THE FEDERALISTS—
CREATORS AND CRITICS
OF THE UNION
1780-1801

PROBLEMS IN AMERICAN HISTORY

EDITOR

LOREN BARITZ

State University of New York, Albany

THE FIRST PARTY SYSTEM: Federalists and Republicans
William N. Chambers

THE LEADERSHIP OF ABRAHAM LINCOLN
Don E. Fehrenbacher

THE AMERICAN CONSTITUTION
Paul Goodman

THE AMERICAN REVOLUTION
Richard J. Hooker

THE FEDERALISTS—Creators and Critics of the Union 1780-1801
Stephen G. Kurtz

AMERICA IN THE COLD WAR
Walter LaFeber

THE ORIGINS OF THE COLD WAR, 1941-1947
Walter LaFeber

AGITATION FOR FREEDOM: The Abolitionist Movement
Donald G. Mathews

THE NATURE OF JACKSONIAN AMERICA
Douglas T. Miller

AMERICAN IMPERIALISM IN 1898
Richard H. Miller

TENSIONS IN AMERICAN PURITANISM
Richard Reinitz

THE GREAT AWAKENING
Darrett B. Rutman

WORLD WAR I AT HOME
David F. Trask

THE CRITICAL YEARS,
AMERICAN FOREIGN POLICY, 1793-1825
Patrick C. T. White

THE FEDERALISTS—
CREATORS AND CRITICS
OF THE UNION
1780-1801

EDITED BY

Stephen G. Kurtz, Director

Institute of Early American History and Culture,
Williamsburg, Virginia

John Wiley & Sons, Inc.

New York • London • Sydney • Toronto

Library of Congress Catalogue Card Number: 75-178144

ISBN 0-471-51114-5 (paper)
ISBN 0-471-51112-9 (cloth)

Printed in the United States of America.

10 9 8 7 6 5 4 3 2 1

SERIES PREFACE

This series is an introduction to the most important problems in the writing and study of American history. Some of these problems have been the subject of debate and argument for a long time, although others only recently have been recognized as controversial. However, in every case, the student will find a vital topic, an understanding of which will deepen his knowledge of social change in America.

The scholars who introduce and edit the books in this series are teaching historians who have written history in the same general area as their individual books. Many of them are leading scholars in their fields, and all have done important work in the collective search for better historical understanding.

Because of the talent and the specialized knowledge of the individual editors, a rigid editorial format has not been imposed on them. For example, some of the editors believe that primary source material is necessary to their subjects. Some believe that their material should be arranged to show conflicting interpretations. Others have decided to use the selected materials as evidence for their own interpretations. The individual editors have been given the freedom to handle their books in the way that their own experience and knowledge indicate is best. The overall result is a series built up from the individual decisions of working scholars in the various fields, rather than one that conforms to a uniform editorial decision.

A common goal (rather than a shared technique) is the bridge of this series. There is always the desire to bring the reader as close to these problems as possible. One result of this objective is an emphasis on the nature and consequences of problems and events, with a de-emphasis of the more purely historiographical issues. The goal is to involve the student in the reality of crisis, the inevitability of ambiguity, and the excitement of finding a way through the historical maze.

Above all, this series is designed to show students how experienced historians read and reason. Although health is not contagious, intellectual engagement may be. If we show students something significant in a phrase or a passage that they otherwise may have missed, we will have accomplished part of our objective. When students see something that passed us by, then the process will have been made whole. This active and mutual involvement of editor and reader with a significant human problem will rescue the study of history from the smell and feel of dust.

Loren Baritz

Preface

New paperback volumes of supplemental readings appear with such regularity that no teacher or student is able to survey them all, and few apparently care to. At present there are at least five such volumes covering the Federalist era waiting to compete with this one for course adoption. Although some books of readings have been carefully constructed and edited, others lack the marks of scholarly attention that should be expected and instead, are what have come to be called "nonbooks," pieced hurriedly together out of the honest labors of others. In this book I have assembled a coherent history of the Federalists that spans the period from the Revolution to the triumph of their political opponents in 1800 in the form of private letters, public papers, and interpretive articles. It is a combination of primary and secondary sources that I have found best in teaching my own students—confidential letters and anonymously published essays that reveal what men wanted to accomplish and what they feared, public statements that represent the best cases they could construct for important policy decisions, and interpretations of their acts and motives by experienced scholars. These readings are intended primarily for college students but should be useful as well to graduate students concerned with the early national period of our history.

While recognizing the limitations and unattractive features of Federalist behavior, I freely admit that I find more wisdom than folly in these men. My basic assumption is that the major decisions they made between 1785 and 1794 were the right ones. Since they had created "a more perfect union" through the adoption of the Constitution and the economic measures championed by Hamilton, I view the policies pursued during the remaining years of their ascendency as attempts to buttress and protect them in both the domestic and foreign policy fields. Jefferson and Madison broke away from the Nationalists or Federalists between 1790 and 1792 after they became increasingly concerned over the sectional bias and economic drift of administration policies. They pointed to the funding system as the great engine of Federalist statecraft and summarized their political convictions as those of persons whom Jefferson termed "monocrats," or adherents of strong executive government. The documents reprinted here bear out the accuracy of Jefferson's analysis, since the

Federalists generally believed in the utility and worthiness of the profit system, of speculation, and of expanding economic opportunity through the exercise of government power. Their notions of democracy and aristocracy were also such as to make them suspicious of the wisdom of the great mass of their fellow citizens and of a good many of their chosen representatives as well. So long as George Washington remained on the scene they could usually rally popular support behind the government and its policies, but his passing stripped them of an important symbol of national destiny or, as Hamilton callously admitted, an essential aegis. Simplistic though it may appear, thousands of men and women, particularly in the southern states, seem to have supported-Federalist candidates and policies largely because Washington had associated himself with them.

The headnotes that accompany the letters, essays, and articles are intended to explain the circumstances under which they were written, to identify writers and recipients, and often to caution against the bias or self-interest of the author. Most of the major figures associated with the history of Federalism are represented in this volume. One obvious exception is Timothy Pickering, Secretary of State during a critical time that spanned the administrations of Washington and Adams. Yet I have not found his presence essential, for, dedicated and energetic as he was, I have concluded that his influence was not proportionate either to the importance of his office or to his unusual genius for inflaming animosities. On the other hand, it may appear that there is more of Hamilton than the case warrants, but I can only admit that although this might have been my own judgment when I began this task, it is not the judgment with which I completed it. How ironic that no national monument to this man exists. His burial place is marked by a simple, stone tomb a few yards from the financial center of the nation, a sharp commentary on the reluctance of Americans to admit to their capitalist tradition and to their distance from arcadian delights that Hamilton found so uninspiring.

STEPHEN G. KURTZ

CONTENTS

Introduction

Chapter I   The Nationalist Movement toward Consoldiation, 1780-1786

1. E. James Ferguson, Counterrevolution in Finance   1
2. Dependence upon Foreign Loans—Robert Morris to Benjamin Franklin, Philadelphia, January 11, 1783   16
3. Morris's Resignation as a Political Tactic—Robert Morris to the President of Congress, Philadelphia, January 24, 1783   18
4. Two Parties: One Local and One Continental—Alexander Hamilton to George Washington, Philadelphia, April 8, 1783   20
5. The Dangers of Involving the Army in Political Affairs— George Washington to Alexander Hamilton, Newburgh, N.Y., April 16, 1783   23
6. Trade at a Very Low Ebb—Stephen Higginson to John Adams, Boston, August 8, 1785   25
7. Licentiousness and Feebleness Threaten Society—John Jay to Thomas Jefferson, New York, October 27, 1786   27

Chapter II   Adoption and Ratification of the Constitution, 1787-1788

1. Madison Outlines A Plan of Union—James Madison to Edmund Randolph, New York, April 8, 1787   29
2. Debates in the Constitutional Convention, June 26, 1787 to September 17, 1787   33
3. The Federalist Papers, addressed by Hamilton, Madison, and Jay to the People of the State of New York between October 27, 1787 and May 28, 1788   43
4. Speeches in the Ratifying Conventions of Pennsylvania and Virginia, October 1787-June 1788   54
5. Jackson T. Main, Why Did the Antifederalists Fail?   61

Contents

Chapter III   The Hamiltonian Program and Its Immediate
              Effects, 1789-1793

1. Hamilton's Reports on the Public Credit, A National
   Bank, and Manufacturers with his Opinion on the Constitutionality of the Bank, January 1790-February 1791   77
2. The Funding System, A Blessing to Creditors—Stephen
   Higginson to Henry Knox, Boston, April 7, 1790   95
3. Virginia Opposition to the Funding System—Washington
   to David Stuart, New York, June 15, 1790   97
4. Hamilton's Defense and Counterattack—Alexander
   Hamilton to Edward Carrington, Philadelphia, May
   26, 1792   99
5. Rising Anger among the Federalists—Oliver Wolcott, Jr.
   to Oliver Wolcott, Sr., Philadelphia, February 8, 1793
   and Chauncey Goodrich to Oliver Wolcott, Jr., Hartford, February 17, 1793   102

Chapter IV   The French Revolution and Internal Security,
             1793-1796

1. A Warning Against French Theories—*Discourses on
   Davila*, Numbers 11 and 12, by John Adams   107
2. French Intrigues in South Carolina—Governor William
   Moultrie to President George Washington, Columbia,
   South Carolina, December 7, 1793   112
3. The President's Report on the Whiskey Rebellion, Speech
   to Congress, November 19, 1794   114
4. Private Reactions to the Whiskey Rebellion—Fisher
   Ames to Christopher Gore, Philadelphia, December 17,
   1794   119
5. Continued French Activity in the Back County—Mem-
   orandum of Oliver Wolcott, Jr. to the President, May
   19-21, 1796   121

Chapter V   Federalist Foreign Policy under Washington, 1794-1796

1. Settling the Mississippi Navigation Problem with Spain— Thomas Pinckney to Secretary of State Edmund Randolph, San Lorenzo, Spain, October 28, 1795   125

2. Jay's Unofficial Instructions—Alexander Hamilton to John Jay, Philadelphia, May 6, 1794   129

3. Hamilton's Opinion of a League of Neutrals—Alexander Hamilton to Secretary of State Randolph, Philadelphia, July 8, 1794   133

4. Hamilton's Defense of the British Treaty—"Camillus" Essay Number 1, July 22, 1795   134

5. Fisher Ames's Speech in the House of Representatives, April 28, 1796   137

6. Joseph Charles, The Political Consequences of the Jay Treaty   142

Chapter VI   The Adams Administration, 1797-1801

1. Adams Calls for Defense Measures—Message to Congress, Philadelphia, May 16, 1797   157

2. A Summary Statement of American Grievances—Pinckney, Marshall, and Gerry to Talleyrand, Paris, April 3, 1798   164

3. President Adams Fans the Fires—Public Letter of John Adams to the Soldier-Citizens of New Jersey, May 31, 1798   171

4. The Federalist Case for the Alien and Sedition Laws— Fisher Ames to Christopher Gore, Dedham, Massachusetts, December 18, 1798   173

5. The Virginia and Kentucky Resolutions Condemned, Sedition Act Defended—John Marshall and Henry Lee, *Address of the Minority in the Virginia Legislature*, 1799   176

Contents

6. Hamilton's Plans for Strengthening the Union—Alexander Hamilton to Johnathan Dayton, New York, February, 1799   180

7. Stephen G. Kurtz, President Adams Chooses Peace   185

Postscript: John C. Miller, the Decline of the Federalists

Bibliography

Chapter I

The Nationalist Movement toward
Consolidation
1780 - 1786

1   FROM   *E. James Ferguson*
                   Counterrevolution in Finance

The French alliance of 1778 tipped the scales in favor of the American states and was recognized by contemporaries as a decisive factor in the struggle for independence. Many months of frustration and near-despair lawy between France's entry into the war in June 1778 and the surrender of Cornwallis at Yorktown more than three years later, however. Savannah fell to Sir Henry Clinton's invading army during the last days of 1779, and the great port city of Charleston five months later. Moving across South Carolina,

SOURCE. E. James Ferguson. *The Power of the Purse: a History of American Public Finance, 1776-1790*. Chapel Hill: University of North Carolina Press, 1961, pp. 109-124. Reprinted by permission of the publisher (and The *Institute of Early American History and Culture, Williamsburg*)

an army under the command of Lord Charles Cornwallis carried devastation into North Carolina and Virginia during the months which ensued. Not until Yorktown itself did Britain's strategy of cutting the southern states off from the rest of the United States appear ill-conceived.

If the majority of Americans were not directly touched by the war, those with the most to hazard in terms of earthly goods were, and by 1780 they had serious doubts about the ability of a poorly supported government (under the informal arrangements that prevailed until the Articles of Confederation were adopted) to meet the challenge of inflation and insolvency in addition to that of the critical military situation. A government that depended on state requisitions could not, in the view of men of affairs, hope to underwrite the cost of prosecuting the war to a successful conclusion. It was seen that whatever independence might be won on the battlefield would be diluted by mounting financial and military dependence upon France.

It was under these circumstances that a determined coterie of merchants, bankers, land speculators, lawyers, and military leaders launched a movement under the leadership of the great Philadelphia merchant, Robert Morris, which they hoped would free the Congress of its dependence upon jealous state legislatures. Their efforts centered upon the establishment of a national import tax or impost which was seen as the necessary first step in rescuing American credit abroad, meeting interest payments on debts already contracted, and providing the basis for domestic credit upon which the expansion of trade and commerce would depend. The failure of this step toward consolidated government on the part of the Nationalists, together with a host of other related problems, led directly to a renewed and more sweeping reform of the federal structure so successful that it has lasted for nearly two centuries. In order to comprehend the Federalists—why they so strongly favored union at the expense of state authority and how they were able to move so swiftly and surely toward toward national consolidation after the adoption of the Constitution—an examination of the earlier and abortive reform movement is necessary. What we have usually labeled Hamiltonianism had its beginnings in the shadow of war's vexations and fears.

War had forced the deliberative body known as the Second Continental Congress to assume the duties and responsibilities of a duly constituted national government and to contract large debts in carrying them out. As the war draggged on it became increasingly clear that the matter of who should pay those debts would be critical in determining where political power would ultimately lie, dispersed widely among the states or concentrated in the hands of a relative few. It could be seen that the nature of social institutions as well as the directions which economic development would take would be greatly influenced by the outcome of the struggle over public finance. Fears of excessive democracy on the one side were balanced by fears of aristocracy on the other. No scholar of the Revolution and Confederation has done more to reveal the close connection between public debt and political and social power than E. James Ferguson from whose superb study of this central theme this selection is taken.

The dismal state of public affairs in 1780 delivered the political initiative to conservative spokesmen, who had been in eclipse sinc the early phases of the Revolution. When the approaching break with Britain portended radical alterations in the *status quo,* a faction supporting a strong government and the preservation of the existing order had emerged. The drastic measures which popular state governments employed to prosecute the war confirmed the views of those who had such leanings, but there was no opportunity to direct the course of public affairs until the apparent failure of the war effort in 1780. The emergency brought men of conservative temper to the fore in several important states; soon they were to dominate Congress. The aims and motives of this group, which we shall call the *Nationalists,* were similar even in detail to those of the Federalists who later drafted the Constitution and enacted Hamilton's funding program. Such Federalists as Washington, Hamilton, and Madison played a role in the earlier movement, whose presiding genius was the great merchant, Robert Morris.

The war for independence reached its nadir in 1780, when it was doubtful whether the nation would continue the struggle. British armies swept through the south virtually unopposed, while General Gates fled at Camden, and Benedict Arnold was exposed as a traitor. Congress and the state governments were nearly destitute. The Continental army eked out an existence by impressments and was sometimes in danger of having to disband for lack of supplies. Many persons thought of "abandoning the cause, not from disaffection, but from despair," while others pondered ways of reaching an "accommodation" with the enemy.

Civilian morale was at low ebb. The nation had been too long at war, and much of the enthusiasm of 1776 had worn off, giving way to indifference, preoccupation with gaining wealth, and, in some quarters, a contempt of the American government. The old patriot Christopher Marshall, offended by most of what he saw, stayed in his house, and mourned the "abomination of the times." Good Whigs, viewing the passion for making money, wondered whether they did not merit a share in the profits of this "diabolical war." Military officers resented the fortunes acquired by men of their own social standing in civilian life. The common people raged against profiteers and government officers. Farmers counted their certificates and felt a sense of injustice. In some states, notably Pennsylvania, political rivalries crippled the administration. The Deane-Lee affair continued to boil up in Congress with each new disclosure of corruption or waste in the federal service. The time was ripe for a change in leadership.

It was understandable that the impetus came from the propertied class. Especially in the middle states, it was the common people and the backcountry farmers, rather than the aristocracy, who supported the leadership of Congress. New England and Virginia had always dominated major Congressional policies, and although the Adamses and the Lees could scarcely be called radical in their social ideas, the measures they advocated were radical in their effects. By promoting the overflow of colonial governments, pushing through independence against the will of the aristocratic leaders of the middle colonies, and drafting a federal constitution which reserved sovereignty to the states, Congress gave scope and encouragement to the social changes that came with the Revolution.

Congress's financial measures also suited the tastes of the common people, whose views ran to such measures as paper money, legal tender, price-fixing laws, embargoes, and anti-monopoly legislation. Paper money was unavoidable, and it was the usual practice of governments to legislate in economic matters; nevertheless, propertied men believed that the weight of restriction fell mainly upon them. They burned with resentment at their subordination to radical committees. In an age when the tenets of laissez-faire were increasingly accepted as natural law, they considered themselves the victims of class legislation.

Dissatisfaction with the existing political order was most prevalent in the propertied class, but by 1780 the idea of strengthening the central government was supported by a considerable and diversified body of opinion. Four years before, this would have been unthinkable. With Britain as their example, most patriots of 1776 had conceived of central government as at best an oppressive force and by its nature a check upon self-rule. Although Congress emerged as an agency for prosecuting the war, the revolutionists had no intention of laying the foundations of a strong central government. Freedom from Britain signified to most Americans that each state would henceforth be free to conduct its affairs without hindrance.

The Articles of Confederation expressed this Revolutionary emphasis upon defense of local rights against central authority. The Articles were designed to safeguard liberty; the Union was a league of states, presided over by a dependent Congress. Its authority was limited in many ways, but of all the restraints devised to forestall usurpation of power, the denial to Congress of the right to tax was the most fundamental. No maxim of political philosophy was so widely accepted in Revolutionary times as that the "power which holds the purse-strings absolutely, must rule." Popular control of taxation was deemed the very foundation of representative government and the only protection of the rights of the citizens. Under the Articles of Confederation the states remained in a position to check arbitrary proceedings by withholding revenue from Congress—just as the states' own citizens could similarly curb the states' power. Agreement on this principle was so nearly universal that although proponents of stronger government took part in drafting the Articles of Confederation, they never proposed that Congress should be given authority to collect taxes.

That a weak central government was a handicap in waging war was acknowledged and accepted as a calculated risk. The extent of the risk was not appreciated, however, during the first few years of the Revolution. Until paper money was exhausted, the limitations on Congress's powers were not thoroughly tested. "It was easy times to the government while Continental money lasted," and Congress proceeded with its affairs without depending on the states. Late in 1779 the decision to stop emissions signalized the virtual end of this resource and exposed to full view the weakness of Congress under the Articles of Confederation.

The ensuing crisis in public affairs led many to re-examine the postulates of their thinking and to wonder whether "political and civil Liberty can be enjoyed amidst the Din of Arms, in their utmost platonic Extent." The violence wrought by popular governments upon their own citizens suggested new approaches to a definition of liberty. There was also some realization that the active support of propertied men must be enlisted to maintain the war. "While the war was carried on by emissions. . .the poor were of equal use in government with the rich," mused Thomas Paine. "But when the means must be drawn from the country. . .unless the wealthier part throw in their aid, public measures must go heavily on." People whose partisanship was not unshakable began listening to conservatives who spoke less of liberty and more about the need for financial stability and strong government. Also, because paper money and tender laws were evidently futile, there was less objection to a trial of the conservative formula of sound money and unrestrained private enterprise.

The swing in popular sentiment produced conservative majorities in several important states, notably Massachusetts, Pennsylvania, and Virginia. New delegates altered the composition of Congress. The Adams-Lee alliance was fractured at the northern end by the advent of Oliver Wolcott of Connecticut, John Sullivan of New Hampshire, and Ezekiel Cornell and James Mitchell Varnum of Rhode Island. Richard Henry Lee left Congress, and the Virginia delegation was guided until 1783 by Theodorick Bland, Joseph Jones, and James Madison, who joined with Daniel Carroll and John Hanson of Maryland to give the southern states a conservative representation.

The change of personnel was only partly responsible for the shaping of new policies: the old methods had failed, and there was scant prospect of reinvigorating them. It no longer seemed possible for Congress to discharge the responsibility it had assumed. After he had arrived in Philadelphia, almost every delegate favored enlarging Congressional powers. Even New Englanders, alert to the slightest portents of despotism, were disgusted with the ineffectiveness of the federal system and admitted that practical affairs sometimes required actions not described in the "political catechism" of good republicans.

A new harmony was soon visible in Congress. Conservatives began saying this was the best Congress since the first and that "party intrigue" and "old prejudices" were being dispelled by "mild spirits" and "sensible men" who put the nation's welfare above factional advantage. Writing from Philadelphia, Samuel Huntington, the President of Congress observed: "There Seems a Spirit rising in this part of the Country to exert themselves in the common cause greater than I have Seen for Some years." But this new unity, although it owed something to the pressure of adversity, had a partisan basis. Two years later Joseph Reed remarked that the old Whigs were disappearing from public life. "Most of those who were much distinguished, and known in times of our greatest difficulty," he lamented, "are now in private stations."

The revisionist group which was to rule Congress until the end of the war was conservative, mercantile, and nationalist in its aims. The group was strongest in the middle states, where it incorporated elements of the displaced colonial aristocracy. Independence had caused a breach in the social order, and, as one observer declared, the previously dominant classes aspired to a pre-eminence which the people now refused to grant them. Moreover, the Revolution had cut the aristocratic classes loose from the security of the British connection, with only their own resources to depend on. A propertied minority, they felt perpetually menaced in the presence of an agrarian majority. Many of them were fundamentally Tories, but even those who sincerely backed the Revolution felt that the experiment in liberty had got out of hand. Lamenting the absence of "public Checks upon the reserved licentiousness of the People," they considered themselves as living under mob rule. They sought security in the establishment of a central government which would protect property and minority rights.

The war itself created another group which was vitally concerned with the enlargement of federal powers—the "public creditors." Up to 1783, the public creditors consisted of the holders of loan certificates, who alone received interest on their securities from the federal government. Eager to assume responsibility for the loan certificate debt, Congress refused to surrender any part of it to the states. Unfortunately, there were insufficient funds to honor this commitment, and in 1780 Congress was obligated to suspend payment of the interest due in paper money. Interest payable in bills of exchange was continued until March 1782, when it too was stopped. Long before the final default the public creditors were lobbying for increased federal powers. Since creditors were likely to be propertied men residing in states north of Maryland, they were in part identical with the aristocracy of the middle states which desired strong central government on other grounds. Drawn from the same powerful and influential ranks of the population were the enlightened merchants of the time, who, along with many intellectuals, regarded a powerful national state as a positive good.

Grimly satisfied that paper money was approaching its destined end, the Nationalists proposed a clean sweep of such radical paraphernalia as tender laws, price regulation, embargoes, and anti-monopoly laws. Once this "detestable tribe" of restrictions was put away they predicted that the country would find new sources of vigor in the self-interested actions of private men.

As "correct principles" were applied in the economic sphere, the Nationalists hoped to inject authority and some degree of managerial efficiency into the government. During 1780 and 1781, the outlines of their policy materialized in acts of Congress. The army was reorganized along lines recommended by Washington. The "militia system" of short-term enlistments was discarded in favor of enlistments for three years or the duration of the war. A significant step was taken when officers who served to the end of the war were promised pensions for life—an act offensive to republican thought, especially in New England where it aroused anxiety that a military caste take root in America.

Another triumph over "prejudice" was scored in the reorganization of the federal administrative departments. Fearful of delegating authority, Congress had hitherto given executive functions only to committees of its own members or to mixed boards made up of members and hired officials. The system was inefficient but persisted until late in 1780, when a sufficient retreat from republican principles took place to permit the establishment of separate executive departments. War, foreign affairs, naval matters, and finance were placed under the direction of individuals, not members of Congress. As the future showed, the forebodings of those who then opposed such extensive delegation of authority were to some extent justified. There was greater efficiency, but the heads of departments wielded an influence that threatened for a time to reduce Congress to a secondary role. Congress entered a phase of "executivism," in which the federal assembly was to a considerable degree dominated by the men appointed to manage its affairs.

These reforms appeased the conservative instinct of authority and efficient management. They were but peripheral, however, to the one reform upon which all else depended. This related to finance.

Any real effort to strengthen the central goverment, restore its financial solvency, and rationalize federal administration had to begin with settling adequate revenues upon Congress. Requisitions had been unproductive; in any case the Nationalists opposed them in principle because they could not in the nature of things afford a basis for centralized authority. Unable to admit this point too openly, they usually argued the less dangerous point that the requisition system was and always would be faulty because it could not supply Congress with an assured income which would support its credit. In contracting foreign and domestic loans, they said, Congress had to act as a responsible agent; but without an income subject to its sole control, it could not really guarantee payment to its creditors. The only thing that would do was a federal tax.

Early in 1781 a proposal for a federal tax was offered to the states. Congress had been mulling over various schemes of finance for nearly a year and at length resolved to ask for an "impoṣt," or import duty, of 5 percent on goods imported into the country. A special minister was being sent to Europe at this time in quest of loans, and it was supposed that they would be more easily obtained if Congress could guarantee security in the form of a revenue subject to its sole control. As originally conceived, therefore, the impost was to provide an income to discharge foreign loans. In its final wording, however, the resolution did not restrict the income to the discharge of loans then being sought, but instead pledged it to the payment of the interest and principal of all debts contracted during the war, both domestic and foreign. The power to collect this revenue was to be coextensive with the existence of the federal debt—in other words, permanent.

That the impost was designed to be a permanent addition to Congress's powers was further confirmed by the wording of the resolution. An early draft had asked the states to "pass laws granting" the duty to Congress. This phrase was changed to "vest a power in Congress." Equally significant was the failure to specify whether the states or Congress were to control the collectors. Wary of reviving memories of the disputes with Britain, Congress did not spell out an arrangement under which federal collectors would act within the states, but the subsequent history of the impost leaves no doubt that collection was to be by federal officers.

A few members thought that the impost could be disguised as a simple revenue measure. Then it would become effective after ratification by nine states. The states, however, at once recognized it as an amendment to the Articles and ratified it only on condition that it be approved by every state in the Union. The impost had a long road to travel, but as one state after another endorsed it in 1781 and 1782, its chances of adoption seemed good. Congress waited eagerly to try new powers.

As the Nationalists in Congress formulated their objectives,they discovered their leader in Robert Morris. He embodied in his person the constituent elements of the Nationalist group, and his genius was to shape their movements. A rich merchant and security holder, he had married into an aristocratic family. As a member of Congress he had associated himself with the conservative faction in Pennsylvania, refusing to vote for the Declaration of Independence. His aims were primarily mercantile rather than political, but in the acrimonious party battle that developed in Pennsylvania during the war, he became an acknowledged leader of the conservative faction which fought the radical Constitutionalists for control of the state.

In the spring of 1781, when Congress began selecting the men to head its administrative departments under the new plan, Morris was the inescapable choice for the Department of Finance. Congress had need of an executive whose personal standing and credit would bolster its weak directives. Morris had a mastery of Continental business that was virtually unsurpassed, and his fortune was one of the greatest in the country. Above all, he had the confidence of the mercantile and propertied interests whose aid was vital to the prosecution of the war.

When tendered his appointment, Morris made two stipulations. He required that Congress expressly sanction his continuance in private business while holding office—undoubtedly a rejoinder to the criticism of his previous service with the federal government. This demand was not hard for Congress to accept, but Morris's second condition aroused grave misgivings. He claimed the right not only to appoint all officers in his own department, but also to dismiss any officer in any branch of the government who handled public property. Only in this way, said Morris, could he cleanse the stables of federal administration.

The terms implied that Morris's authority would penetrate every branch of the administration and even the army. Congress deliberated more than a month and once voted down the proposition, but "Mr. Morris was inexorable, Congress at his mercy," and at length his stipulations were met. Actually, Congress had for years leaned ever more definitely towards granting decisive authority to its executive officers. The Congress of 1781 went the whole distance.

Morris soon possessed the greatest influence of any man in the country except, perhaps, George Washington, Whatever the subject under consideration in Congress-whether military matters, foreign affairs, or relations with the states-the main problems usually related to finance. Morris was expert and full of expedients. Under the spell of its own helplessness, Congress all but relinquished the initiation of policy to the Financier. His formal powers were increased. In the name of economy,the Department of Marine was placed under the Financier; the Board of Admiralty and the several navy boards were abolished and their functions transferred to the Office of Finance. All the proceeds of foreign loans were placed in his hands, and he was given discretionary power to import or export goods on the account of the United States. He was authorized to supply the army by contract and to dispose of specific supplies by sale to private individuals. In recognition of the fact that negotiations with foreign nations mainly concerned loans and material aids, he was empowered to correspond with the foreign ministers of the United States; thus diplomatic functions were added to his chores. After the lapse of a few months, General William Irvine wrote that "the most trifling thing can not be done in any department but through Mr. Morris."

Not long afterward, one of Morris's detractors observed that since his appointment the business of Congress had been extremely simplified. "Mr. Morris having relieved them from all business of deliberation in executive difficulty with which money is in any respect connected . . . they are now very much at leasure to read despatches, return thanks, pay and receive compliments &c. For form's sake some things go thither to receive a sanction, but it is the general opinion that it is form only."

Morris's personal influence was strengthened by the appointment of his friend and business associate, Robert R. Livingston, as Secretary of Foreign Affairs. Gouverneur Morris, who was not a relative but a close friend, became Assistant Financier. General Philip J. Schuyler was a candidate for the post of Secretary of War, and it was said that if he were named to the office, Morris and his associates would hold the chief positions in all the executive departments. As it was, Richard Peters, a friend who had once begged Morris for admission into the "privateer circle," served as active head of the Department of War for a lengthy period before General Benjamin Lincoln took over.

His enemies were alarmed at what they considered his overweening ambition and continued to make snide allusion to his remaining in private trade, but Morris's conduct of the Office of Finance leaves no doubt that his personal goals were couched in the larger purposes of effecting reforms which he deemed beneficial to the country. Announcing his appointment to friends, he took high ground: "Pressed by all my friends, acquaintances, and fellow-citizens, and still more pressed by the *necessity*, the *absolute necessity* of a change in our moneyed system to work salvation, I have yielded, and taken a load on my shoulder." In his letter accepting the position, he informed Congress: "It is not from vanity that I mention the expectations which the public seem to have formed from my appointment." Although such effusions were discounted, they had considerable validity, for Morris considered himself, and was in fact, the leader of a party with a definite program of action.

Like the class of progressive merchants with whom he was associated, Morris had scant sympathy with agrarian tradition. For him the goal of the Revolution was the creation of a national state which would rise to "power, consequence, and grandeur." This idea was inseparably joined with the conception of a political regime which would foster business enterprise and at the same time leave business free of restrictions. Morris was accustomed to define liberty primarily in economic terms. "It is inconsistent with the principles of liberty," he argued, "to prevent a man from the free disposal of his property on such terms as he may think fit." He looked forward to the moment when, by the removal of all economic restraints, the people would be put in possession of "that freedom for which they are contending."

Freedom of trade, however, was but part of his goal. Like many of the Revolutionary generation, he was imbued with the idea that the United States was standing on the threshold of its development. With Gouverneur Morris he believed that "Nothing remained but Vigor Organization & Promptitude to render this a considerable Empire." He and his associates admired the commercial and industrial progress of European nations, particularly Great Britain. Anticipating a similar development in the United States, they could scarcely wait to experiment with the magical properties of commercial banks and marine insurance companies. They were deeply impressed by the sheer power of British public finance, which had withstood the shocks of two costly wars, and they contrasted the sound fiscal policy of Britain with the vagaries of public finance in America. To them the Revolution meant a break with the agrarian past and the growth of commercial and industrial enterprise in the United States—a process in which they hoped to play a significant role."

Democracy was no part of the pattern. In their private letters, Morris and his associates avowed their contempt for the people and their impatience with popular government. They ascribed the behavior of the common people to such motives as passion, greed, and an incapacity to generalize above limited experience. They complained that popular governments were slow and perverse in action, distracted by petty conflicts of interest. There is no order that he has a will of its own," wrote Hamilton. "The inquiry constantly is what will *please,* not what will *benefit* the people." Arrogating to themselves a higher knowledge of natural law and public affairs, they dismissed their political foes as men of diminutive intellect and paltry motives, "vulgar souls whose narrow optics can see but the little circle of selfish concerns." They considered themselves men of "patriotic mind seeking the great good of the whole on enlightened principles."

Morris and his associates were quite aware that the United States was a singularly democratic country and that the majority of people did not subscribe to their aims. As Superintendent of Finance, Morris set himself the task of "doing that infinite variety of things which are to be done in an infant government, placed in such delicate circumstances that the people must be wooed and won to do their duty to themselves and pursue their own interest." He proposed to draw by degrees "the bands of authority together, establishing the power of Government over a people impatient of control, and confirming the Federal Union . . . by correcting defects in the general Constitution."

He proposed first of all to demonstrate managerial efficiency, showing what might have been accomplished had "Continental men" not held the reins. "Regularity" was to be introduced into fiscal affairs: henceforth federal requisitions on the states were to demand specie, not paper money. Federal officers were to keep orderly accounts and submit periodic reports. At the first opportunity, Morris intended to bring about a settlement of Congress's accounts with individual citizens and the states. When the government knew what its debts were and the amount of its income, a basis would exist for rational planning.

These reforms were preliminary to the restoration of "public credit," and he hoped to initiate the process by keeping his own administration solvent. Morris was most earnest about this because his personal affairs as a merchant were mingled with his official engagements, and for the sake of his own finances it was essential that he pay the bills he contracted as Financier. To sweep aside the clutter of the past, he refused to pay federal debts contracted before January 1, 1782, which he considered the effective date of his administration. From that date forward he accepted responsibility, intending to prove that the government could remain solvent if correct administrative methods were employed. Economies could be expected from the discharge of superfluous personnel and supplying the army by contract. Morris planned to expand government funds by creating a bank and by utilizing in behalf of the government all the anticipatory devices customary among merchants.

Such fiscal reforms were the proper work of a financial administrator and of sufficient importance to have absorbed Morris's whole energy. They were but instrumental, however, to his larger goal of recasting the structure of the Union. Illustrative of Morris's methods were his plans for the Bank of North America, which he submitted to Congress three days after taking office. On the ground that the Bank would aid his conduct of the finances, he requested a federal charter of incorporation. As outlined to Congress, the main function of the Bank was to hold government funds, make loans to the government, and discount its notes. Morris contended that by the sale of shares to individuals, the

Bank would draw private capital in support of the government's operations. Although these services were sufficient justification of the Bank's existence, they were but the beginning of Morris's designs. The Bank was to be capitalized at only $400,000 specie; Morris hoped to increase its capital to the extent that much of the private wealth in the country would be invested in its stock. Its circulating notes would then provide a medium of exchange for the entire nation. He intended to bring about an early retirement of all federal and state currencies, replacing them with bank notes, and thereby put an end to the evils of agrarian paper money. Thus enlarged, the Bank would become a citadel of the Union. Morris advised John Jay of his desire to "unite the several States more closely together in one general money connexion, and indissolubly to attach many powerful individuals to the cause of our country by the strong principle of self-love and the immediate sense of private interest."

The same interweaving of financial and political reform is evident in Morris's plans for dealing with the federal debt. In one aspect, the debt represented potential capital for business development. Morris once told Congress that if the debt were properly funded—that is, if the payment of interest and principal was secured by adequate revenues—the market value of securities would rise, causing wealth to flow "into those hands which could render it most productive." Deposited in the Bank of North America and other financial institutions, the revitalized securities would constitute backing for a national system of currency and credit. "A due provision for the public debts would at once convert those debts into a real medium of commerce." Pursuant to these ends, Morris proposed in 1782 that existing federal securities be taken in exchange for new securities, which would be backed by (as yet nonexistent) federal taxes. Like Hamilton at a later date, he had to refute the notion that a discrimination be made between original and present holders. Needless to say, Morris advocated acceptance of all securities at full value without discrimination.

The economic functions of a public debt went hand in hand with its political uses. Invigorated by the establishment of federal taxes and held by propertied men in all parts of the country, the public debt would be a bond of union. "It is . . . an advantage peculiar to domestic loans," he explained to Congress, "that they give stability to Government by combining together the interests of moneyed men for its support and consequently in this Country a domestic debt would greatly contribute to that Union, which seems not to have been sufficiently attended to, or provided for, in forming the national compact."

Morris's plan of action anticipated the major features of the later Federalist program. As the leader of the first conservative movement in national politics, he addressed himself to his task.

2

Dependence upon Foreign Loans

Robert Morris to Benjamin Franklin, Philadelphia, January 11, 1783

Robert Morris had been Superintendent of Finance for two years when he confessed his inability to stabilize the nation's credit in the letter which follows. A man of wide experience in both political and mercantile affairs, Morris had served in the Continental Congress and had signed the Declaration with misgivings, he had almost miraculously managed to provide Washington's forces with supplies sufficient to maintain them and although often attacked for private speculations while serving in a public capacity, had escaped with his reputation intact when asked to assume the heavy burden of restoring order to chaotic finances. By January of 1783 he had applied every expedient conceivable even including the circulation of notes backed only by his personal credit and the establishment under government auspices of a private bank, the Bank of North America, which was intended to provide the services of a national bank. Foreign loans negotiated by Franklin at Paris and by

SOURCE. Francis Wharton, ed., *Revolutionary Diplomatic Correspondence of the United States,* Volume VI, Washington: Government Printing Office, 1889, pp. 203 - 204.

John Adams in Holland helped to achieve the limited success which flowed from Morris's vigorous efforts.

Enclosed you have a general statement of the public account until the year 1781, on which you will observe that the army was fed principally, though scantily, by the specific supplies called for at different previous periods, and that there remained in the treasury near three hundred thousand dollars, being part of the money which Colonel Laurens brought with him from France. I also enclose to you the copy of a letter written to Congress on the 21st of October and of its several enclosures, which will need no commentary; or if it did, I would only add, that I have been obliged to sell part of the goods which arrived here from Holland, in order to raise so much money as would save my sinking credit from destruction. I would go into a detail of the various measures pursued to stimulate the exertions of the states, but to do this with accuracy would be to give a tedious history of my whole administration. Whatever expedient could suggest itself which might have that desirable effect, I have tried, and I do assure you that when I look back at the scenes I have passed through they strike my own mind with astonishment. As soon as I can get the accounts made up I will transmit to you the total of our expenditures; but to transmit, or even relate, our hazards and difficulties would be impossible.

Even at this moment I am making further exertions to bring our unwieldy system into form and ward off impending evils; but what the success may be, Heaven only knows. Imagine the situation of a man who is to direct the finances of a country almost without revenue (for such you will perceive this to be) surrounded by creditors whose distresses, while they increase their clamors, render it more difficult to appease them; an army ready to disband or mutiny; a government whose sole authority consists in the power of framing recommendations. Surely it is not necessary to add any coloring to such a piece, and yet truth would justify more than fancy would paint. The settlement of accounts, long and intricate beyond comprehension, becomes next to impossible from the want of that authority, which is on the verge of annihilation, from those confusions which nothing can dissipate except the complete settlement of accounts and an honest provision for payment.

Upon discovering the situation of our affairs in the manner

already mentioned, I laid them before Congress. You will know the result. The Secretary of Foreign Affairs will, doubtless, transmit their act; to which I must add this further communication, that I expect my bills will amount to a million within a month from this date. There are cases where nothing worse can be apprehended from a measure than what would inevitably happen without it, and our present position is one of them. An immediate command of money is alike necessary to our present existence and future prospects. In Europe, when this letter arrives, you will know decidedly whether we are to expect peace or war. We must prepare for the latter. By so doing we may forward negotiations for peace, and at the worst will only have incurred some additional expense; whereas by neglecting it we risk of being taken unawares, and paying very dearly the penalties of neglect . . . On this occasion your sovereign will expect your most vigorous exertions, and your country will, I trust, be indebted to you in a degree for her political existence.

3

Morris's Resignation as a Political Tactic
Robert Morris to the President of Congress,
Philadelphia, January 24, 1783

The letter below is a letter of resignation but not quite. The intention was clearly to stir Congress to take action on his projects for funding the debt and to bring outside pressures, namely the army, to bear upon the situation. Peace rumors from France as well as the absence of pay in miliary pockets had brought the morale of Washington's officers to the lowest ebb since the winter encampment at Morristown. As Alexander Hamilton, one of the best-placed and most eager of the Nationalists admitted to General Washington some weeks later, Morris had not handled this situation altogether well—Congress

SOURCE. *Ibid.* pp. 228-229

had blunted his intent by keeping the letter secret, and Morris, in finally reguesting that it be made public, revealed his scheme in a way pleasing to his worst enemies. Morris did not resign until September 1784.

As nothing but the public danger would have induced me to accept my office, so I was determined to hold it until the danger was past, or else to meet my ruin in the common wreck. Under greater difficulties than were apprehended by the most timid, and with less support than was expected by the least sanguine, the generous confidence of the public has accomplished more than I presumed to hope.

Congress will recollect that I expressly stipulated to take no part in past transactions. My attention to the public debts, therefore, arose from the conviction that funding them on solid revenues was the last necessary work of our glorious Revolution. The accomplishment of this necessary work is among the objects nearest my heart, and to effect it I would sacrifice time, property, and domestic bliss.

Many late circumstances have so far lessened our apprehensions from the common enemy that my original motives have almost ceased to operate. But other circumstances have postponed the establishment of public credit in such manner that I fear it will never be made. To increase our debts while the prospect of paying them diminishes, does not consist with my ideas of integrity. I must, therefore, quit a situation which becomes utterly insupportable. But lest the public measures might be deranged by any precipitation, I will continue to serve until the end of May. If effectual measures are not taken by that period to make permanent provision for the public debts of every kind, Congress will be pleased to appoint some other man to be the superintendent of their finances. I should be unworthy of the confidence reposed in me by my fellow citizens if I did not explicitly declare that I will never be the minister of injustice.

4

Two Parties: One Local and One Continental
Alexander Hamilton to George Washington, Philadelphia,
April 8, 1783

Hamilton at the age of twenty-eight was already an experienced and extremely able actor on the stage of great events when he wrote this letter summarizing the situation at Philadelphia. As former aide and confidant to the General he could speak freely; his association with Robert Morris, Gouverneur Morris, Madison, and others of the leading Nationalists was close; and his basic outlook upon political and economic matters led him easily to the unionist or consolidationist position. Having retired from the Continental Army after Yorktown, Hamilton had studied law and been admitted to the bar where he found his principal source of livelihood throughout his brief life. At the time of writing Hamilton was serving a term as one of New York's representatives in Congress.

. . . There are two classes of men Sir in Congress of very Different views—one attached to state, the other to Continental politics. The last have been strong advocates for funding the public debt upon solid securities, the former have given every opposition in their power and have only been dragged into the measures which are now near being adopted by the clamours of the army and other public creditors. The advocates for Continental funds have blended the interests of the army with other Creditors from a conviction, that no funds for partial purposes will go through those states to whose citizens the United States are largely indebted—or if they should be carried through from impression of the moment would have the necessary stability; for the influence of those unprovided for would always militate against a provision for others, in exclusion of them. It is in vain to

SOURCE. Henry C. Lodge, ed., The Works of Alexander Hamilton,Volume IX, New York: G.P. Putnam's Sons, 1904. pp. 332-337.

tell men who have parted with a large part of their property on the public faith that the services of the army are entitled to a preference. They would reason from their interest and their feelings. These would tell them that they had as great a title as any other class of the community to public justice, and that while this was denied to them, it would be unreasonable to make them bear their part of a burden for the benefit of others. . .

But the question was not merely how to do justice to the creditors, but how to restore public credit. Taxation in this Country, it was found, could not supply a sixth part of the public necessities. The loans in Europe were far short of the balance and the prospect every day diminishing. The Court of France telling us in plain terms she could not even do as much as she had done— Individuals in Holland and every where else refusing to part with their money on the precarious tenure of the mere faith of this country, without any pledge for the payment either of principal or interest.

In this situation what was to be done? It was essential to our cause that vigorous efforts should be made to restore public credit—it was necessary to combine all the motives to this end, that could operate upon different descriptions of persons in the different states. The necessity and discontents of the army presented themselves as a powerful engine.

But Sir these Gentlemen would be puzzled to support their insinuations by a single fact. It was indeed proposed to appropriate the intended impost on trade to the army debt and what was extraordinary by Gentlemen who had expressed their dislike to the principle of the fund. I acknowledge I was one that opposed this; for the reasons already assigned and for these additional ones— *That* was the fund on which we most counted—to obtain further loans in Europe it was necessary we should have a fund sufficient to pay the interest of what had been borrowed and what was to be borrowed. The truth was these people in this instance wanted to play off the army against the funding system.

As to Mr. Morris, I will give Your Excellency a true explanation of his conduct. He had been for some time pressing Congress to endeavour to obtain funds, and had found a great backwardness in the business. He found the taxes unproductive in the different states—he found the loans in Europe making a very slow progress— he found himself pressed on all hands for supplies; he found himself in short reduced to this alternative either of making engagements which he could not fulfill or declaring his resignation in case funds were not established by a given time. Had he followed the first course the bubble must soon have burst—he must have sacrificed his credit and his character, and public credit already in a ruinous condition would have lost its last support. He wisely judged it better to resign; this might increase the embarrassments of the moment, but the necessity of the case it was to be hoped would produce the proper measures; and he might then resume the direction of the machine with advantage and success. He also had some hope that his resignation would prove a stimulus to Congress.

He was however ill-advised in the publication of his letters of resignation. This was an imprudent step and has given a handle to his personal enemies, who by playing upon the passions of others have drawn some well meaning men into the cry against him. But Mr. Morris certainly deserves a great deal from his country. I believe no man in this country but himself could have kept the money-machine a going during the period he has been in office. From every thing that appears his administration has been upright as well as able. . .

The matter with respect to the army which has occasioned most altercation in Congress and most dissatisfaction in the army has been the half pay. The opinion on this head have been two. One party was for referring the several lines to their states to make such commutation as they should think proper—the other for making the commutation by Congress and funding it on continental security. I was of this last opinion and so were all those who will be represented as having made use of the army as puppets. Our principal reasons were 1st by referring the lines to their respective states, those which were opposed to the half pay would have taken advantage of the officers necessities, to make the commutation far short of an equivalent. 2dly. The inequality which would have arisen in the different states when the officers came to compare (as has happened in other cases) would have been a new source of discontent. 3dly. such a reference was a continuance of the old wretched state system, by which the ties between Congress and the army have been diverted from the common treasury and wasted; a system which Your Excellency has often justly reprobated.

I have gone into these details to give You a just idea of the parties in Congress. I assure you upon my honor Sir I have given you a candid state of facts to the best of my judgment. The men against whom the suspicions you mention must be directed are in general the most sensible the most liberal, the most independent and the most respectable characters in our body as well as the most unequivocal friends to the army. In a word they are the men who think continentally.

5

The Dangers of Involving the Army in Political Affairs

George Washington to Alexander Hamilton, Newburgh, New York, April 16, 1783

Aside from the questions of public finance and commerce there was no pressure more keenly felt by members of the Confederation Congress at Philadelphia as the war drew to a close than that created by a restive and resentful army whose officers and men were in a rebellious mood in the Spring of 1783. Officers, in particular, resented the broken promises of many years concerning the terms of their service, and but for the prestige and good sense of their commanding general they might well have set for the United States the dangerous precedent of attempting to intimidate the government with the threat of mutiny. In mid-March Washington had intervened decisively against intriguers, largely by staring them down; yet he was keenly aware of the injustices which his men had borne and, as this excerpt from his reply to Hamilton reveals, was not willing to see the matter of back pay and broken promises settled in a way that would promote the cause of a stronger union.

SOURCE. Harold C. Syrett and Jacob E. Cooke, eds., *The Papers of Alexander Hamilton,* Vol. III, New York: Columbia University Press, 1962, pp. 329-331.

*Washington, at his best, displayed political sagacity as well as the moral
integrity always associated with him. This letter tells us something of*

My last to you was written in a hurry. . . . My meaning
however, was only to inform, that there were different sentiments
in the Army and as well as in Congress, respecting Continental
and State Funds; some wishing to be thrown upon their respective
States rather than the Continent at large, for payment and that, if
an idea should prevail generally that Congress, or part of its
members of Ministers, bent upon the latter, should *delay* doing
them justice, or *hazard* it in pursuit of their favourite object; it
might create such divisions in the Army as would weaken, rather
than strengthen the hands of those who were disposed to support
Continental measures—and might *tend* to defeat the end they
themselves had in view by endeavouring to involve the Army.

For these reasons I said, or meant to say, the Army was a
dangerous Engine to work with, as it might be made to cut both
ways—and, considering the Sufferings of it, would, more than
probably, throw its weight into that Scale which seemed most
likely to preponderate towards its immediate relief, without
looking forward (under the pressure of present wants) to future
consequences with the eyes of Politicians. . . .

That no man can be more opposed to State funds and local
prejudices than myself, the whole tenor of my conduct has been
one continual evidence of. No man perhaps has had better
opportunities to *see* and to *feel* the pernicious tendency of the latter
than I have—and I endeavor (I hope not altogether ineffectually)
to inculcate them upon the Officers of the Army upon all proper
occasions. . . .Justice must be done them. . . .

6

Trade at a Very Low Ebb
Stephen Higginson to John Adams, Boston, August 8, 1785

As an illustration of precisely where it was that the shoe pinched, this letter from Boston merchant—and wartime privateer owner—Stephen Higginson to the first American minister to the British court is illuminating. The importance attached to Adams's mission to London was such that Adams himself considered it the highest responsibility he had thus far accepted. He and others deeply concerned with the fishing trade and maritime opportunities were well aware that future prospects would remain dim in the face of continuing British hostility to allowing former colonists a share of empire profits. Such hopes as Adams carried with him to London were soon broken on the rock of British indifference, creating or enforcing one more pressure toward strong central government. Both Higginson and Adams became warm supporters of the new regime inaugurated in 1789.

Though I have not the honour of a personal acquaintance with you, I shall, at the desire of a number of Gentlemen in Trade, take the liberty of stating to you briefly the situation of our Commerce, and of making a few observations relative thereto. The importation of foreign merchandise into this State since the peace has so much exceeded the value of our exports, that our Cash has of necessity been exported in great quantities; and though we are now from that cause almost drained of Money, we have yet a very great balance against us without any means of discharging it. By the operation of the British Acts of Navigation we are deprived of a good part of the means of remitting which we formerly enjoyed, and the rest is by the effects of the same Acts rendered less extensive and beneficial than before; our Oil was formerly a good and valuable Article to remit direct to London, our [New England] Rum when exported to Newfoundland, Quebec, and Nova

SOURCE. "Letters of Stephen Higginson," American Historical Association, *Report, 1896,* Volume I, Washington: Government Printing Office, 1897, pp. 719-725.

Scotia furnished us with large Sums in Bills upon Britain, and our new ships when they obtained freight in the British Islands for London and were there sold, served very well as remittance—these several means of remitting with advantage to Europe we have lost . . . we have since the peace remitted very largely in Rice and Tobacco, perhaps more than in our own [New England] exports, but for want of Cash, without which no great quantities of these Articles can be purchased, we shall lose the benefit of exporting them . . .in this view of the matter the trade to [New Foundland] and Quebec is very important also to our Cod-Fishery, since a great proportion of the Fish caught will ever be unfit for any other Market but the West Indies, and our Exports to the Islands must depend upon our having markets for our Imports from hence.

It is perhaps equally important to the British that their Fishery at [New Foundland] should be supplied with Rum and provisions from hence, or the French by having that advantage may very soon vie with if not supplant them in the Fishery; and when they shall be able to supply their own [West Indian] islands they will, by excluding us from them, very much depress our Fishery and encourage their own. This would very much increase their naval strength and prove a great source of national wealth—we seem to have a common interest with the British in checking the French Fishery. . . . If anything beside can check the ardour of the French in pushing their fishery, it must be the local and exposed situation of their Settlements, and the danger from thence of losing all their labour and expence, in case of a War before they shall have acquired such naval strength as to be able to protect them.

The Trade of Massachusetts is now at a very low Ebb and still declining, every branch of it is very much embarrassed and the Whale Fishery almost at an end, another season will probably finish it. Our people embarked with Spirit in this Fishery at the peace, they pushed it with great exertion and success the two seasons past; but being deprived of a Market that will support a living price they have in general quitted the Business already. . . Many of our merchants and Politicians have great expectations from the late Acts of this State imposing heavy Duties upon foreign Vessels and Goods imported in them, others are fearful that none but disagreeable consequences can result from them, at best I think they are but an experiment and the effect very uncertain. . .

Congress are not yet empowered to regulate Trade, nor have they any Funds given them for supporting the public Credit; so great is the jealousy of the States, and so excessive their attachment to local and partial interest, that there is no probability of their giving very soon to Congress the necessary powers for either purpose—nothing short of severe sufferings and sad experience will teach them the necesssity of doing it. Even in this State no Funds can be raised for our own purpose but such as are drawn from Commerce, and this Source is daily lessening. Our prospects therefore, as it relates both to our national Government and our Commerce, is far from being a bright one, and the most sanguine hopes we entertain of a change for the better is from your negotiations with Britain; if this fails, despair and discontent will very generally appear in our Seaport Towns.

7

Licentiousness and Feebleness Threaten Society
John Jay to Thomas Jefferson, New York, October 27, 1786

In the summer of 1786 violence broke out in the hill country of western Massachusetts directed by angry farmers against hard times, landlords, foreclosures, and the Commonwealth's judges. Shays' Rebellion confirmed the worst fears of men of conservative stamp who had been anticipating an outbreak of democratic licentiousness for several years. Debtor relief measures had been paid scant attention by the Massachusetts legislature, but to the former Chief Justice of New York violence signalled the need for a thorough revision of the structure of government in the face of anarchy. In October 1786 Jay was serving his third year as Secretary of the Department of Foreign Affairs after distinguished political and judicial service in New York and national appointments in Paris and Madrid. His views were also shaped by the weakness of his position in negotiating with Spain unsuccessfully for navigation rights on the Mississippi. Like Adams in London, Jay found it

SOURCE. Henry P. Johnston, ed., *The Correspondence and Public Papers of John Jay,*Volume III, New York: G.P. Putnam's Sons, 1891, pp. 212-213.

difficult to win concessions when backed by a goverment without coercive power. Jefferson, when he received Jay's letter, was in Paris as Franklin's successor. There he saw things from a somewhat different perspective.

The inefficacy of our goverment becomes daily more and more apparent. Our treasury and our credit are in a sad situation; and it is probable that either the wisdom or the passions of the people will produce changes. A spirit of licentiousness has infected Massachusetts, which appears more formidable than some at first apprehended. Whether similar symptoms will not soon mark a like disease in several other States is very problematical.

The public papers herewith sent contain everything known about these matters. A reluctance to taxes, an impatience of government, a rage for property and little regard to the means of acquiring it, together with a desire of equality in all things, seem to actuate the mass of those who are uneasy in their circumstances. To these may be added the influence of ambitious adventurers, and the speculations of the many characters who prefer private to public good, and of others who expect to gain more from wrecks made by tempests than from the produce of patient and honest industry. . .

Much, I think, is to be feared from the sentiments which such a state of things is calculated to infuse into the minds of the rational and well-intented. In their eyes, the charms of liberty will daily fade; and in seeking for peace and security, they will too naturally turn towards systems in direct opposition to whose which oppress and disquiet them.

If faction should long bear down law and goverment, tyranny may raise its head, or the more sober part of the people may even think of a king.

In short, my dear sir, we are in a very unpleasant situation. Changes are necessary; but what they ought to be, what they will be, and how and when produced, are arduous questions. I feel for the cause of liberty, and for the honour of my countrymen who have so nobly asserted it, and who, at present so abuse its blessings. If it should not take root in this soil, little pains will be taken to cultivate it in any other.

CHAPTER II
ADOPTION AND
RATIFICATION OF THE
CONSTITUTION
1787 to 1788

1

Madison Outlines a Plan of Union
James Madison to Edmund Randolph, New York,
April 8, 1787

*Between May 1787 and the late summer of 1788 the great issues which
had come to the fore during the years of war and loose confederation were
debated and fought over in the Constitutional Convention at Philadelphia.
The degree of political sophistication exhibited by those who engaged in these
debates was remarkable, nor was this sophistication preponderantly on one
side of the question only. After a generation of close analysis scholars are*

SOURCE. Gaillard Hunt, ed., *The Writings of James Madison*, Volume II, New York:
G.P. Putnam's Sons 1901, pp. 337-340.

certain that ability, education, and wealth were about evenly divided between Nationalists or Federalists and their opponents upon whom they successfully fixed the label Antifederalists or just plain "Antis." So complex is the problem of deciding who acted what part for what reason that discussion of the question has been left to one of the outstanding historians of the Confederation period, Jackson T. Main, whose conclusions complete this chapter. Our focus is upon the Federalists and our primary responsibility to demonstrate why they acted as they did, but there is good reason for ending an examination of the ratification struggle with a reminder that adoption of the Constitution was by an extremely narrow margin and that we cannot even be sure that a majority of the citizenry approved what became the highest law in the land with the Federalist victories in state capitals.

The documents comprising the bulk of Chapter II include selections from what may be termed preparatory correspondence, convention debates, and the great essays known as The Federalist Papers. *Thoughtful reading of the contemporary documents will disclose a dominant theme: the attempt to allay the widespread fear that establishment of a strong national government would destroy the bases of local liberty and individual freedom. It was intuitively understood that the best offense is a good defense. understood that the best offense is a good defense.*

In April 1787 James Madison was attending sessions of the Confederation Congress in New York where a safe haven had been finally found for delegates who had been threatened with musketry by enraged Pennsylvania troops in the summer of 1783. Like others of his colleagues, Madison would be expected to attend sittings of Congress at the same time that the Convention was meeting in Philadelphia during the summer of 1787. There was not longer a question, however, about where priorities lay. Madison was the first delegate to the Convention to arrive in Philadelphia where his claims to pre-eminence among the founders of the United of the United States were to be firmly established. Unlike his collaborator Alexander Hamilton and a good many others of the Nationalist group, Madison had not served in a military capacity during the Revolution but had instead risen steadily through a series of state and national political positions.

In outlining the basic plan which is described in this letter to Randolph, Madison was also carefully courting Virginia's powerful governor. Edmund Randolph, another former military aide to Washington, inherited great landed wealth and one of Virginia's most aristocratic names and as a distinguished lawyer wielded great influence among leaders of the largest of the states. Some weeks later he was to sponsor the so-called "Virginia Plan" for a new constitution, the frame upon which the final structure was built.

I am glad to find that you are turning your thoughts towards the business of May next. My despair of your finding the necessary leisure, as signified in one of your letters, with the probability that some leading propositions at least would be expected from Virginia, had engaged me in a closer attention to the subject than I should otherwise have given. . .

I think with you, that it will be well to retain as much as possible of the old Confederation, though I doubt whether it may not be best to work the valuable articles into the new system, instead of engrafting the latter on the former. I am also perfectly of your opinion, that, in framing a system, no material sacrifices ought to be made to local or temporary prejudices. . . . I am not sure that it will be practicable to present the several parts of the reform in so detached a manner to the States, as that a partial adoption will be binding. Particular States may view different articles as conditions of each other, and would only ratify them as such. Others might ratify them as independent propositions. The consequence would be that the ratifications of both would go for nothing. . .In truth, my ideas of a reform strike so deeply at the old Confederation, and lead to such a systematic change, that they scarcely admit of the expedient.

I hold it for a fundamental point, that an individual independence of the States is utterly irreconcilable with idea of an aggregate sovereignty. I think, at the same time, that a consolidation of the States into a simple republic is not less unattainable than it would be inexpedient. Let it be tried then whether any middle ground can be taken, which will at once support a due supremacy of the national authority, and leave in force the local authorities so far as they can be subordinately useful.

The first step to be taken is, I think, a change in the principle of representation. According to the present form of the Union, an equality of suffrage, if not just towards the larger members of it, is at least safe to them, as the liberty they exercise of rejecting or executing the acts of Congress, is uncontrollable by the nominal sovereignty of Congress. Under a system which would operate without the intervention of the States, the case would be materially altered. A vote from Delaware would have the same effect as one from Massachusetts or Virginia.

Let the national Government be armed with a positive and complete authority in all cases where uniform measures are necessary, as in trade, etc. Let it also retain the powers which it now possesses.

Let it have a negative, in all cases whatsoever, on the Legislative acts of the States, as the King of Great Britain heretofore had. This I conceive to be essential and the least possible abridgement of the State sovereignties. Without such a defensive power, every positive power that can be given on paper will be unavailing. It will also give stability to the States. There has been no moment since the peace at which the Federal assent would have been given to paper money, etc.

Let this national supremacy be extended also to the Judiciary department. If the Judges in the last resort depend on the States, and are bound by their oaths to them and not the Union, the intention of the law and the interests of the nation may be defeated by the obsequiousness of the tribunals to the policy or prejudices of the States. The admiralty jurisdiction may be fully submitted to the National Government.

A Government formed of such extensive powers ought to be well organized. The Legislative department may be divided into two branches. One of them to be chosen everyyears by the Legislatures or the people at large; the other to consist of a more select number, holding their appointments for a longer term, and going out in rotation. Perhaps the negative on the State laws may be most conveniently lodged in this branch. A Council of Revision may be superadded, including the great ministerial officers.

A national Executive will also be necessary. I have scarcely ventured to form my own opinion yet, either of the manner in which it ought to be constituted, or of the authorities with which it ought to be clothed.

An article ought to be inserted expressly guaranteeing the tranquillity of the States against internal as well as external dangers.

To give the new system its proper energy, it will be desirable to have it ratified by the authority of the people, and not merely by that of the Legislatures. . .

The change in the principle of representation will be relished by a majority of the States, and those too of most influence. The northern States will be reconciled to it by the *actual* superiority of their populousness; the Southern by their *expected* superiority on this point. This principle established, the repugnance of the large States to part with power will in a degree subside, and the smaller States must ultimately yield to the predominant will. It is also already seen by many, and must by degrees be seen by all, that, unless the Union be organized efficiently on republican principles, innovations of a much more objectionable form may be obtruded, or . . .the partition of the Empire, into rival and hostile confederacies will ensue.

2

Debates in the Constitutional Convention

On Friday May 25 the Convention was formally organized with the election of Washington as presiding officer. Had James Madison not followed his habit of taking careful notes of what transpired between that day and the final session of September 17, our knowledge of the unvarnished sentiments of the Founders would be scanty. It was immediately decided that the meetings would be private—a tribute to the turbulence of eighteenth-century audiences— and the notes taken by six other delegates are fragmentary. Jefferson asked Madison to publish his Convention journal a few years later as a corrective to Federalist policies that appeared heretical, but Madison wisely declined partly because his own views had changed enough for the journal to have been a source of embarrassment. The selections which follow have been taken from his journal which was not published until 1840. The themes which are emphasized by selection illustrate important aspects for Federalist thinking about federalism, state rights, stability in government, and sectional log-rolling.

SOURCE. Charles C. Tansill, ed., *Documents Illustrative of the Formation of the Union of the American States,* Washington: Government Printing Office, 1927, 279-282, 297-302, 589-594.

TUESDAY, JUNE 26, 1787: THE NEED FOR STABILITY

Mr. Ghoram [Mass.] moved to fill the blank with "six years," one third of the members to go out every second year.

Mr. Wilson [Pa.] 2nded the motion.

Genl. Pinckney [S.C.] opposed six years in favor of four years. The States he said had different interests. Those of the Southern and of S. Carolina in particular were different from the Northern. If the Senators should be appointed for a long term, they wd. settle in the State where they exercised their functions; and would in a little time be rather the representatives of that than of the State appointg. them.

Mr. Read [Del.] movd. that the term be nine years. . .one third going out triennially. He wd. still prefer "during good behavior," but being little supported in that idea, he was willing to take the longest term that could be obtained.

Mr. Broom [Del.] 2nd the motion.

Mr. Madison [Va.] In order to judge of the form to be given to this institution, it will be proper to take a view of the ends to be served by it. These were first to protect the people agst. their rulers; secondly to protect the people agst. the transient impressions into which they themselves might be led. A people deliberating in a temperate moment. . .would first be aware, that those chargd. with the public happiness might betray their trust. An obvious precaution agst. this danger wd. be to divide the trust between different bodies of men, who might watch and check each other. . . . It wd. next occur to such a people, that they themselves were liable to temporary errors, through want of information as to their true interest, and that men chosen for a short term. . .might err from the same cause. This reflection wd. naturally suggest that the Govt. be so constituted, as that one of its branches might have an opportunity of acquiring a competent knowledge of the public interests. . .that as different interests necessarily result from the liberty to be secured, the major interest might under sudden impulses be tempted to commit injustice on the minority. In all civilized Countries the people fall into different classes having a real or supposed difference of interests. There will be creditors and debtors, farmers, merchants, and manufacturers. There will be particularly the distinction of rich and poor. . . We cannot however be regarded even at this time, as one homogeneous mass, in which every thing that affects a part will affect in the same manner the whole. . .An increase of population will of necessity increase the proportion of those who will labour under all the hardships of life, and secretly sigh for a more equal distribution of its blessings. . .According to the equal laws of suffrage, the power will slide into the hands of the former. No agrarian [land equalization] attempts have yet been made in this Country, but symptoms of a leveling spirit, as we have understood, have sufficientlly appeared in certain quarters to give notice of the future danger. How is the danger to be guarded agst. on republican principles?. . .Among other means, by the establishment of a body in the Govt. sufficiently respectable for its wisdom and virtue, to aid on such emergences, the preponderance of justice by throwing its weight into that scale. Such being the objects of the second branch in the proposed Govt. he thought a considerable duration ought to be given to it. . .

Mr. Sherman [Conn.] Govt. is instituted for those who live under it. . .The more permanency it has the worse if it be a bad Govt. Frequent elections are necessary to preserve the good behavior of rulers. . .He wished to have provision made for steadiness and wisdom in the system to be adopted; but he thought six or four years would be sufficient. . .

Mr. Hamilton [N.Y.] He did not mean to enter particularly into the subject. He concurred with Mr. Madison in thinking we were now to decide forever the fate of Republican Government; and that if we did not give to that form due stability and wisdom, it would be disgraced and lost among ourselves, disgraced and lost to mankind for ever. He acknowledged himself not to think favorably of Republican Government; but addressed his remarks to those who did think favorably of it, in order to prevail on them to tone their Government as high as possible. He professed himself to be as zealous an advocate for liberty as any man whatever and trusted he should be as willing a martyr to it though he differed as to the form in which it was most eligible. . . He rose principally to remark that [Mr. Sherman] seemed not to recollect that one branch of the proposed Govt. was so formed as to render it particularly the guardians of the poorer order of Citizens. . .Under the British system as well as the federal, many of the great powers appertaining to Govt. . . were not in the hands of the

Govt. there. . .Of late the Govermt. had entirely given way to the people, and had in fact suspended many of its ordinary functions in order to prevent those turbulent scenes which had appeared elsewhere. He asks [Mr. Sherman] whether the State [of Connecticut] at this time dare impose and collect a tax on the people? To these causes, and not to the frequency of elections, the effects, as far as it existed ought to be chiefly ascribed.

FRIDAY, JUNE 29, 1787: THE ROLE OF THE STATES IN THE UNION

Doctr. Johnson [Conn.] The controversy must be endless whilst Gentlemen differ in the grounds of their arguments; those on one side considering the States as districts of people composing one political Society; those on the other considering them as so many political societies. The fact is that the States do exist as political Societies, and a Govt. is to be formed for them in their political capacity, as well as for the individuals composing them. Does it not seem to follow that if the States as such are to exist they must be armed with some power of self-defense. This is the idea of [Col. George Mason of Va.] who appears to have looked to the bottom of the matter. Besides the Aristocratic and other interests, which ought to have the means of defending themselves, the States have their interests as such, and equally entitled to like means. On the whole he thought that . . the two ideas embraced on different sides, instead of being opposed to each other, ought to be combined; that in *are* branch the *people* ought to be represented, in the *other* the *States*.

Mr. Ghoran [Mass.] The States as now confederated have no doubt a right to refuse to be consolidated. . .But he wished the small States which seemed most ready to object, to consider which are to give up most, they or the larger ones. He conceived that a rupture of the Union wd. be an event unhappy for all, but surely the large States would be least unable to take care of themselves and to make connections with one another. The weak therefore were most interested in establishing some general system for maintaining order. . .What would be the situation of Delaware in case of a separation of the States? Would she not lie at the mercy of Pennsylvania? Would not her true interest lie in being consolidated with her. . .as will put it out of the power of Pena. to oppress her?. . .Masst. was originally three colonies. . .and every distinction is now forgotten. The case was similar with Connecticut and Newhaven. The dread of union was reciprocal. . .In like manner N. Jersey had been made one society out of two parts. Should a separation of the States take place, the fate of N. Jersey wd. be worst of all. She has no foreign commerce and can have but little. Pa. and N. York will continue to levy taxes on her consumption. . .He shd. consider it as his duty if his colleagues viewed the matter in the same light he did, to stay here as long as any other State would remain with them, in order to agree on some plan that could with propriety be recommended to the people. . .

Mr. Madison [Va.] agreed with Docr. Johnson, that the mixed nature of the Govt. ought to be kept in view; but thought too much stress was laid on the rank of the States as political societies. . .Under the proposed Govt. the powers of the States would be much farther reduced. . .It will in particular have the power, without the consent of the State Legislatures, to levy money directly on the people themselves. . .

He entreated the gentlemen representing the small States to renounce a principle wch. was confessedly unjust, which cd. never be admitted. . .He prayed them to ponder well the consequences of suffering the Confederacy to go to pieces. . .Let each state depend on itself for its security, and let apprehensions arise of danger from distant powers or from the neighboring States, and the languishing condition of all the States, large as well as small, wd. soon be transformed into vigorous and high toned Govt. His great fear was that their Govts. wd. then have too much energy, that these might not only be formidable in the large to the small States, but fatal to the internal liberty of all. The same causes that have rendered the old world the Theatre of incessant wars and have banished liberty from the face of it, would soon produce the same effects here. The weakness and jealousy of the small States wd. quickly introduce some regular military force agst. sudden danger from their powerful neighbors. The example wd. be followed by others, and wd. soon become universal. . .Throughout all Europe, the armies kept up under the pretext of defending, have enslaved the people. . .The insular situation of G. Britain was the principal cause of her being an exception to the general fate of Europe. . .These consequences he conceived ought to be apprehended whether the States should run into a total separation from each other or shd. enter into partial confederacies. Either event wd. be truly deplorable; and those who might be accessary to either, could never be forgiven by their Country, nor themselves.

Mr. Hamilton [N.Y.]. . .It has been said that if the smaller States renounce their *equality,* they renounce at the same time their *liberty.* The truth is, it is a contest for power, not for liberty, Will the men composing the small States be less free than those comprising the larger. The State of Delaware having 40,000 souls will *lose power* if she has 1/10 only of the votes allowed to Pa. having 400,000: but will the people of Del. be *less free,* if each citizen has an equal vote with each citizen of Pa. He admitted that common residence within the same State would produce a certain degree of attachment; and that this principle might have a certain influence in public affairs. He thought however that this might by some precautions be in a great measure excluded, and that no material inconvenience could result from it, as there could not be any ground for combination among the States whose influence was most dreaded. . .Some of the consequences of a dissolution of the Union, and the establishment of partial confederacies, had been pointed out. He would add another of a most serious nature. Alliances will immediately be formed with different rival and hostile nations of Eurupe, who will foment disturbances among ourselves and make us parties to their own quarrels. Foreign Nations having American dominions are and must be jealous of us. . .It had been said that respectability in the eyes of foreign Nations was not the object at which we aimed; that the proper object of republican Government was domestic tranquility and happiness. This was an ideal distinction. No Government could give us tranquility and happiness at home which did not possess sufficient stability and strength to make us respectable abroad. This was the critical moment for forming such a Government. We should run every risk in trusting to future amendments. . . It is a miracle that we were now here exercising our tranquil and free deliberations on the subject. It would be madness to trust to future miracles. . . . on the subject. It would be madness to trust to future miracles. . .

WEDNESDAY, AUGUST 22, 1787: SLAVERY

Mr. Sherman [Conn.] was for leaving the clause as it stands. He disapproved of the slave trade; yet as the States were now possessed of the right to import slaves, as the public good did not require it to be taken from them, and as it was expedient to have as few objections as possible to the proposed scheme of Government, he thought it best to leave the matter as we find it. He observed that the abolition of Slavery seemed to be going on in the U.S. and that the good sense of the several States would probably by degrees compleat it. He urged on the Convention the necessity of despatching its business.

Col. Mason [Va.] This infernal trafic originated in the avarice of British Merchants. The British Govt. constantly checked the attempts of Virginia to put a stop to it. The present question concerns not the importing States alone but the whole Union. The evil of having slaves was experienced during the late war. Had slaves been treated as they might have been by the Enemy, they would have proved dangerous instruments in their hands. . .Maryland and Virginia he said had already prohibited the importation of slaves expressly. N. Carolina had done the same in substance. All this would be in vain if S. Carolina and Georgia be at liberty to import. The Western people are already calling out for slaves for their new lands. . .Slavery discourages arts and manufactures. The poor despise labor when performed by slaves. They prevent the immigration of Whites, who really enrich and strengthen a Country. They produce the most pernicious effect on manners. Every master of slaves is born a petty tyrant. They bring the judgement of heaven on a Country. . . By an inevitable chain of causes and effects providence punishes national sins, by national calamities. He lamented that some of our Eastern brethren had from a lust of gain embarked in this nefarious traffic. . .He held it essential in every point of view that the Genl. Govt. should have power to prevent the increase of slavery.

Mr. Ellsworth [Conn.] As he had never owned a slave could not judge the effects of slavery on character. He said however that if it was to be considered in a moral light we ought to go farther and free those already in the Country—As slaves also multiply so fast in Virginia and Maryland that it is cheaper to raise them than import them, wilst in the sickly rice swamps foreign supply is necessary; if we go no farther than is urged, we shall be unjust towards S. Carolina and Georgia. Let us not intermeddle. As population increases poor laborers will be so plenty as to render slaves useless. Slavery in time wil not be a speck in our Country. Provision is already made in Connecticut for abolishing it. And the abolition has already taken place in Massachusetts. . .

Mr. Pinckney [S.C.] If slavery be wrong, it is justified by the example of all the world. He cited the case of Greece and Rome and other ancient states; the sanction given by France, England, Holland and other modern States. In all ages one half of mankind have been slaves. If the S. States were let alone they will probably of themselves stop importations. He wd. himself as a Citizen of S. Carolina vote for it. An attempt to take away the right as proposed will produce serious objections to the Constitution which he wished to see adopted.

Gen. C. C. Pinckney [S.C.] declared it to be his firm opinion that if himself and all his colleagues were to sign the Constitution and use their personal influence, it would be of no avail towards obtaining the assent of their constituents. S. Carolina and Georgia cannot do without slaves. As to Virginia she will gain by stopping the importations. Her slaves will rise in value, and she has more than she wants. It would be unequal to require S.C. and Georgia to confederate on such terms. . .He contended that the importation of slaves would be for the interest of the whole Union. . . . The more slaves, the more produce. . .the more consumption. . .the more revenue for the common treasury. He admitted it be reasonable that slaves should be dutied. . . Mr. Sherman [Conn.] observed that the clause had been agreed to and therefore could not be committed.

Mr. Randolph [Va.] was for committing in order that some middle ground might, if possible, be found. He could never agree to the clause as it stands. He wd. sooner risk the constitution. He dwelt on the dilemma to which the Convention was exposed. By agreement to the clause, it would revolt the Quakers, the Methodists, and many others in the States having no slaves. On the other hand, two States might be lost to the Union. Let us then, he said, try the chance of a commitment.

On the question for committing the remaining part of Sect. 4

and 5 of article 7: N.H. no; Mass, absent; Conn. ay; N.J. ay; Pa. no; Del. no; Va. ay; Md. ay; N.C. ay; S.C. ay; Ga. ay.

MONDAY, SEPTEMBER 17, 1787: AN ACT OF FAITH

The engrossed Constitution being read, Docr. Franklin rose with a speech in his hand, which he had reduced to writing for his own conveniency, and which Mr. Wilson [Pa.] read in the following words.

Mr. President, I confess that there are several parts of this constitution which I do not at present approve, but I am not sure I shall never approve them: For having lived long, I have experienced many instances of being obliged by better information, or fuller consideration, to change opinions even on important subjects, which I once thought right, but found to be otherwise. It is therefore that the older I grow, the more apt I am to doubt my own judgement, and to pay more respect to the judgement of others. Most men indeed as well as most sects in Religion, think themselves in possession of all truth, and the wherever others differ from them it is so far error. . .But though many private persons think almost as highly of their own infallibility as that of their sect, few express it so naturally as a certain french lady, who in dispute with her sister, said, "I don't know how it happens, sister, but I meet with no body but myself, that's always in the right. . ."

In these sentiments, Sir, I agree to this Constitution with all its faults, if they are such; because I think a general Government necessary for us, and there is no form of Government but what may be a blessing to the people if well administered, and believe farther that this is likely to be well administered for a course of years, and can only end in Despotism, as other forms have done before it, when the people shall become so corrupted as to need despotic Government, being incapable of any other. . . . If every one of us in returning to our Constituents were to report the objections he has had to it, and endeavor to gain partizans in support of them, we might prevent its being generally received, and thereby lose all the salutary and great advantages resulting naturally in our favor among foreign Nations as well as among ourselves, from our real or apparent unanimity. . .On the whole, sir, I can not help expressing a wish that every member of the Convention who may still have objections to it, would with me, on this occasion doubt a little of his own infallibility, and to make manifest our unanimity, put his name to this instrument. He then moved that the Constitution be signed by the members and offered the following as a convenient form, viz. "Done in Convention by the unanimous consent of *the States* present the 17th of Sept. In witness whereof we have hereunto subscribed our names."

This ambiguous form had been drawn up by Mr. G[ouverneur] M[orris] in order to gain the dissenting members, and put into the hands of Docr. Franklin that it might have the better chance of success. . . [A last minute motion was made to increase the size of the House ofRepresentatives by allowing one representative for each 30,000 persons as opposed to 40,000. The President of the Convention, George Washington, commended the amendment as well as the Constitution generally, and the amendment was adopted.]

The Constitution being signed by all the members except Mr. Randolph, Mr. Mason, and Mr. Gerry, who declined giving it the sanction of their names, the Convention dissolved itself by an Adjournment sine die. . . .

3

The Federalist Papers
Addressed by Hamilton, Madison, and Jay to the People of the State of New York between October 27, 1787 and May 28, 1788

Any attempt to comprehend and interpret the Constitution of the United States must include study of the eighty-five essays composed by Alexander Hamilton, James Madison, and John Jay in their attempt to influence the outcome of the intense struggle for ratification in New York State. The plan to undertake this ambitious project was made by Hamilton, according to Jacob, E. Cooke, editor with Harold C. Syrett of Hamilton's papers and the editor of the edition of The Federalist from which these selections have been taken. The first seventy-seven essays appeared in New York City newspapers in installments, the remaining eight with the others in book form at the end of May 1788.

Defenders of the Constitution were thrown on the defensive by virulent attacks against a plan which opponents insisted would erode the liberties of individual citizens and the freedom of the states while fastening dangerous monarchical and aristocratic institutions upon them. The tone of The Federalist *is sober and reassuring. The defects of government under the Articles of Confederation have been catalogued by the authors and the advantages of the new regime argued with great skill. Clearly, Alexander Hamilton was less satisfied with the interpretation of the Constitution exhibited by* The Federalist *than was Madison, althought most of the men who helped frame it held reservations about its adequacy. Future developments showed Hamilton attempting to move toward greater strength at the center, Madison toward less.*

While no student of the Federalist *essays will agree that selections from*

SOURCE. Jacob E. Cooke, ed., *The Federalist*, Cleveland and New York: The World Publishing Company, pp. 56-65, 471-480, 523-530. Reprinted by permission of Wesleyan University Press

numbers ten, seventy, and seventy-eight adequately present the case for the Constitution as made by its advocates, few would wish to leave any one of the three out of a short list. They are, as Professor Clinton Rossiter notes in the introduction to his own edition of The Federalist Papers *(New York: The New American Library of World Literature, Incorporated, Mentor Books, 1961, p. xvii) among the most frequently reprinted, and the three problems posed and answered here—the probable effects of basing political activity upon the claims of competing interest groups, of establishing a strong executive, and of creating an independent judiciary—well represent Federalist thinking about the citizen and the state, the new central government and the individual states. All of the essays in the series were printed over the pseudonym, "Publius." New York ratified on July 26, 1788 by the narrow margin of 30 to 27.*

Number 10: Advantages of a Democratic Republic
JAMES MADISON

Among the numerous advantages promised by a well constructed Union, none deserves to be more accurately developed than its tendency to break and control the violence of faction. The friend of popular governments, never finds himself so much alarmed for their character and fate, as when he contemplates their propensity to this dangerous vice. He will not fail therefore to set a due value on any plan which, without violating the principles to which he is attached, provides a proper cure for it. . .It will be found indeed, on a candid review of our situation, that some of the distresses under which we labor, have been erroneously charged on the operation of our governments; but it will be found, at the same time, that other causes will not alone account for many of our heaviest misfortunes; and particularly, for that prevailing and increasing distrust of public engagements, and alarm for private rights, which are echoed from one end of the continent to the other. These must be chiefly, if not wholly, effects of the unsteadiness and injustice, with which factious spirit has tainted our public administrations.

By faction I understand a number of citizens, whether amounting to a majority or minority of the whole, who are united and actuated by some common impulse or passion, or of interest, adverse to the rights of other citizens, or to the permanent and aggregate interests of the community.

There are two methods of curing the mischiefs of faction: the one, by removing its cause; the other, by controling its effects. There are again two methods of removing the causes of faction: the one by destroying the liberty which is essential to its existence; the other, by giving to every citizen the same opinions, the same passions, and the same interests.

It could never be more truly said than of the first remedy, that it is worse than the disease. Liberty is to faction, what air is to fire, an aliment without which it instantly expires. But it could not be less folly to abolish liberty, which is essential to political life, because it nourishes faction, that it would be to wish the annihilation of air, which is essential to animal life, because it imparts to fire its destructive agency.

The second expedient is as impracticable, as the first would be unwise. As long as the reason of man continues fallible and he is at liberty to exercise, it, different opinions will be formed. As long as the connection subsists between his reason and his self-love, his opinions and his passions will have a reciprocal influence on each other; and the former will be objects to which the latter will attach themselves. The diversity in the faculties of men from which the rights of property originate, is not less an insuperable obstacle to a uniformity of interests. The protection of these faculties is the first object of Government. From the protection of different and unequal faculties of acquiring property, the possession of different degrees and kinds of property immediately results: and from the influence of these on the sentiments and views of the respective proprietors, ensues a division of the society into different interests and parties.

The latent causes of faction are thus sown in the nature of man; and we see them every where brought into different degrees of activity, according to the different circumstances for civil society. A zeal of different opinions concerning religion, concerning Government and many other points, as well of speculation as of practice; an attachment to different leaders ambitiously contending for pre-eminence and power; or to persons of other descriptions whose fortunes have been interesting to the human passions, have in turn divided mankind into parties, inflamed them with mutual animosity, and rendered them much more disposed to vex and oppress each other, than to co-operate for their common good. So strong is this propensity of mankind to fall into mutual animosities, that where no substantial occasion presents itself, the most frivolous and fanciful distinctions have been sufficient to kindle their unfriendly passions, and excite their most violent conflicts. But the most common and durable source of factions, has been the various and unequal distribution of property. Those who hold, and those who are without property, have ever formed distinct interests in society. Those who are creditors, and those who are debtors, fall under a like discrimination. A landed interest, a manufacturing interest, a mercantile interest, a monied interest, with many lesser interests, grow up of necessity in civilized nations, and divide them into different classes, actuated by different sentiments and views. The regulation of these various and interfering interests forms the principal task of modern Legislation, and involves the spirit of party and faction in the necessary and ordinary operations of Government.

No man is allowed to be a judge in his own cause; because his interest would certainly bias his judgment, and, not improbably, corrupt his integrity. With equal, nay with greater reason, a body of men, are unfit to be both judges and parties, at the same time; yet, what are many of the most important acts of legislation, but so many judicial determinations, not indeed concerning the rights of single persons, but concerning the rights of large bodies of citizens; and what are the different classes of legislators, but advocates and parties to the causes which they determine? Is a law proposed concerning private debts? It is a question to which the creditors are parties on one side, and the debtors on the other. Justice ought to hold the balance between them. Yet the parties are and must be themselves the judges; and the most numerous party, or, in other words, the most powerful faction must be expected to prevail. Shall domestic manufactures be encouraged, and in what degree, by restrictions on foreign manufactures? are questions which would be differently decided by the landed and manufacturing classes; and probably by neither, with a sole regard to justice and the public good. The apportionment of taxes on the various descriptions of property, is an act which seems to require the most exact impartiality; yet, there is perhaps no legislative act in which greater opportunity and temptation are given to a predominant party, to trample on the rules of justice. Every shilling with which they over-burden the inferior number, is a shilling saved to their pockets.

It is in vain to say, that enlightened statesmen will be able to adjust these clashing interests, and render them all subservient to the public good. Enlightened statesmen will not always be at the helm: Nor, in many cases, can such an adjustment be made at all, without taking into view indirect and remote considerations, which will rarely prevail over the immediate interest which one party may find in disregarding the rights of another, or the good of the whole.

The inference to which we are brought is, that the *causes* of faction cannot be removed; and that relief is only to be sought in the means of controlling its *effects*.

If a faction consists of less than a majority, relief is supplied by the republican principle, which enables the majority to defeat its sinister views by regular vote: it may clog the administration, it may convulse the society; but it will be unable to execute and mask its violence under the forms of the Constitution. When a majority is included in a faction, the form of popular government on the other hand enables it to sacrifice to its ruling passion or interest, both the public good and rights of other citizens. To secure the public good, and private rights, against the danger of such a faction, and at the same time to preserve the spirit and form of popular government, is then the great object to which our enquiries are directed: Let me add that it is the great desideratum, by which alone this form of government can be rescued form the opprobrium under which it has so long labored, and be recommended to the esteem and adoption of mankind.

By what means is this object attainable? Evidently by one of two only. Either the existence of the same passion or interest in a majority at the same time, must be prevented; or the majority, having such co-existent passion or interest, must be rendered, by their number and local situation, unable to concert and carry into effect schemes of oppression. If the impulse and the opportunity be suffered to coincide, we well know that neither moral nor religious motives can be relied on as an adequate control. They are not found to be such on the injustice and violence of individuals, and lose their efficacy in proportion to the number combined together; that is, in proportion as their efficacy becomes needful.

From this view of the subject, it may be concluded that a pure Democracy, by which I mean a Society, consisting of a small number or citizens, who assemble and administer the Government in person, can admit of no cure for the mischiefs of faction. A common passion or interest will, in almost every case, be felt by a majority of the whole; a communication and concert results from the form of Government itself; and there is nothing to check the inducements to sacrifice the weaker party, or an obnoxious individual. Hence it is, that such Democracies have ever been spectacles of turbulence and contention; have ever been found incompatible with personal security, or the rights of property; and have in general been as short in their lives, as they have been violent in their deaths. Theoretic politicians, who have patronized this species of Government, have erroneously supposed, that by reducing mankind to a perfect equality in their political rights, they would at the same time, be perfectly equalized and assimilated in their possessions, their opinions, and their passions.

A Republic, by which I mean a Government in which the scheme of representation takes place, opens a different prospect, and promises the cure for which we are seeking. Let us examine the points in which it varies from pure Democracy, and we shall comprehend both the nature of the cure, and the efficacy which it must derive from the Union.

The two great points of difference between a Democracy and a Republic are, first, the delegation of the Government, in the latter, to a small number of citizens elected by the rest; secondly, the greater number of citizens, and greater sphere of country, over which the latter may be extended.

The effect of the first difference is, on the one hand to refine and enlarge the public views, by passing them though the medium of a chosen body of citizens, whose wisdom may best discern the true interest of their country, and whose patriotism and love of justice, will be least likely to sacrifice it to temporary or partial considerations. . .On the other hand, the effect may be inverted. Men of factious tempers, of local prejudices, or of sinister designs, may by intrigue, by corruption or by other means, first obtain the suffrages, and then betray the interests of the people. The question resulting is, whether small or extensive Republics are most favorable to the election of proper guardians of the public weal: and it is clearly decided in favor of the latter by two obvious considerations.

In the first place it is to be remarked that however small the Republic may be, the Representatives must be raised to a certain

number, in order to guard against the cabals of a few; and that
however large it may be, they must be limited to a certain
number, in order to guard against the confusion of a multitude.
Hence the number of Representatives in the two cases, and being
proportinally greatest in the small Republic, it follows, that if the
proportion of fit characters, be not less, in the large than in the
small Republic, the former will present a greater option, and
consequently a greater option, and consequently a greater probability of a fit choice. probability of a fit choice..

NUMBER 70: NECESSITY OF A STRONG EXECUTIVE
ALEXANDER HAMILTON

There is an idea, which is not without its advocates, that a
vigorous executive is inconsistent with the genius of republican
government. The enlightened well wishers of this species of
government must at least hope that the supposition is destitute of
foundation; since they can never admit its truth, without at the
same admitting the condemnation of their own principles. Energy
in the executive is a leading character in the definition of good
government. It is essential to the protection of the community
against foreign attacks: It is not less essential to the steady
administration of the laws, to the protection of property against
those irregular and high handed combinations, which sometimes
interrupt the ordinary course of justice, to the security of liberty
against the enterprises and assaults of ambition, of faction, and of
anarchy. Every man the least conversant in Roman story knows
how often that republic was obliged to take refuge in the absolute
power of a single man, under the formidable title of dictator, as
well against the intrigues of ambitious individuals. . .as against
the invasions of external enemies. . . .

There can be no need however to multiply arguments or
examples on this head. A feeble executive implies a feeble execution of the government. A feeble execution is but another
phrase for a bad execution: And a government ill executed,
whatever it may be in theory, must be in practice a bad government. . . .

The ingredients, which constitute energy in the executive, are first unity, secondly duration, thirdly an adequate provision for its support, fourthly competent powers.

The circumstances which constitute safety in the republican sense are, 1st. a due dependence on the people, secondly a due responsibility. . . .

That unity is conducive to energy will not be disputed. Decision, activity, secrecy, and dispatch will generally characterise the proceedings of one man, in a much more eminent degree, than the proceedings of any greater number; and in proportion as the number is increased, these qualities will be diminished.

This unity may be destroyed in two ways; either by vesting the power in two or more magistrates of equal dignity and authority; or vesting it ostensibly in one man, subject in whole or in part to the control and co-operation of others, in the capacity of counsellors to him. Of the first the two consuls of Rome may serve as an example; of the last we shall find examples in the constitutions of several of the states. New York and New Jersey, if I recollect right, are the only states, which have entrusted the executive authority wholly to single men. . . .

Wherever two or more persons are engaged in any common enterprize or pursuit, there is always danger of difference of opinion. If it be a public trust or office in which they are cloathed with equal dignity and authority, there is peculiar danger of personal emulation and even animosity. From either and especially from all these causes, the most bitter dissentions are apt to spring. Whenever these happen, they lessen the respectability, weaken the authority, and distract the plans and operations of those whom they divide. If they should unfortunately assail the supreme executive magistracy of a country, consisting of a plurality of persons, they might impede or frustrate the most important measures of the government, in the most critical emergencies of the state. And what is still worse, they might split the community into the most violent and irreconcilable factions, adhering differently to the different individuals who composed the magistracy.

Men often oppose a thing merely because they have had no agency in planning it, or because it may have been planned by those whom they dislike. But if they have been consulted and have happened to disapprove, opposition then becomes in their estimation and indispensable duty of self love. They seem to think themselves bound in honor, and by all the motives of personal infallibility to defeat the success of what has been resolved upon contrary to their sentiments. . . .

Upon the principles of a free government, inconveniencies from the source just mentioned must necessarily be submitted to in the formation of the legislature; but it is unnecessary and therefore unwise to introduce them into the constitution of the executive. It is here too that they may be most pernicious. In the legislature, promptitude of decision is oftener an evil than a benefit. The differences of opinion, and the jarrings of parties in that department of the government, though they may sometimes obstruct salutary plans, yet often promote deliberation and circumspection; and serve to check execess in the majority. When a resolution too is once taken, the opposition must be at an end. That resolution is law, and resistance to it punishable. But no favourable circumstance palliate or atone for the disadvantages of dissention in the executive department. . . . They constantly counteract those qualities in the executive, which are the most necessary ingredients in its composition, vigour and expedition, and this without any counterbalancing good. In the conduct of war, in which the energy of the executive is the bulwark of the national security, every thing would be to be apprehended from its plurality. . . .

But one of the weightiest objections to a plurality in the executive, and which lies as much against the last as the first plan, is that it tends to conceal faults, and destroy responsibility. Responsibility is of two kinds, to censure and to punishment, The first is the most important of the two; especially in an elective office. Man, in public trust, will much oftener act in such a manner as to render him unworthy of being any longer trusted, than in such a manner as to make him obnoxious to legal punishment. But the multiplication of the executive adds to the difficulty of detection in either case. . . .

It is evident from these considerations, that the plurality of the excutive tends to deprive the people of the two greatest securities they can have for the faithful exercise of any delegated power; first, the restraints of public opinion, which lose their efficacy as well on account of the division of the censure attendant on bad measures among a number, as on account of the uncertainty on whom it ought to fall; and secondly, the opportunity of discovering with facility and clearness the misconduct of the persons they trust in order either to their removal from office, or to their actual pusnishment, in cases which admit of it. . . .

NUMBER 78: AN INDEPENDENT JUDICIARY
ALEXANDER HAMILTON

. . .The complete independence of the courts of justice is peculiarly essential in a limited constitution. By a limited constitution I understand one which contains certain specified exceptions to the legislative authority; such for instance as that it shall pass no bills of attainder, no *ex post facto laws,* and the like. Limitations of this kind can be preserved in practice no other way than through the medium of the courts of justice; whose duty it must be to declare all acts contrary to the manifest tenor of the constitution void. Without this, all the reservations of particular rights or privileges would amount to nothing.

Some perplexity respecting the right of the courts to pronounce legislative acts void, because contrary to the constitution, has arisen from an imagination that the doctrine would imply a superiority of the judiciary to the legislative power. It is urged that the authority which can declare the acts of another void, must necessarily be superior to the one whose acts may be declared void. As this doctrine is of great importance in all the American constitutions, a brief discussion of the grounds on which it rests cannot be unacceptable.

There is no position which depends on clearer principles, than that every act of a delegated authority, contrary to the tenor of the commission under which it is exercised, is void, No legislative act therefore contrary to the consitution can be valid. To deny this would be to affirm that the deputy is greater than his principal; that the servant is above the master; that the representatives of the people are superior to the people themselves; that men acting by virtue of powers may do not only what their powers do not authorize, but what they forbid.

If it be said that the legislative body are themselves the constitutional judges of their own powers, and that the construction they put upon them is conclusive upon the other departments, it may be answered, that this cannot be the natural presumption, where it to is not be collected from any particular provisions in the constitution. It is not otherwise to be supposed that the constitution could intend to enable the representatives of the people to substitute their *will* to that of their constituents. It is far more rational to suppose that the courts were designed to be an intermediate body between the people and the legislature, in order, among other things, to keep the latter within the limits assigned to their authority. The interpretation op laws is the profer and peculiar province of the courts. A constitution is in fact, and must be, regarded by the judges as a fundamental law. It therefore belongs to them to ascertain its meaning as well as the meaning of any particular act proceeding from the legislative body. If there should happen to be irreconcileable variance between the two, that which has the superior obligation and validity ought of course to be preferred; or in other words, the constitution ought to be preferred to the statute, the intention of the people to the intention of their agents.

Nor does this conclusion by any means suppose a superiority of the judicial to the legislative power. It only supposes that the power of the people is superior to both; and that where the will of the legislature declared in its statutes, stands in opposition to that the people declared in the constitution, the judges ought to be governed by the latter, rather than the former. They ought to regulate their decisions by the fundamental laws, rather than by those which are not fundamental. . . .

That inflexible and uniform adherence to the rights of the constitution and of individuals, which we perceive to be indispensable in the courts of justice, can certainly not be expected from judges who hold their offices by a temporay commission. Periodical appointments, however regulated, or by whomsoever made, would in some way or other be fatal to their necessary independence. If the power of making them was committed to either the executive or legislature, there would be danger of an improper complaisance to the branch which possessed it; if to both, there would be an unwillingness to hazard the displeasure of either; if to the people, or to person chosen by them for the special purpose, there would be too great a disposition to consult popularity, to justify a reliance that nothing would be consulted but the constitution and the laws. . . .

Upon the whole there can be no room to doubt that the convention acted wisely in copying from the models of those constitutions which have established *good behaviour* as the tenure of their judicial offices in point of duration; and that so far from being blameable on this account, their plan would have been enexcuseably defective if it had wanted this important feature of good government. The experience of Great Britain affords an illustrious comment on the excellence of the institution.

4

Speeches in the Ratifying Conventions of Pennsylvania and Virginia October 1787 - June 1788

Both Madison's notes of the debates in the Federal Convention and the Federalist Papers are essential reading for anyone attempting to understand how the men who adopted the Constitution also interpreted it, but an examination of the records of debates in the state ratifying conventions are more revealing than either. Later in life Madison declared that it had been the state conventions where the people were most closely represented that had breathed life into the Constitution. Fortunately, the records of the state conventions were collected by Jonathan Elliot in 1830 and a second edition published by request of both houses of Congress six years later at a time of increasing concern over the matter of states' rights and Federal authority. From this second edition these brief selections have been taken.

The first introduces James Wilson of Pennsylvania, an immigrant from Scotland whose knowledge of the law and of British and American constitutional history placed him in a very select company of contemporary scholar-statesmen. Washington named him to the first Supreme Court , and except for he speculation and bankruptcy which brought him, like Robert Morris, to disgrace, he would be well known to Americans, who have not been

---

SOURCE: Jonathan Elliot, ed., *The Debates in the Several State Conventions on the Adoption of the Federal Constitution,* 2nd edition, Philadelphia: J.B. Lippincott and Company, 1863, Volume II, pp. 434-437, 498-499, Volume III, pp. 618-622, 652.

particulary charitable about such failings. Here Wilson explains why a bill of rights had been omitted from the new Constititution and emphasizes both the sovereignty of the people in American and enumerated powers granted to the federal government.

Madison, in the second selection, faces the issue which has so often plagued the history of American federalism—the problem of sectional interests and the existence of slavery. Governor Edmund Randolph's decision to vote for ratification after his refusal to sign his name to the work of the Convention in Philadelphia owed much to the enterprise and courage of Madison who, more than any other, had borne the weight of Patrick Henry's scornful attacks in debate. Before the decade of the 1790's had passed all three had reversed their fields, a tribute to the pragmatic temper of American political life.

PHILADELPHIA, JAMES WILSON: THE SOVEREIGNTY OF THE PEOPLE

[October 28, 1787] This will be a proper time for making an observation or two on what may be called the preamble to this Constitution. I had occasion, on a former day, to mention that the leading principle in the politics, and that which pervades the American constitutions, is, that the supreme power resides in the people. This Constitution, Mr. President, opens with a solemn and practical recognition of that principle: "We, the *people of the United States,* in order to form a more perfect union, establish justice, etc., *do ordain* and establish this Constitution for the United States of America." It is announced in *their* name—it receives its political existence from *their* authority: they ordain and establish. What is the necessary consequence? Those who ordain and establish have the power, if they think proper, to repeal and annul. A proper attention to this principle may, perhaps, give ease to the minds of some who have heard much concerning the necessity of a bill of rights.

Its establishment, I apprehend, has more force than a volume written on the subject. It renders this truth evident—that the people have a right to do what they please with regard to the government. I confess I feel a kind of pride in considering the striking difference between the foundation on which the liberties of this country are declared to stand in this Constitution and the footing on which the liberties of England are said to be placed. The Magna Charta of England is an instrument of high value to the people of that country. But, Mr. President, from what source does that instrument derive the liberties of the inhabitants of that kingdom? Let it speak for itself. The king says, *"We* have *given* and *granted* to all archbishops, bishops, abbots, priors, earls, barons, and to all the freemen of this realm, these liberties following,to be kept in our kingdom of England forever." When this was assumed as the leading principle of that government, it was no wonder that the people were anxious to obtain bills of rights, and to take every opportunity of enlarging and securing their liberties. But here, Sir, the fee-simple remains in the people at large, and by this Constitution they do not part with it.

I am called upon to give a reason why the Convention omitted to add a bill of rights to the work before you. . . I cannot say, Mr. President, what were the reaons of every member of that Convention for not adding a bill of rights. I believe the truth is, that such an idea never entered the mind of many of them. I do not recollect to have heard the subject mentioned till within about three days of the time of our rising; and even then there was no direct motion offered for any thing of the kind. . . . A proposition to adopt a measure that would have supposed that we were throwing into the general government every power not expressly reserved by the people, would have been spurned at, in that house, with the greatest indignation. Even in a single government, if the powers of the people rest on the same establishment as is expressed in this Constitution, a bill of rights is by no means a necessary measure. In a government possessed of enumerated powers, such a measure would be not only unnecessary, but preposterous and dangerous. Whence comes this notion, that in the United States there is no security without a bill of rights? [Wilson pointed out that at least six of the state constitutions contained no bills of rights.] . . . this enumeration, sir, will serve to show by experience, as well as principle, that, even in single governments, a bill of rights is not an essential or necessary measure. But in a government consisting of enumerated powers, such as is proposed for the United States, a bill of rights would not only be unnecessary, but, in my humble judgment, highly imprudent. In all societies there are many powers and rights which cannot be particularly enumerated. A bill of rights annexed to a constitution is *an enumeration of the powers reserved.* If we attempt an enumeration, every thing that is not enumerated is presumed to be given. The consequence is, that an imperfect enumeration would throw all implied power into the scale of the government, and the rights of the people would be rendered incomplete. But of the two, it is much safer to run the risk on the side of the constitution; for an omission in the enumeration of the powers of government is neither so dangerous nor important as an omission in the enumeration of the rights of the people. . . .

To every suggestion concerning a bill of rights, the citizens of the United States may always say, We reserve the right to do what we please.

[December 11, 1787] I know very well all the common-place rant of state sovereignties, and that government is founded in original compact. If that position was examined, it will be found not to accede very well with the true principle of free government. It does not suit the langugage or genius of the system before us. I think it does not accord with experience, so far as I have been able to obtain information from history. . . . This Constitution may be found to have defects in it; hence amendments may become necessary; but the idea of a government founded on contract destroys the means of improvement. We hear it every time the gentlemen are up, "Shall we violate the Confederation, which directs every alteration that is thought necessary to be established by the state legislatures only?" Sir, those gentlemen must ascend to a higher source; the people fetter themselves by no contract. If your state legislatures have cramped themselves by compact, it was done without the authority of the people, who alone possess the supreme power. . . . The expressions declare, in a practical manner, the principle of this Constitution. It is ordained and established by the people themselves; and we, who give our votes for it, are merely proxies of our constituents. We sign it as their attorneys, and, as to ourselves, we agree to it as individuals.

RICHMOND, JAMES MADISON: THE DANGERS IN REJECTION

[June 24, 1788] It is a most awful thing that depends on our decision—no less than whether the thirteen states shall unite freely, peaceably, and unanimously, for security of their common happiness and liberty, or whether every thing is to be put in confusion and disorder. Are we to embark in this dangerous enterprise, uniting various opinions to contrary interests, with the vain hope of coming to an amicable concurrence?

It is worthy of our consideration that those who prepared the paper on the table found difficulties not to be described in its formation; mutual deference and concession were absolutely necessary. Had they been inflexibly tenacious of their individual opinions, they would never have concurred. Under what circumstances was it formed? When no party was formed, or particular proposition made, and men's minds were calm and dispassionate. Yet, under these circumstances, it was difficult, extremely difficult, to agree to any general system.

Suppose eight states only should ratify, and Virginia should propose certain alterations, as the previous condition of her accession. If they should be disposed to accede to her proposition, which is the most favorable conclusion, the difficulty attending it will be immense. Every state which has decided it, must take up the subject again. They must have not only the mortification of acknowledging that they had done wrong, but the difficulty of having a reconsideration of it among the people, and appointing new conventions to deliberate upon it. . . . The gentlemen who, within this house, have thought proper to propose previous amendments, have brought no less than forty amendments, a bill of rights which contains twenty amendments, and twenty other alterations, some of which are improper and inadmissible. Will not every state think herself equally entitled to propose as many amendments? And suppose them to be contradictory! I leave it to this Convention whether it be probable that they can agree, or agree to any thing but the plan on the table; or whether greater difficulties will not be encountered than were experienced in the progress of the formation of the Constitution. . . .

It gives me infinite pain to reflect that all the earnest endeavors of the warmest friends of their country to introduce a system promotive of our happiness, may be blasted by a rejection, for which I think . . . that previous amendments are but another name. . . . . With respect to the proposition of the honorable gentleman to my left (Mr. Wythe), gentlemen apprehend that, by enumerating three rights, it implied there were no more. . . . Can the general government exercise any power not delegated? If an enumeration be made of our rights, will it not be implied that every thing omitted is given to the general government? Has not the honorable gentleman himself admitted that an imperfect enumeration is dangerous? Does the Constitution say that they shall not alter the law of descents, or do those things which would subvert the whole system of the state laws. . . .

With respect to *the amendments* proposed by he honorable gentleman, it ought to be considered how far they are good. . . . One amendment he proposes is, that any army which shall be necessary shall be raised by the consent of two thirds of the states. I most devoutly wish that there may never be an occasion for having a single regiment. There can be no harm in declaring that standing armies, in time of peace, are dangerous to liberty, and ought to be avoided, as far as it may be consistent with the protection of the community. But when we come to say that the national security shall depend, not on a majority of the people of America, but that it may be frustrated by less than one third of the people of America, I ask if this be a safe or proper mode. What parts of the United States are most likely to stand in need of this protection? The weak parts, which are the Southern States. . . .

The regulation of *commerce,* he further proposed, should depend on two thirds of both houses. I wish I could recollect the history of this matter; but I cannot call it to mind with sufficient exactness. But I well recollect the reasoning of some gentlemen on that subject. . . . It was observed that the Northern States were most competent to their own safety. Was it reasonable, they asked, that they should bind themselves to the defence of the Southern States, and still be left at the mercy of the minority for commercial advantages? Should it be in the power of the minority to deprive them of this and other advantages, when they were bound to defend the whole Union, it might be a disadvantage for them to confederate. . . .

I was struck with surprise when I heard him express himself alarmed with respect to the emancipation of slaves. Let me ask, if they should ever attempt it, if it will not be a usurpation of power. There is no power to warrant it, in that paper. If there be, I know it not. . . . Can any one believe that the American councils will come into a measure which will strip them of their property, and discourage and alienate the affections of five thirteenths of the Union? Why was nothing of this sort aimed at before? I believe such an idea never entered into any American breast. . . I am persuaded that the gentlemen who contend for previous amendments are not aware of the dangers which must result. Virginia, after having made opposition, will be obliged to recede from it. . . .

RICHMOND, GOVERNOR EDMUND RANDOLPH: THE DANGERS OF REJECTION

[June 25, 1788] Mr. Chairman, one parting word I humbly supplicate. The suffrage which I shall give in favor of the Constitution will be ascribed, by malice, to motives unknown to my breast. But, although for every other act of my life I shall seek refuge in the mercy of God, for this I request his *justice* only. Lest, however, some future annalist should, in the spirit of party vengeance, deign to mention my name, let him recite these truths— that I went to the federal Convention with the strongest affection for the Union; that I acted there in full conformity with this affection; that I refused to subscribe, because I had, as I still have, objections to the Constitution, and wished a free inquiry into its merits; and that the accession of eight states reduced our deliberations to the single question of *Union or no Union.*

5

Why Did the Antifederalist Fail?
Jackson T. Main

As the cult of the Constitution has developed since 1789 it has been more and more widely assumed that the Founding Fathers were united in their wisdom and that there could have been no other outcome to their efforts than adoption of the instrument of their handiwork. It is perfectly clear, however, that they themselves regarded the new fundamental law as only the best of fallible compromises. The fact that an amending process was included in the constitution is proof enough of their discontents, and even the glimpse into their letters and public utterances afforded here is suffi- cient to indicate that adoption came only after skillful and determined political activity more often associated with passage of a tariff act than so august a document as a constitution. Historians have been presented with the question, why did the Nationalists or Federalists succeed in so radically changing the structure of federalism and why did their opponents fail? By concentrating on the Antifederalists, historian Jackson T. Main has arrived at answers which have stood up well to the criticisms of his colleagues. The final selection in this chapter constitutes the greater portion of the concluding chapter to his study, The Antifederalists.

It will never be known whether a majority of the voters—to say nothing of all the people—opposed ratification. It seems likely that the Antifederalists outnumbered the Federalists by as much as four to one in Rhode Island and South Carolina, and that they were slightly more than a majority in Massachusetts and Virginia. Probably the two sides were nearly equal in New Hampshire in June 1788, although there had been an Antifederal majority earlier. On the other hand, almost all of the citizens in Georgia,

SOURCE. Jackson T. Main, The *Antifederalists: Critics of the Constitution,* Chapel Hill: University of North Carolina Press for the Institute of Early American History and Culture, 1961, pp. 249-266, 280-281. Reprinted by permission of the publisher and the Institute of Early American History and Culture, Williamsburg.

New Jersey, and Delaware were Federalists. The situation in the remaining three states is uncertain; probably the Federalists had a clear majority in them, though perhaps not as large as the margin of victory in the ratifying conventions suggests. If we try to form an estimate of the entire white population, the two sides appear to have been nearly equal in numbers. Of course in 1787-1788 this was of no importance: what counted then was the ratification by nine states. Since the Federalists were a minority in at least six and probably seven states, they ought surely to have been defeated. Yet they came from behind to win.

A number of factors help to account for this. One of them, perhaps, was delay in the circulation of newspapers and letters. The Antifederalists complained that the residents of a state might not even know that opposition existed, and that this delay was an intentional effort on the part of the postal authorities to prevent the people from being informed. The Antifederalists also claimed that they were prevented from communicating promptly with one another in their efforts to organize and to combat misrepresentation. Most of the protests concerned the delivery of newspapers. As far as private mail is concerned, George Clinton complained vigorously of poor service, with some reason if the dates he gave are correct, and continued, "I can only add, that while the new Constitution was in agitation, I have discovered that many letters written to me, have never been delivered, and that others especially those which came by private conveyances appeared to have been opened on their passage." There were other complaints of slow mail too. Whether these delays were intentional or accidental cannot be proven, but they handicapped the Antifederalists.

The pro-Constitution attitude of the newspapers was undoubtedly much more important. The number of papers which opposed ratification or even of those which presented both sides impartially was very few. This was natural, for the city people were overwhelmingly Federal, and the printers were influenced by local opinion as well as by their own convictions; moreover, it was profitable to agree with the purchasers and the advertisers. In some cases pressure was used to enforce comformity: in Philadelphia the *Herald* was obliged to discontinue its coverage of the ratifying convention when almost one hundred readers stopped their subscriptions; in New York City the *Morning Post* published a number of Antifederal articles until January 9, after which they suddenly ceased to appear; in Boston the *American Herald* lost subscribers and untimately moved out of the city. The Federalist domination of news coverage permitted them not only to obtain more space for their own publications but to conceal or distort the facts. The objections of the Antifederalists were sometimes twisted so as to make them appear foolish; at other times it was denied that there was any opposition at all to the Constitution. In Pennsylvania it was claimed that Patrick Henry was working for ratification; in Charleston readers were informed that thirty-nine fortieths of the New Yorkers favored adoption; in Rhode Island, readers were presented with an article which purported to originate in Richmond. "Out of all the members as yet returned to the Convention, *there are only three or four against the Constitution;* and it is the general opinion, that there will scarcely be found ten men in the whole state, who when they meet here in June, will set their opinions in competition with those of all the great and good patriots in America, and thus suffer themselves to be branded with the *odious and disgraceful* appellation of antifederalists."

Issues of the *New-Hampshire Spy* are fairly typical. On October 9 a gentleman reputed to have made a tour of New England was quoted as having heard not a single dissenting voice in the four states; in New York no opposition was expected, and even Clinton favored the Constitution. On the 27th appeared an often-reprinted story concerning George Mason's reputed unpopularity in Alexandria; three days later it was asserted that Mason was suffering "contempt and neglect" and that Patrick Henry favored ratification. On November 23, another frequently printed falsehood related that Washington had been on his feet for two hours at a time in the Federal Convention speaking in favor of every part of the Constitution. On December 7 the *Spy* informed its readers that "it is currently reported, that there are only two men in Virginia, who are not in *debt,* to be found among the enemies of the federal constitution." Subsequent issues gave false reports concerning Federal strength; on May 27, 1788, it was asserted that a majority of twenty was expected in Virginia and on the 31st the same margin was predicted in North Carolina. Evidently some Federalists believed their own propaganda; one of them wrote that even the Shaysites were for adoption! There is no way of determining how effective this misinformation was. When news arrived that opposition did exist, the public reaction to exposure of previous falsehoods may sometimes have undone what had been accomplished. Yet it must have been discouraging for the Antifederalists to keep reading such gloomy reports in the newspapers, and it is even possible that some regions never knew that opposition existed-this was actually the case in Luzerne County, Pennsylvania. The ability of the Federalists to outmaneuver their opponents was due in part to superior organization. The Antifederalists had not been able to unite, even within a particular state, in order to concert their efforts, until the creation of the Federal Republican Committee in New York, Everywhere they were too late. Thus a Pennsylvania Quaker sent Antifederal pamphlets to Maryland and Georgia in April, after the contest had ended in both states; his only hope was that another convention would be called. On the other hand the Federalists were consistently ahead of the game from the time when, in September, the "gentlemen" of Philadelphia rode out to harangue "the rabble." Certainly their correspondence shows far better co-operation. Perhaps this evidence is deceptive and indicates only that more of their letters have survived; yet the results are to be seen in their better distribution of campaign propaganda and information.

Still another advantage of the Federalists was the superior prestige of some of their leaders. In many of the states this advantage was very great. In New Hampshire all of the noted Revolutionary leaders were Federalists; in Massachusetts a majority of the prominent men favored ratification; in Connecticut almost all; and in New Jersey, Delaware, and Georgia all or nearly all backed the proposed Constitution. The weight of prestige was also on the Federalist side in South Carolina, Maryland, and Virginia. While it is true that some Federalists probably did more harm than good because their views and aspirations were known or suspected-among them Robert Morris, Hamilton, and Gouverneur Morris-yet there remained many whose opinions were trusted and whose intentions were known to be honorable. Preeminent among them were Franklin (though his age told against him) and Washington. The latter was assured by friends that his influence was decisive, and this was not just flattery, for observers on both sides agreed, and the Antifederalists paid him the honor of newspaper attacks. The truth is that he was trusted, with reason, and his guarantee that the Constitution was a good one carried weight.

The influence of these men of wealth and prestige was exerted in various ways, not, it seems, by bribery, for had efforts of that sort been made there would surely have been revelations of it, but rather by example and persuasion. Thus Nathaniel Barrell of York was informed from Boston that "you will meet the most pointed opposition from all your friends here." Antifederalists who proved immune to arguments were occasionally treated with scorn or ridicule, but more often, evidently, they were wined and dined, as in South Carolina where Aedanus Burke complained that the Charlestonians kept open house. Everywhere there was talk. In some cases the men of small property and little prestige may have been impressed by the great ones, but more susceptible to conversion were Antifederal merchants, lawyers, planters, and well-to-do leaders in general, who were persuaded to coalesce with their Federal equivalents.

The course of events also favored the Federal cause. Ratification got off to a quick-albeit somewhat forced-start by the actions of Delaware, Pennsylvania, New Jersey, Georgia, and Connecticut. This momentum was never entirely lost. The fact that every one of the five ratified by large margins was important in Massachusetts, and the outcome there was influential elsewhere. By the time the states controlled by the Antifederalists held their conventions eight states had already ratified. By pressing for a conclusion where victory was assured and staving off defeat in other cases (as in New Hampshire), the Federalists were able to extract the utmost benefit from circumstances. They took advantage of local forces and issues: the activities of the Boston artisans, the threat of secession in southern New York, the Indian menace in frontier Georgia, and the British posts in the northwest are examples.

Finally there was the promise of amendments without which the Constitution could never have been ratified. The Antifederalists included many persons who would under no circumstances accept ratification, but there also many whose hostility was less intense, who in fact believed that the Constitution was fundamentally a good one, whose defects could be removed by amendment. The Federalists did not have to worry about those who wholly rejected the Constitution; they needed only enough votes for ratification-a dozen or so here, a handful there. They themselves did not admit the need for any alterations. Publicly they preached that the Constitution was perfect, and wherever they had control (as in

South Carolina) they proposed no amendments. But when the technique of conceding amendments to the opposition first proved its value in Massachusetts, winning over some waverers and enabling others who had already been convinced to violate their instructions with a clear conscience, it became the most valuable weapon in the Federal arsenal.

Fundamentally, the Antifederalists faced an insuperable difficulty in that they agreed upon the need for political changes. Although the Constitution was too radical a departure from the Confederation to meet their views, it was a substantial effort toward political reform. This fact persuaded large numbers of people to support the new plan despite its shortcomings. As George Bryan put it, "When the federal Constitution was proposed to the people, the Desire of increasing the powers of Congress was great and this Object had a mighty Influence in its Favor." Thus a few Antifederalists—just enough—felt that the Constitution was better than "anarchy and confusion," and the promise of amendments was enough to quiet their fears.

The final result was that he Federalits did surprisingly well in the election and then succeeded in converting convention minorities into majorities. All told, at least sixty delegates, perhaps as many as seventy-five, who were chosen as Antifederalists, ended by voting for ratification. To study these men, who they were and where they came from, is to explain much about the nature of Antifederalism. Two facts emerge which are of especial significance: the converts came from the regions near the coast and from the upper socio-economic stratum of society.

Of some fifty-six delegates who are known to have changed sides, the majority represented areas in the east or in the transition zone between east and west. These geographical terms are to be understood in the [following] ways . . . by "east" is meant, in Massachusetts, the towns near the coast, in New York, those along the southern Hudson; by transition is meant, for example, the "border" parishes of South Carolina. Although converts to Federalism were made everywhere, for the most part these accessions represented a drawing together—a coalescing—of delegates from regions near the great commercial centers and along the paths of commerce, of the solidifying of strength in localities already Federal and the extension of Federal influence into adjacent areas. In Virginia, the process is represented by the shift of Edmund

Randolph of Henrico, the second, by that of William Ronald of Powhatan. Similar illustrations in Massachusetts are Charles Turner of Scituate and William Symmes of Andover, and in New York, Samuel Jones of Queens and Zephaniah Platt of Dutchess. So too the Federal tide in Rhode Island rose slowly from Providence and Newport to engulf the other bay towns, and in North Carolina swept inland form the sounds.

The second major fact about the converts is that they included many of the Antifederal leaders, men of superior wealth, position, and prestige. In some states the party was already decapitated. The apostasy of its leaders often influenced the event in other states. In Massachusetts, the prominent Revolutionary leaders Nathan Dane and Samuel Osgood, who were not chosen to the ratifying convention, were at first opposed to the Constitution, but changed their minds. The shift of Hancock and Samuel Adams is well known. James Sullivan apparently also changed. Charles Turner, William Symmes, Nathaniel Barrell, and John Sprague (of Lancaster) all voted in favor. Of this group, the first was a respected Congregational minister and one-time senator, the second was a lawyer, the third was a wealthy son of a tory, and the last was a well-to-do lawyer who had opposed Shays although he lived in the heart of the Shaysite country. In addition, there are indications that Charles Jarvis, a Boston doctor, and John Winthrop, a wealthy merchant, were at first uncertain, then voted for ratification; Samuel Holten of Danvers, a prominent and well-to-do doctor, failed to vote; while Capt. Isaac Snow of Harpswell, a shipowner, accepted the Constitution after amendments. In New York, the dozen who changed on the final vote included a merchant, a judge, and three wealthy landowners. Of similar significance were the stand taken by Edmund Randolph, when he emerged from his gyrations, the statement of the prominent Charleston doctor Fayssoux, the shifts of Humphrey Marshall and William Ronald in Virgina, of William Williams in Connecticut, of William Paca in Maryland, and of John Chesnut (merchant), Henry Pendleton (judge), the Reverend Mr. Cummins, and Alexander Tweed in South Carolina. Comparable, too, were the refusal of Abraham Clark to actively oppose the Constitution in New Jersey, the similar attitude of Thomas Johnson in Maryland, and the ultimate decision of Governor John Collins in Rhode Island that further resistance was useless.

About half of the delegates who changed sides were obscure men of only local repute, followers rather than leaders, whose conversion was not likely to influence many others, The other half, however, included a number of large property owners-indeed about a third of the total were well-to-to. There were three doctors, five merchants, as shipowner, at least four large landowners, and no less than ten lawyers. The Federalists could appeal to such men with particular success because of the nature of the Constitution. If the new government favored the well-to-do, as some Antifederalits maintained, this was hardly an objection to those who were of the "better sort" themselves. They might dislike an aristocracy in theory, but in practice, rule by the educated, wellbred, wellborn few was appealing. Insofar as the Constitution helped to guard against popular uprisings, they were all for it—the Warrens and their friends, for example, had not defended Shays's Rebellion. This is not to suggest that all men of property were impressed by such arguments—some were repelled by them; yet the Constitution may have seemed less menacing to those who would probably help to administer it, some of whom were basically inclined to favor the few rather than the many. Many, probably most, of the converts were hard-money advocates, who supported financial policies opposite to those which the rank and file of Antifederalists preferred. Moreover, more than most Antifederalists they were impressed with the need for change, perhaps because they lived nearer the commercial centers and were influenced by the mercantile point of view. From the first, therefore, they were less antagonistic to the Constiution, its faults seemed fewer, its virtues more numerous. Their objections were more readily removed by arguments, or, when that failed, by the promise of amendments. Thus Silas Lee, of Biddeford, Maine, believed from the first that the Articles were inadequate; his correspondents included staunch Federalists, and the was ultimately persuaded that the Constitution, once amended, would serve to avoid the anarchy and confusion which the Federalists prophesied.

An analysis of the Antifederalists who changed their vote suggests that Federalism attracted particularly the economic elite and also those who were connected with commerce. These key generalizations must now be tested against all that has been learned about the great controversy. Historians who have studied the division which took place in 1787-88 have arrived at very different conclusions: some have defended the sectional hypothesis as an explanation for political conflicts, other have suggested class antagonisms, or the presence or lack of vision, age, or religion. The first essential in reaching a conclusion is therefore to remove some of the errors.

The difference was not one of age. It is true that some of the "old patriots" were getting on, as Charles Warren says, and that many were Antifederal—he lists ten who were over forty and contrasts them with nine Federalists who were younger. But a few selected examples do not prove a point. In Pennsylvania the Antifederalists were older by two years, but in New York there was no difference at all; in South Carolina the median age of eleven Antifederalists was 33, of thirty-two Federalists only 29; in Massachusetts the average Antifederalist was 52, the Federalist 51. All told, the Federalits were about two years younger than their antagonists. It is hard to see how this could have made any difference.

One explanation for the nature of the division stems from Charles Francis Adams's observation that "among the opponents of the Constitution are to be ranked a great majority of those who had most strenuously fought the battle of independence." Unless the statement was meant to apply only to Massachusetts, it is not correct. Among the signers of the Declaration of Independence, Federalists outnumbered the Antifederalists nearly three to one, and of the latter, half finally voted for ratification; thus the margin becomes no less than six to one. It is true that many of the signers were not enthusiastic about the Declaration and that all those who signed reluctantly became Federalists; but even when these are eliminated Adams's remark is inaccurate.

Differences in religion also fail to provide a solution, whatever their importance in the earlier history of the country or their influence upon other issues. Some Antifederalists criticized the Constitution because it did not secure freedom of conscience; the omission would affect, presumably, the dissenting sects. But others objected to it because it tolerated all alike; this would affect those denominations which aspired to control the state. A majority of Congregationalists were perhaps in favor of ratication (certainly the ministers were); yet there does not seem to have been any clear-cut alignment of Congregationalists behind the Constitution: thus while Connecticut favored adoption, central and western

Massachusetts did not. The situation in regard to the Baptists is instructive. Those in Philadelphia were Federal, and in New York City a convention of Baptists of the middle states recommended ratification. Baptists in eastern North Carolina and in eastern South Carolina were also Federal. In New Jersey there were twenty-seven Baptist churches, but few Antifederalists. On the other hand, the Virginia Baptist Association voted unanimously against ratification. In Massachusetts most of the Baptists lived in the interior and were Antifederal, but the few who were in the east, including the prominent Isaac Backus, were Federal. Elsewhere the Baptists were usually small farmers and were Antifederal. Obviously, the opinions of Baptists depended upon where they lived or what their other interests were, and the same was true of their religious or racial groups. Presbyterians of southern New York, eastern Pennsylvania, and Shenandoah Valley were Federalists, but those of other sections were not. In North Carolina most of them were Antifederal, but W.R. Davie, a lawyer who represented the town of Halifax, was a Federalist. The Presbyterians were the strongest denomination in Federal New Jersey. Two other religious groups were fairly consistent in their Federalism: the Quakers in Pennsylvania and the Episcopalians; yet in the west they were often in the opposite camp. Antifederalist Charles Clay of Bedford County, Virgina, was an Episcopalian minister. German sects divided irregularly. As Dorpalen discovered, they were for or against the Constitution for reasons other than their religion or national origin; he found that in Pennsylvania many Germans of whatever creed joined the Federalists but that in the South they were Antifederal because they resided in the backcountry. In short the alignment on the Constitution was not affected significantly by religion.

On the other hand there is a good deal of evidence to show that the division followed class lines. There was no working class to any extent, but there did exist an antagonism between small and large property holders. It is true that such conflicts were tempered by exceptionally high vertical mobility, but there were nevertheless significant economic and social differences, well recognized at the time, that were continually reflected in political disputes. In the debate over the Constitution, several types of evidence are available to prove the existence of a division along class lines. First, there is the testimony of contemporaries. In Massachusetts the statements of King, Knox, Jackson, Thatcher, Sewall, Minot, Singletary, Lewis Morris, and Randal have been cited. Both East and Harding give other examples. In New Hampshire, Sullivan, Madison, Atherton, and Tobias Lear testified that the Federalists were men of greater wealth. Hugh Ledlie referred to the Connecticut Federalists as men of "superior rank," while David Humphreys listed clergy, lawyers, physicians, merchants, and army officers. In Rhode Island, General Varnum observed that "the wealth and resources of this state are chiefly in the possession of the well-affected." Similarly in New York, both sides noted a difference, the Federalists with pride, the Antifederalists with alarm. The Pennsylvanian George Bryan discussed class differences, while Benjamin Rush contrasted the "people" and "their rulers." Observers in the South noted the same distinction, as Arthur Bryan did when he discovered that in South Carolina the "second class of people" were especially inclined to Antifederalism; Burke contrasted the "rich leading men" with "the Multitude." Timothy Bloodworth felt that the aristocracy favored adoption in North Carolina. Lord Dorchester was informed that "the partizans in favour of the new system hold the greater share of landed and personal property." John Quincy Adams also felt that there was a general class division over the Constitution. Even in Maryland, John Francis Mercer believed that the contest was between "wealthy men" or "the *few*" and "the People" or "the *many*," and another observer there believed that ratification was secured by the aristocracy, not the "common class." Some proof by implication may be drawn from the fact that Antifederalists generally criticized the Constitution for its undemocratic features, while in contrast a considerable number of Federalists did not approve of the upsurge of the democracy and praised the Constitution as a check on popular majorities.

Another type of evidence is based on a study of individuals whose politics are known, especially members of the ratifying conventions. Such a study clearly reveals a class alignment. If it be conceded that there was some sort of a difference between "Esq." and "Mr." as used in New England, then it is evident that the Federalists outranked their opponents by a significant margin; they constituted nearly three and one-half times as many esquires. Second, it is probably true in New England and certainly true in the South that there was a correlation between socio-economic status and army rank. In every state for which information is available, except New York, the higher ranking officers were Federal by a margin of more than two to one. On the other hand there were about the same number of lesser ranking officers on either side, lieutenants tending toward Antifederalism. Third, the holders of a college degree almost always came from the upper income groups and they were Federal by a margin of more than three to one. Fourth, certain professions carried with them superior prestige and usually higher income. Merchants were Federal by a five to one margin, lawyers and judges by well over two to one, shipowners, ship captains, and large manufacturers by over seven to one.

The highest political offices were at that time principally held by men of wealth and status (even aside from the property qualifications), and taking as representative of these offices the governors, state senators, and members of Congress, it appears that the Federalist held well over twice as many such posts in states where close contests occurred. Among the governors and former governors whose political opinions are known, twenty-seven were Federal and eleven were Antifederal, and of the latter, five changed sides. Men who had served in Congress were Federal by a four to one margin.

The political preference of the members of state senates is of particular interest. They were numerous (over eight hundred served at various times from 1775 to 1788) and influential because their approval was essential for the passage of all laws. The great majority of them were well-to-do- merchants, lawyers, or large landholders. Among those whose opinions are known, nearly two-thirds voted for ratification. This may be attributed to their superior education and wider experience, or to the fact that as men of political knowledge they recognized the need for change. But economic status had something to do with it too. The wealthier senators supported the Constitution by a margin of over three to one; those who were merely well-to-do favored it two to one; but those of only moderate means opposed it by a small margin. The wealthier the senator, the more apt he was to be a Federalist.

Indeed, men of wealth in general, in or out of the conventions, were usually Federalists. Almost all of them in New Jersey, Delaware, and Georgia apparently favored ratification, and nearly all in Connecticut and Maryland. In the remaining eight states, among almost three hundred men definitely known to have possessed considerable fortunes, nearly three-fourths were Federal. Yet in these states the majority of the population was against the Constititution.

Other evidence to the same effect may be stated briefly. In Pennsylvania, the Federalist delegates to the ratifying convention owned, on the average, half again as much land and other taxable property as the Antifederalists. In Massachussetts, Federal towns were wealthier. In Rhode Island, Federal towns contained far more slaves than did the Antifederal. Another type of property, public securities, was also unequally distributed, for much of the debt, worth millions of dollars, was concentrated in centers of Federalist strength. Observers agreed that creditors, both public and private, tended to be Federal, while debtors were ordinarily Antifederal. Finally, the areas which supported Federalism, including the towns and the rich river valleys, contained most of the men who were well-to-do and a great proportion of the whole wealth of the country.

Still a third type of evidence in support of a class division is based upon a correlation between the alignment on ratification and that on earlier issues which involved conflicts between rich and poor, large and small property owners. Allowing for the inevitable exceptions, the Antifederalists had in the past supported the more democratic state constitutions which increased the political power of the majority, whereas the Federalists had preferred to restrain or "manage" the democracy; the Antifederalists had supported paper money, lower interest rates, legal tender clauses, valuation and instalment and stay laws, and other measures favorable to debtors; they had attempted also to reduce the state debts so as to render taxes less burdensome to the majority, while the Federalists upheld the creditor interest and favored the taxes necessary to pay the debts at par. Similarly the Antifederalists, in combating the loyalists, opposing the Bank of North America, obstructing enforcement of the British treaty, striving for lower court fees, and checking the increase of power in government, had defended the interest of the many against the few. The struggle over the Constitution was in part a continuation of a long history of social conflicts which extended far back into colonial times.

All of this evidence proves that there was a division along lines of class. It does not, however, prove that the struggle over ratification can be explained exclusively in terms of class conflict. There are several states in which the concept obviously does not hold. In Georgia both wealthy planters and yeomen farmers agreed on ratification. In North Carolina and Virginia a large number of planters were Antifederal, and in the interior of the latter state, two large sections inhabited by small farmers favored ratification. Maryland does not fit the theory, nor do Delaware and New Jersey. Delegates from small farmer strongholds in Connecticut, New Hampshire, Pennsylvania, and even Massachusetts (parts of Hampshire County) were Federal.

But the most serious of all objections to an interpretation based exclusively on an alignment along class lines is the complete absence of a division of opinion in the towns. Where there should have been the most feeling, the least existed. . . .

But after all of these facts have been taken into account, we can return to the major generalization: that the struggle over the ratification of the Constitution was primarily a contest between the commercial and the non-commercial elements in the population. This is the most significant fact, to which all else is elaboration, amplification, or exception. The Federalists included the merchants and the other town dwellers, farmers depending on the major cities, and those who produced a surplus for export. The Antifederalists were primarily those who were not so concerned with, or who did not recognize a dependence upon, the mercantile community and foreign markets. Such people were often isolated from the major paths of commerce and usually were less well-to-do because they produced only enough for their own purposes. Because of this basic situation, a majority of the large property holders were Federal, but this division along class lines did not exist in the towns and not everywhere in the country. It was real enough however to find reflections in the political ideas of both sides. Because the Federalists dominated the towns and the rich valleys, they included most of the public and private creditors, great landowners, lawyers and judges, manufacturers and ship-owners, higher ranking civil and military officials, and college graduates. Although the Antifederalists derived their leadership from such men, the rank and file were men of moderate means, with little social prestige, farmers often in debt, obscure men for the most part.

Antifederal thought was shaped by the composition and objectives of the party, but was modified by the social and political attitudes of the articulate leaders through whom it was expressed. Only a few of these leaders came from the small farmers or truly represented them. They frequently defended views somewhat less democratic than those of their constituents, and they were often out of sympathy with the economic demands of the rank and file, especially in the case of paper money and debtor relief legislation. As a result, Antifederalism as formulated by its most prominent spokesmen sometimes lacks the democractic overtones we have attributed to it.

But the democratic implication existed. As a body of political thought, Antifederalism had a background in English and American political theory long before the Constitution was drafted. Its principles were embodied in the Articles of Confederation; later they were elaborated in the controversy over the impost. Always the emphasis was on local rule and the retention of power by the people, which were democratic tenets in that age. Such a body of thought could of course be used by special interest groups; its bare political doctrine was put forth in opposition to the impost by the merchants of Rhode Island and Massachusetts. But it was always more congenial to the many than the few. Throughout the 1780's, whenever the question of sovereignty arose, the same men representing the same interests rehearsed the arguments they were to employ in debating the Constitution. Although the Antifederalist position was employed to mask special interests, it was fundamentally anti-aristocratic; whoever used its arguments had to speak in terms which implied, if they did not clearly define, a democratic content. It was therefore peculiarly congenial to those who were tending toward democracy, most of whom were soon to rally around Jefferson. The Antifederalists, who lost their only major battle, are forgotten while the victors are remembered, but it is not so certain which is the more memorable.

CHAPTER III
THE HAMILTONIAN
PROGRAM AND ITS
IMMEDIATE EFFECTS
1789 - 1793

1

Hamilton's Reports on the Public Credit,
National Bank, and Manufactures with his Opinion
on the Constitutionality of the Bank
January 1790 - February 1791

Hamilton was the prime mover of the establishment by law of the program
ever since associated with the Federalists in power. Acting very much as
though he were Washington's prime minister, believing that consolidation of
the Revolutionary debt was the key to economic growth and that the national

SOURCE. Harold C. Syrett and Jacob E. Cooke, eds., *The Papers of Alexander Hamilton,* New York: Columbia University Press 1961, - Volume VI, pp. 65-67, 73-74, 77-78, 80-81, 106-107; Volume VII, pp. 305-306, 307, 309, 310, 338, 341; Volume X, pp. 230, 236, 291, 293, 294-295; Volume VIII, pp. 97-99.

rather than the state governments must control the process, Hamilton made a powerful case for the promotion of commerce and manufacturing under the aegis of government. In asking for the establishment of a tariff for the protection of manufactures, for the establishment of a national bank, and for the federal government's assumption of the debts of the states, the administration made a host of enemies as well as ardent friends. What had become of a former emphasis upon enumerated powers? Alarmed Antifederalists, as they witnessed the speculation fever commence with the flow of money into Philadelphia and New York, doubted Hamilton's premise that agriculture would gain immeasurably in the long run.

The documents comprising this chapter present the case for and to a lesser degree, the case against Hamilton's conception of capitalism and society. After so great an effort to submerge the causes of sectional division, the administration seemed deliberately bent upon exacerbating them in the opinion of James Madison and his fellow southerners in particular. By the Spring of 1792 charges of betrayal were becoming commonplace on both sides of the line Hamilton had drawn. If the still universal respect for Washington and the general indifference to political matters felt by the majority of isolated citizens did much to prevent divisiveness, the seeds of party growth had already been planted. seeds of party growth had already been planted.

The first of Hamilton's famous reports addressed to the Speaker of the House of Representatives proposed what has to come to be known familiarly as the Funding and Assumption System. Hamilton's insistence upon exchanging depreciated paper at face value for new interest bearing bonds and the unwillingness of his supporters in Congress to make adjustments which would compensate original holders of this wartime and Confederation paper, left angry scars. The history of the passage of the bill authorizing the assumption of state debts has always included Jefferson's own account of his naive complicity, although recent research indicates that his intervention was unnecessary to passage. Sectional feeling was immediately aroused as indicated by the fact that nineteen of the twenty votes cast unsuccessfully against the bill establishing the Bank were southern votes. Congress could not be induced, however, to erect tariff walls for the promotion of manufacturing. The low tariff of July 1789 was rather a revenue measure which, together with the excise tax on distilleries, provided income sufficient for the government's needs when added to that derived from land sales. The Report on Manufactures stands as a testimonial to the Federalist belief that government may be used to alter the nature of society. The opinion which Washington asked Hamilton to submit to him on the Bank's constitutionality is a classic statement of the Constitution's flexibility or elasticity just as Jefferson's opposing opinion is a classic statement of the doctrine of limited powers to which the advocates of states' rights often resorted.

REPORT ON PUBLIC CREDIT, JANUARY 9, 1790

The Secretary of the Treasury, in obedience to the resolution of the House of Representatives, of the twenty-first day of September last, has, during the recess of Congress, applied himself to the consideration of a proper plan for the support of the Public Credit, with all the attention which was due to the authority of the House, and to the magnitude of the object. . . .

With an ardent desire that his well-meant endeavors may be conducive to the real advantage of the nation, and with the utmost deference to the superior judgment of the House, he now respectfully submits the result of his enquiries and reflections, to their indulgent construction.

In the opinion of the Secretary, the wisdom of the House, in giving their explicit sanction to the proposition which has been stated, cannot but be applauded by all, who will seriously consider, and trace through their obvious consequences, these plain and undeniable truths.

That exigencies are to be expected to occur, in the affairs of nations, in which there will be a necessity for borrowing.

That loans in times of public danger, especially from foreign war, are found an indispensable resource, even to the wealthiest of them.

And that in a country, which, like this, is possessed of little active wealth, or in other words, little monied capital, the necessity for that resource, must, in such emergencies, be proportionately urgent. . . .

It is agreed on all hands, that that part of the debt which has been contracted abroad, and is denominated the foreign debt, ought to be provided for, according to the precise terms of the contracts relating to it. The discussions, which can arise, therefore, will have reference essentially to the domestic part of it, or to that which been contracted at home. It is to be regretted, that there is not the same unanimity of sentiment on this part, as on the other.

The Secretary has too much deference for the opinions of every part of the community, not to have observed one, which has, more than once, made its appearance in the public prints, and which is occasionally to be met with in conversation. It involves this question, whether a discrimination ought not to be made between original holders of the public securities, and present possessors, by purchase. Those who advocate a discrimination are for making a full provision for the securities of the former, at their nominal value; but contend, that the latter ought to receive no more than the cost to them, and the interest: And the idea is sometimes suggested of making good the difference to the primitive possessor.

In favor of this scheme, it is alleged, that it would be unreasonable to pay twenty shillings in the pound, to one who had not given more for it than three or four. And it is added, that it would be hard to aggravate the misfortune of the first owner, who, probably through necessity, parted with his property at so great a loss, by obliging him to contribute to the profit of the person, who had speculated on his distresses.

The Secretary, after the most mature reflection on the force of this argument, is induced to reject the doctrine it contains, as equally unjust and impolitic, as highly injurious, even to the original holders of public securities; as ruinous to public credit.

It is inconsistent with justice, because in the first place, it is a breach of contract; in violation of the rights of a fair purchaser.

The nature of the contract in its origin, is, that the public will pay the sum expressed in the security, to the first holder, or his *assignee*. The *intent* in making the security assignable, is, that the proprietor may be able to make use of his property, by selling it for as much as it *may be worth in the market*, and that the buyer be *safe* in the purchase.

Every buyer therefore stands exactly in the place of the seller, has the same right with him to the identical sum expressed in the security, and having acquired that right, by fair purchase, and in conformity to the original *agreement* and *intention* of the government, his claim cannot be disputed, without manifest injustice.

That he is to be considered as a fair purchaser, results from this:

Whatever necessity the seller may have been under, was occasioned by the government in not making a proper provision for its debts. The buyer had no agency in it, and therefore ought not to suffer. He is not even chargeable with having taken an undue advantage. He paid what the commodity was worth in the market, and took the risks of reimbursement upon himself. He of course gave a fair equivalent, and ought to reap the benefit of the hazard; a hazard which was far from inconsiderable, and which, perhaps, turned on little less than a revolution in government.

That the case of those, who parted with their securities from necessity, is a hard one, cannot be denied. But whatever complaint of injury, or claim of redress, they may have, respects the government solely. They have not only nothing to object to the persons who relieved their necessities, by giving them the current price of their property, but they are even under an implied condition to contribute to the reimbursement of those persons. They knew, that by the terms of the contract with themselves, the public were bound to pay to those, to whom they should convey their title, the sums stipulated to be paid to them; and, that as citizens of the United States, they were to bear their proportion of the contribution for that purpose. This, by the act of assignment, they tacitly engage to do; and if they had an option, they could not, with integrity or good faith, refuse to do it, without consent of those to whom they sold. . . .

The impolicy of a discrimination results from two considerations; one, that it proceeds upon a principle destructive of the *quality* of the public debt, or the stock of the nation, which is essential to its capacity for answering the purposes of money—that is the *security* of *transfer*; the other, that as well on this account, as because it includes a breach of faith, it renders property in the funds less valuable; consequently induces lenders to demand a higher premium for what they lend, and produces every other inconvenience of a bad state of public credit. . . .

But there is still a point in view in which it will appear perhaps even more exceptionable, than in either of the former. It would be repugnant to an express provision of the Constitution of the United States. This provision is, that "all debts contracted and engagements entered into before the adoption of that Constitution shall be as valid against the United States under it, as under the confederation." which amounts to a constitutional ratification of the contracts respecting the debt, in the state in which they existed under the confederation. And resorting to that standard, there can be no doubt, that the rights of assignees and original holders, must be considered as equal. . . .

The Secretary concluding, that a discrimination, between the different clauses of creditors of the United States, cannot with propriety be *made,* proceeds to examine whether a difference ought to be permitted to *remain* between them, and another description of public creditors—Those of the states individually.

The Secretary, after mature reflection on this point, entertains a full conviction, that an assumption of the debts of the particular states by the union, will be a measure of sound policy and substantial justice.

It would, in the opinion of the Secretary,contribute, in an eminent degree, to an orderly, stable and satisfactory arrangement of the national finances.

Admitting, as ought to be the case, that a provision must be made in some way or other, for the entire debt; it will follow, that no greater revenues will be required, whether that provision be made wholly by the United States, or partly by them, and partly by the states separately.

The principal question then must be, whether such a provision cannot be more conveniently and effectually made, by one general plan issuing from one authority, than by different plans originating in different authorities. . . .

If all the public creditors receive their dues from one source, distributed with an equal hand, their interest will be the same. And having the same interests, they will unite in the support of the fiscal arrangements of the government: As these, too, can be made with more convenience, where there is no competition: These circumstances combined will insure to the revenue laws a more ready and more satisfactory execution.

If on the contrary there are distinct provisions, there will be distinct interests, drawing different ways. That union and concert of views, among the creditors, which in every government is of great importance to their security, and to that of public credit, will not only not exist, but will be likely to give place to mutual jealousy and opposition. And from this cause, the operation of the system which may be adopted, both by the parti- cular states, and by the union,with relation to their respective debts, will be in danger of being counteracted.

There are several reasons, which render it probable, that the situation of the state creditors would be worse, than that of the creditors of the union, if there be not a national assumption of the state debts. Of these it will be sufficient to mention two; one, that a principal branch of revenue is exclusively vested in the union; the other, that a state must always be checked in the imposition of taxes on articles of consumption, from the want of power to extend the same regulation to the other states, and from the tendency of partial duties to injure its industry and commerce. Should the state creditors stand upon a less eligible footing than the others, it is unnatural to expect they would see with pleasure a provision for them. The influence which their dissatisfaction might have, could not but operate injuriously, both for the creditors and the credit, of the United States.

Hence, it is even the interest of the creditors of the union, that those of the individual states should be comprehended in a general provision. Any attempt to secure to the former either exclusive or peculiar advantages, would materially hazard their interests.

Neither would it be just, that one class of the public creditors should be more favoured than the other. The objects for which both descriptions of the debt were contracted, are in the main the same. Indeed a great part of the particular debts of the States has arisen from assumptions by them on account of the union. And it is most equitable, that there should be the same measure of retribution for all. . . .

Persuaded as the Secretary is, that the proper funding of the present debt, will render it a national blessing: Yet he is so far from acceding to the position, in the latitude in which it is sometimes laid down, that "public debts are public benefits, "a position inviting to prodigality, and liable to dangerous abuse,— that he ardently wishes to see it incorporated, as a fundamental maxim, in the system of public credit of the United States, that the creation of debt should always be accompanied with the means of extinguishment. This he regards as the true secret for rendering public credit immortal. And he presumes, that it is difficult to conceive a situation, in which there may not be an adherence to the maxim. At least he feels an unfeigned solicitude, that this may be attempted by the United States, and that they may commence their measures for the establishment of credit with the observance of it.

Under this impression, the Secretary proposes, that the net product of the post-office, to a sum not exceeding one million of dollars, be vested in commissioners, to consist of the Vice-President of the United States or President of the Senate, the Speaker of the House of Representatives, the Chief Justice, Secretary of the Treasury, and Attorney-General of the United States, for the time being, in trust, to be applied, by them, or any three of them, to the discharge of the existing public debt, either by purchases of stock in the market, or by payments on account of the principal, as shall appear to them most advisable, in conformity to the public engagements; to continue so vested, until the whole of the debt shall be discharged. . . .

SECOND REPORT ON THE PUBLIC CREDIT, DECEMBER 13, 1790

In obedience to the order of the House of Representatives of the ninth day of August last, requiring the Secretary of the Treasury to prepare and report on this day such further provision as may, in his opinion, be necessary for establishing the public Credit The said Secretary further respectfully reports That from a conviction (as suggested in his report No. 1 herewith presented) That a National Bank is an Institution of primary importance to the prosperous administration of the Finances, and would be of the greatest utility in the operations connected with the support of the Public Credit, his attention has been drawn to devising the plan of such an institution, upon a scale, which will intitle it to the confidence, and be likely to render it equal to the exigencies of the Public.

Previously to entering upon the detail of this plan, he entreats the indulgence of the House, towards some preliminary reflections naturally arising out of the subject, which he hopes will be deemed, neither useless, nor out of place. Public opinion being the ultimate arbiter of every measure of Government, it can scarcely appear improper, in deference to that, to accompany the origination of any new proposition with explanations, which the superior information of those, to whom it is immediately addressed, would render superfluous.

It is a fact well understood, that public banks have found admission and patronage among the principal and most enlightened commercial nations. They have successfully obtained in Italy, Germany, Holland, England and France, as well as in the United States. And it is a circumstance, which cannot but have considerable weight, in a candid estimate of their tendency, that after an experience of centuries, there exists not a question about their util[ity] in the countries in which they have been so long established. Theorists and men of business unite in the acknowledgement of it.

Trade and industry, wherever they have been tried, have been indebted to them for important aid. And Government has been repeatedly under the greatest obligations to them, in dangerous and distressing emergencies. That of the United States, as well in some of the most critical conjunctures of the late war, as since the peace, has received assistance from those established among us, with which it could not have dispensed. . . .

The following are among the principal advantages of a Bank.

First. The augmentation of the active or productive capital of a country. Gold and Silver, when they are employed merely as the instruments of exchange and alienation, have not been improperly denominated dead Stock; but when deposited in Banks, to become the basis of a paper circulation, which takes their character and place, as the signs or representatives of value, they then acquire life, or, in other words, an active and productive quality. This idea, which appears rather subtle and abstract, in a general form, may be made obvious and palpable, by entering into a few particulars. It is evident, for instance, that the money, which a merchant keeps in his chest, waiting for a favourable opportunity to employ it, produces nothing 'till that opportunity arrives. But if instead of locking it up in this manner, he either deposits it in a Bank, or invests it in the Stock of a Bank, it yields a profit, during the interval; in which he partakes, or not, according to the choice he may have made of being a depositor or a proprietor; and when any advantageous speculation offers, in order to be able to embrace it, has has only to withdraw his money, if a depositor, or if a proprietor to obtain a loan from the Bank, or to dispose of his Stock; an alternative seldom or never attended with difficulty, when the affairs of the institution are in a prosperous train. His money thus deposited or invested, is a fund, upon which himself and others can borrow to a much larger amount. It is a well established fact, that Banks in good credit can circulate a far greater sum than the actual quantum of their capital in Gold and Silver. The extent of the possible excess seems indeterminate; though it has been conjecturally stated at the proportions of two and three to one. . . .

Secondly, Greater facility to the Government in obtaining pecuniary aids, especially in sudden emergencies. This is another and an undisputed advantage of public banks: one, which as already remarked, has been realised in signal instances, among ourselves. The reason is obvious: The capitals of a great number of individuals are, by this operation, collected to a point, and placed under one direction. The mass, formed by this union, is in a certain sense magnified by the credit attached to it: And while this mass is always ready, and can at once be put in motion, in aid of the Government, the interest of the bank to afford that aid, independent of regard to the public safety and welfare, is a sure pledge for its disposition to go as far in its compliances, as can in prudence be desired. There is in the nature of things, as will be more particularly noticed in another place, an intimate connection of interest between the government and the Bank of a Nation.

Thirdly. The facilitating of the payment of taxes. This advantage is produced in two ways. Those who are in a situation to have access to the Bank can have the assistance of loans to answer with punctuality the public calls upon them. This accommodation has been sensibly felt in the payment of duties heretofore laid, by those who reside where establishments of this nature exist. This however, though an extensive, is not an universal benefit. The other way, in which the effect here contemplated is produced, and in which the benefit is general, is the encreasing of the quantity of circulating medium and the quickening of circulation. The manner in which the first happens has already been traced. The last may require some illustration. When payments are to be made between different places, having an intercourse of business with each other, if there happens to be no private bills, at market, and there are no Bank notes, which have a currency in both, the consequence is, that coin must be remitted. This is attended with trouble, delay, expense and risk. If on the contrary, there are bank notes current in both places, the transmission of these by the post, or any other speedy, or convenient conveyance answers the purpose; and these again, in the alternations of demand, are frequently returned, very soon after, to the place from whence they were first sent: Whence the transporation and retransportation of the metals are obviated; and a more convenient and more expeditious medium of payment is substituted. Nor is this all. The metals, instead of being suspended from their usual functions, during this process of vibration from place to place, continue in activity, and administer still to the ordinary circulation; which of course is prevented from suffering either diminution or stagnation. These circumstnaces are additional causes of what, in a practical sense, or to the purposes of business, may be called greater plenty of money. And it is evident, that whatever enhances the quantity of circulating money adds to the ease, with which every industrious member of the community may acquire that portion of it, of which he stands in need; and enables him the better to pay his taxes, as well as to supply his other wants. Even where the circulation of the bank paper is not general, it must still have the same effect, though in a less degree. For whatever furnishes additional supplies to the channels of circulation, in one quarter, naturally contributes to keep the streams fuller elsewhere. This last view of the subject serves both to illustrate the position, that Banks tend to facilitate the payment of taxes; and to exemplify their utility to business of every kind, in which money is an agent. . . . The combination of a portion of the public Debt in the formation of the Capital, is the principal thing, of which an explanation is requisite. The chief object of this is, to enable the creation of a capital sufficently large to be the basis of an extensive circulation, and an adequate security for it. As has been elsewhere remarked, the original plan of the Bank of North America contemplated a capital of ten millions of Dollars, which is certainly not too broad a foundation for the extensive operations, to which a National Bank is destined. But to collect such a sum in this country, in gold and silver, into one depository, may, without hesitation, be pronounced impracticable. Hence the necessity of an auxiliary which the public debt at once presents.

This part of the fund will be always ready to come in aid of the specie. It will more and more command a ready sale; and can therefore expeditiously be turned into coin if an exigency of the Bank should at any time require it. This quality of prompt convertibility into coin, renders it an equivalent for that necessary agent of Bank circulation; and distinguishes it from a fund in land of which the sale would generally be far less compendious and at great disadvantage. The quarter yearly receipts of interest will also be an actual addition to the specie fund during the intervals between them and the half yearly dividends of profits. The objection to combining land with specie, resulting from their not being generally in possession of the same persons, does not apply to the debt, which will always be found in considerable quantity among the monied and trading people.

The debt composing part of the capital, besides its collateral effect in enabling the Bank to extend its operations, and consequently to enlarge its profits, will produce a direct annual revenue of six per centum from the Government, which will enter into the half yearly dividends received by the Stockholders.

When the present price of the public debt is considered, and the effect which its conversion into Bank Stock, incorporated with a specie fund, would in all probability have to accelerate its rise to the proper point, it will easily be discovered, that the operation presents in its outset a very considerable advantage to those who may become subscribers; and from the influence, which that rise would have on the general mass of the Debt, a proportional benefit to all the public creditors, and, in a sense, which has been more than once adverted to, to the community at large. . . ..

The last thing, which will require any explanatory remark, is the authority proposed to be given to the President to subscribe to the amount of two millions of Dollars on account of the Public. The main design of this is to enlarge the specie fund of the Bank, and to enable it to give a more early extension to its operations. Though it is proposed to borrow with one hand what is lent with the other, yet the disbursement of what is borrowed will be progressive, and Bank notes may be thrown into circulation, instead of the gold and silver. Besides, there is to be an annual reimbursement of a part of the sum borrowed, which will finally operate as an actual investment of so much specie. In addition to the inducements to this measure, which results from the general interest of the Government, to enlarge the sphere of the utility of the Bank, there is more particular consideration, to wit, that as far as the dividend on the Stock shall exceed the interest paid on the loan, there is a positive profit.

REPORT ON MANUFACTURES DECEMBER 5, 1791

The Secretary of the Treasury in obedience to the order of the House of Representatives, of the 15th day of January 1790, has applied his attention, at as early a period as his other duties would permit, to the subject of Manufactures; and particularly to the means of promoting such as will tend to render the United States, independent on foreign nations, for military and other essential supplies. And he there [upon] respectfully submits the following Report.

The expediency of encouraging manufactures in the United States, which was not long since deemed very questionable, appears at this time to be pretty generally admitted. The embarrassments, which have obstructed the progress of our external trade, have led to serious reflections on the necessity of enlarging the sphere of our domestic commerce: the restrictive regulations, which in foreign markets abridge the vent of the increasing surplus of our Agricultural produce, serve to beget an earnest desire, that a more extensive demand for that surplus may be created at home: And the complete success which has rewarded manufacturing enterprise, in some valuable branches, conspiring with the promising symptoms, which attend some less mature essays, in others, justify a hope, that the obstacles to the growth of this species of industry are less formidable than they were apprehended to be; and that it is not difficult to find, in its further extension; a full indemnification for any external disadvantages, which are or may be experienced, as well as an accession of resources, favourable to national independence and safety. . . .

It ought readily to be conceded, that the cultivation of the earth—as the primary and most certain source of national supply— as the immediate and chief source of subsistence to man—as the principal source of those materials which constitute the nutriment of other kinds of labor—as including a state most favourable to the freedom and independence of the human mind—one, perhaps, most conducive to the muliplication of the human species—has *intrinsically a strong claim to pre-eminence over every other kind of industry.* But, that it has a title to any thing like an exclusive predilection, in any country, ought to be admitted with great caution. That it is even more productvie than every other branch of Industry requires more evidence, than has yet been given in support of the position. That its real interests, precious and important as without the help of exaggeration, they truly are, will be advanced, rather than injured by the due encouragement of manufactures, may, it is believed, be satisfactorily demonstrated. And it is also believed that the expediency of such encouragement in a general view may be shewn to be recommended by the most cogent and persuasive motives of national policy.

It has been maintained, that Agriculture is, not only, the most productive, but the only productive species of industry. The reality of this suggestion in either aspect, has, however, not been verified by any accurate detail of facts and calculations; and the general arguments, which are adduced to prove it, are rather subtil and paradoxical, than solid or convincing. . . .

Not only the wealth; but the independence and security of a Country, appear to be materially connected with the prosperity of manufactures. Every nation, with a view to those great objects, ought to endeavor to possess within itself all the essentials of national supply. These comprise the means of *subsistence, habitation, clothing,* and *defence.*

The possession of these is necessary to the perfection of the body politic, to the safety as well as to the welfare of the society; the want of either, is the want of an important organ of political life and Motion; and in the various crises which await a state, it must severely feel the effects of any such deficiency. The extreme embarrassments of the United States during the late War, from an incapacity of supplying themselves, are still matter of keen recollection: A future war might be expected again to exemplify the mischiefs and dangers of a situation, to which that incapacity is still in too great a degree applicable, unless changed by timely and vigorous exertion. To effect this change as fast as shall be prudent, merits all the attention and all the Zeal of our Public Councils; 'tis the next great work to be accomplished.

The want of a Navy to protect our external commerce, as long as it shall Continue, must render it a peculiarly precarious reliance, for the supply of essential articles, and must serve to strengthen prodigiously the arguments in favour of manufactures. . . . It is not uncommon to meet with an opin[ion] that though the promoting of manufactures may be the interest of a part of the Union, it is contrary to that of another part. The Northern and southern regions are sometimes represented as having adverse interests in this respect. Those are called Manufacturing, these Agricultural states; and a species of opposition is imagined to subsist between the Manufacturing and Agricultural interests.

This idea of an opposition betweeen those two interests is the common error of the early periods of every country, but experience gradually dissipates it. Indeed they are perceived so often to succour and to befriend each other that they come at length to be considered as one; a supposition which has been frequently abused and is not universally true. Particular encouragements of particular manufactures may be of a Nature to sacrifice the interests of landholders to those of manufacturers; But it is nevertheless a maxim well established by experience, and generally acknolwedged, where there has been sufficient experience, that the *aggregate* prosperity of manufactures, and the *aggregate* prosperity of Agriculture are intimately connected. In the Course of the discussion which has had place, various weighty considerations have been adduced operating in support of that maxim. Perhaps the superior steadiness of the demand of a domestic market for the surplus produce of the soil, is alone a convincing argument of its truth.

Ideas of a contrariety of interests between the Northern and southern regions of the Union, are in the Main as unfounded as they are mischievous. The diversity of Circumstances on which such contrariety is usually predicated, authorises a directly contrary conclusion. Mutual wants constitute one of the strongest links of political connection, and the extent of the[se] bears a natural proportion to the diversity in the means of mutual supply. . . . It is a truth as important as it is agreeable, and one to which it is not easy to imagine exceptions, that every thing tending to establish *substantial* and *permanent order,* in the affairs of a Country, to increase the total mass of industry and opulence, is ultimately beneficial to every part of it. On the Credit of this great truth, an acquiescence may safely be accorded, from every quarter, to all institutions and arrangements, which promise a confirmation of public order, and an augmentation of National Resource.

But there are more particular considerations which serve to fortify the idea, that the encouragement of manufactures is the interest of all parts of the Union. If the Northern and middle states should be the principal scenes of such establishments, they would immediately benefit the more southern, by creating a demand for productions; some of which they have in common with the other states, and others of which are either peculiar to them, or more abundant, or of better quality, than elsewhere. These productions, principally are Timber, flax, Hemp, Cotton, Wool, raw silk, Indigo, iron, lead, furs, hides, skins and coals. Of these articles Cotton and Indigo are peculiar to the southern states; as are hitherto *Lead* and *Coal.* Flax and Hemp are or may be raised in greater abundance there, than in the More Northern states; and the Wool of Virginia is said to be of better quality than that of any other state; a Circumstance rendered the more probable by the reflection that Virginia embraces the same latitudes with the finest Wool Countries of Europe. The Climate of the south is also better adapted to the production of silk.

The extensive cultivation of Cotton can perhaps hardly be expected, but from the previous establishment of domestic Manufacturies of the Article; and the surest encouragement and vent, for the others, would result from similar establishments in respect to them.

If then, it satisfactorily appears, that it is the Interest of the United States, generally, to encourage manufactures, it merits particular attention, that there are circumstances, which Render the present a critical moment for entering with Zeal upon the important business. The effort cannot fail to be materially seconded by a considerable and increasing influx of money, in consequence of foreign speculations in the funds—and by the disorders which exist in different parts of Europe. . . .

OPINION ON THE CONSTITUTIONALITY OF THE BANK, FEBRUARY 23, 1791

The Secretary of the Treasury having perused with attention the papers containing the opinions of the Secretary of State and

Attorney General concerning the constitutionality of the bill for establishing a National Bank proceeds according to the order of the President to submit the reasons which have induced him to entertain a different opinion. . . .

In entering upon the argument it ought to be premised, that the objections of the Secretary of State and Attorney General are founded on a general denial of the authority of the United States to erect corporations. The latter indeed expressly admits, that if there be any thing in the bill which is not warranted by the Constitution, it is the clause of incorporation.

Now it appears to the Secretary of the Treasury, that this *general principle* is *inherent* in the very *definition* of *Government* and *essential* to every step of the progress to be made by that of the United States; namely—that every power vested in a Government is in its nature *sovereign*, and includes by *force* of the *term*, a right to employ all the *means* requisite, and fairly *applicable* to the attainment of the *ends* of such power; and which are not precluded by restrictions and exceptions specified in the constitution; or not immoral, or not contrary to the essential ends of political society.

The principle in its application to Government in general would be admitted as an axiom. And it will be incumbent upon those, who may incline to deny it, to *prove* a distinction; and to shew that a rule which in the general system of things is essential to the preservation of the social order is inapplicable to the United States.

The circumstances that the powers of sovereignty are in this country divided between the National and State Governments, does not afford the distinction required. It does not follow from this, that each of the *portions* of powers delegated to the one or to the other is not sovereign *with regard to its proper objects*. It will only *follow* from it, that each has sovereign power as to *certain things*, and not as to *other things*. To deny that the Government of the United States has sovereign power as to its declared purposes and trusts, because its power does not extend to all cases, would be equally to deny, that the State Governments have sovereign power in any case; because their power does not extend to every case. The tenth section of the first article of the Constitution exhibits a long list of very important things which they may not do. And thus the United States would furnish the singular spectacle of a *political society* without *sovereignty*, or of a people *governed* without *government*.

It would be necessary to bring proof to a proposition so clear as that which affirms that the powers of the federal government, *as to its objects,* are sovereign, there is a clause of its Constitution which would be decisive. It is that which declares, that the Constitution and the laws of the United States made in pursuance of it, and all treaties made or which shall be made under their authority shall be the supreme law of the land. The power which can create the *Supreme law* of the land, in any case, is doubtless sovereign *as to such case.*

This general and indisputable principle puts at once an end to the *abstract* question—Whether the United States have power to erect a *corporation?* that is to say, to give a *legal* or *artificial capacity* to one or more persons, distinct from the natural. For it is unquestionably incident to *sovereign power* to erect corporations, and consequently to *that* of the United States, in *relation to the objects* intrusted to the management of the government. The difference is this—where the authority of the government is general, it can create corporations in *all cases*; where it is confined to certain branches of legislation, it can create corporations only in those cases. . . .

It is not denied, that there are *implied,* as well as *express* powers, and that the former are as effectually delegated as the latter. And for the sake of accuracy it shall be mentioned, that there is another class of powers, which may be properly denominated *resulting* powers. It will not be doubted that if the United States should make a conquest of any of the territories of its neighbours, they would possess sovereign jurisdiction over the conquered territory. This would rather be a result from the whole mass of the powers of the government and from the nature of political society, than a consequence of either of the powers specially enumerated. . . . The jursidiction acquired over such conquered territory would certainly be competent to every species of legislation. . . .

Then it follows, that as a power of erecting a corporation may as well be *implied* as any other thing; it may as well be employed as an *instrument* or *mean* of carrying into execution any of the specified powers, as any other instrument or mean whatever. The only question must be, in this as in every other case, whether the mean to be employed, or in this instance the corporation to be erected, has a natural relation to any of the acknowledged objects or lawful ends of the government. . . .

2

The Funding System, A Blessing to Creditors
Stephen Higginson to Henry Knox, Boston, April 7, 1790

Reactions to the establishment of the funding system were generally favorable among the mercantile community of the larger towns and highly enthusiastic among the most sophisticated of the speculators. The letter below reflects the attitude of New England's mercantile leaders. Stephen Higginson (1743-1828) was already a wealthy man in 1790 as a result of his wartime speculations as a privateer. He rose from obscurity, and by h time of this death was among the richest men in Boston. His correspondent, Henry Knox (1750-1806) was the first Secretary of War and former commander of artillery in Washington's armies. He also had risen from humble beginnings and tied his hopes to daring speculations in land.

The Sentiments you express, as to the future prospects of our Country are very natural, when judging by the past, and reasoning from analogy. In that view of the Subject, there appears too much reason to fear yet farther fluctuations, if not changes, in the tempers, and dispositions of the people toward the Government of the Union. But it appears to me, that a general alteration in the habits and feelings of the people has taken place for the better; and that many new circumstances have arisen; tending to increase the force and respectability of Government, and to give a strong impression of the necessity of its being suported. Habits of industry and frugality are taking place of those of luxury and dissipation, more generally and with more celerity than I expected. It is a growing Idea, that the manners contracted during the War must be done away; and that every Class of Citizens must expect only to thrive by the means commonly successful in a time of peace. With such Sentiments impressed on the minds of the body of the

SOURCE. J. F. Jameson, ed., "Letters of Stephen Higginson," American Historical Association, *Report, 1896,* Washington: Government Printing Office, 1897, Volume 1, pp. 781-782.

people, and the advantages they will derive soon from the System proposed by the Secretary of the Treasury, and from some general commercial Arrangements, which may soon be expected, the situation of individuals will become more easy and eligible, and private happiness be more generally enjoyed. From the same causes, I expect, the Government will be gradually increasing in its energy and dignity, and will daily extend its protection and blessings. The public mind, to judge from this part of the Union, has kept pace with the times; and has been prepared, with wonderful success and facility, for new Events. There seems to be a general conviction, that the Union must be supported, as the alone Source of national Security; and that every burthen necessary to the Object must be cheerfully bourne. If the Secretary's report should be adopted, Government will receive a very great addition of strength, by the joint support of all classes of public Creditors; and will soon be possessed, exclusively, of every source of revenue except direct taxation. This invidious resource will remain to the States, and, by its operation, will produce an effect favorable to the Union. In short the Government of the Union now seems to have a fair prospect. Its measures contemplated have national and right objects in view. They are marked strongly with wisdom and decision; and they will, in my opinion, if adopted with union, and executed with firmness and address, ensure permanent safety and happiness to this people. thus have I given you a concise and general view, of my present impressions, as to the affairs of the Union; and with that confidence, which one candid man ought to feel toward another. . . .

Virginia Opposition to the Funding System
Washington to David Stuart, New York, June 15, 1790

Virginia's reaction to the Hamiltonian program and especially to the plan for assuming the state debt was in direct contrast to that of mercantile Massachusetts. David Stuart (1753-1816), physician and personal friend of the President, had reported resentments and fears brewing from a variety of sources, among them rumors of federal emancipation schemes and the appearance in Virginia of northern speculators who were hurriedly buying up depreciated paper from the uninformed. Washington takes pains to defend his conduct in the letter printed here.

Your letter of the 2nd Instant came duly to hand. . . . Your description of the public Mind, in Virginia, gives me pain. It seems to be more irritable, sour and discontented than (from the information received) it is in any other State in the Union, except Massachusetts; which, from the same causes, but on quite different principles, is tempered like it.

That Congress does not proceed with all that dispatch which people at a distance expect; and which, were they to hurry business, they possibly might; is not to be denied. That measures have been agitated whc. are not pleasing to Virginia; and others, pleasing perhaps to her, but not so to some other States; is equally unquestionable. Can it well be otherwise in a Country so extensive, so diversified in its interests? And will not these different interests naturally produce in an Assembly of Representatives who are to Legislate for, and to assimilate and reconcile them to the general welfare, long, warm and animated debates . . . . our reputation has risen in every part of the Globe; and our credit, especially in Holland, has got higher than that of any Nation in Europe (and where our funds are above par) as appears by *official*

SOURCE. John C. Fitzpatrick, ed., *The Writings of George Washington,* Washington: Government Printing Office, 39 volumes, 1931-1944, Volume XXXI, pp. 49-55.

advices just received. But the conduct we seem to be pursuing will soon bring us back to our late disreputable condition. The introductions of the (Quaker) Memorial respecting Slavery, was to be sure, not only an illjudged piece of business, but occasioned a great waste of time. The final decision thereon, however, was as favourable as the proprietors of that species of property could have expected considering the great dereliction to Slavery in a large part of this Union.

The question of Assumption has occupied a great deal of time, and no wonder; for it is certainly a very important one; and, under *proper* restrictions and scrutiny into Accounts will be found, I conceive, to be just. The Cause in which the expenses of the War was incurred, was a Common Cause, The States (in Congress) declared it so at the beginning and pledged themselves to stand by each other. If then, some States were harder pressed than others, or from particular or local circumstances contracted heavier debts, it is but reasonable when this fact is ascertained (though it is a sentiment I have not made known here) that an allowance ought to be made them when due credit is given others. Had the invaded and hard pressed States believed the case would have been otherwise; opposition in them would very soon, I believe, have changed to submission, and given a different termination to the War.

In a letter of last year to the best of my recollection, I informed you of the motives, which *compelled* me to allot a day for the reception of idle and ceremonious visits. . . Before the custom was established, which now accommodates foreign characters, Strangers, and others who from motives of curiosity, respect to the Chief Magistrate, or any other cause, are induced to call upon me, I *was unable to attend to any other business whatsoever;* for Gentlemen, consulting their own convenience rather than mine, were calling from the time I rose from breakfast, often before, until I sat down to dinner. . . . To please every body was impossible; I therefore adopted that line of conduct whichi combined public advantage with private convenience, and which in my judgment was unexceptionable in itself. That I have not been able to make bows to the taste of poor Colonel Bland, (who, by the by, I believe never saw one of them) is to be regretted . . . would it not have been better to throw the veil of charity over them, ascribing their stiffness to the effects of age, or to the unskillfulness of my teacher, than to pride and dignity of office, which God knows, has no charms for me? for I can truly say I had rather be at Mount Vernon with a friend or two about me, than to be attended at the Seat of Government by the Officers of State and the Representatives of every Power in Europe. . . .

4

Hamilton's Defense and Counterattack
Alexander Hamilton to Edward Carrington, Philadelphia, May 26, 1792

From Hamilton's viewpoint, the open opposition of Jefferson and particularly of Madison, with whom he had so closely worked for a decade, was a betrayal. To Edward Carrington (1748-1810) of Richmond, the Secretary unburdened himself in a letter which he hoped might be circulated to good effect. Carrington was United States Marshal, Collector of Internal Revenue for Virginia, and a trusted lieutenant. He had served as an officer in the Continental Army and was the brother-in-law of another Richmond Federalist, John Marshall. In September 1792 Hamilton took up the fight with Madison directly in a series of able essays over the signature, "Catullus," which may be consulted in the twelfth volume of the Syrett and Cooke edition of Hamilton's papers. An even more detailed defense of the funding and assumption plans may be found in the same volume in the form of questions and answers addressed to the President, pp.229 ff.

Believing that I possess a share of your personal friendship and confidence and yielding to that which I feel towards you— persuaded also that our political creed is the same on *two essential points*, 1st the necessity of *Union* to the respectability and happiness

SOURCE. Harold C. Syrett and Jacob E. Cooke, eds., *The Papers of Alexander Hamilton*, New York: Columbia University Press, 1961 - , Volume XI, pp. 426-445.

of this country, and 2 the necessity of an *efficient* general government to maintain that Union—I have concluded to unbosom myself to you on the present state of political parties and views. . . . Mr. Jefferson is an avowed enemy to a funded debt. Mr. Madison disavows in public any intention to *undo* what has been done; but in a private conversation with Mr. Charles Carroll. . . he favoured the sentiment in Mr. Mercers speech that a Legislature had no right to *fund* the debt by mortgaging permanently the public revenues because they had no right to bind posterity. The inference is that what has been unlawfully done may be undone. . . .

Whatever were the original merits of the funding system, after having been so solemnly adopted, and after so great a transfer of property under it, what would become of the Government should it be reversed? What of the National Reputation? Upon what system of morality can so atrocious a doctrine be maintained? In me, I confess, it excites *indignation and horror!*

What are we to think of those maxims of Government by which the power of a Legislature is denied to bind the Nation by a *Contract* in an affair of *property* for twenty-four years? For this is precisely the case of the debt. What are to become of all the legal rights of property, of all charters to corporations, nay, of all grants to a man, his heirs, and assigns for ever, if this doctrine be true. What is the term for which a government is in capacity to *contract?* Questions might be multiplied without end to demonstrate the perniciousness and absurdity of such a doctrine.

In almost all the questions great and small which have arisen since the first session of Congress, Mr. Jefferson and Mr. Madison have been found among those who were disposed to narrow the Federal authority. The question of a National Bank is one example. The question of bounties to the Fisheries is another . . . [Madison] has lost no opportunity of sounding the alarm with great affected solemnity at encroachment meditated on the rights of the States, and of holding up the bugbear of a faction in the Government having designs unfriendly to Liberty.

This kind of conduct has appeared to me the more extraordinary on the part of Mr. Madison as I know for a certainty it was a primary article in his Creed that the real danger in our system was the subversion of the National authority by the preponderancy of the State Governments. . . .

Mr. Jefferson, it is known, did not in the first instance cordially acquiesce in the new constitution of the U States; he had many doubts and reservations. He left this Country before we had experienced the imbecilities of the former. In France he saw government only on the side of abuses. He drank deeply of the French Philosophy, in Religion, in Science, in politics. He came from France in the moment of a fermentation which he had had a share in exciting. . . . Attempts were made by these Gentlemen in different ways to produce a Commercial Warfare with Great Britain. In this too they were disappointed. . . .

Another circumstance has contributed to widening the breach. 'Tis evident beyond a question, from every movement, that Mr. Jefferson aims with great ardent desire at the Presidential Chair. This too is an important object of the party-politics. It is supposed, from the nature of my former personal and political connexions that I may favor some other candidate. . . .

A word on another point, I am told that serious apprehensions are disseminated in your state as to the existence of a Monarchical party meditating the destruction of State and Republican Government. If it is possible that so absurd an idea can gain ground it is necessary that it should be combatted. I assure you on my *private faith* and *honor* as a Man that there is not in my judgment a shadow of foundation in it. A very small number of men indeed may entertain theories less republican than Mr. Jefferson and Mr. Madison; but I am persuaded there is not a man among them who would not regard as both *criminal* and *visionary* any attempt to subvert the republican system of this Country. . . .

As to the destruction of State Governments, the *great* and *real* anxiety is to be able to preserve the National from the too potent and counteracting influence of these Governments. As to my own political Creed, I give it to you with the utmost sincerity. I am *affectionately* attached to the Republican theory. I desire *above all things* to see the *equality* of political rights exclusive of all *hereditary* distinction firmly established by a practical demonstration of its being consistent with the order and happiness of society.

As to State Governments, the prevailing bias of my judgment is that if they can be circumscribed within bounds consistent with the preservation of the National Government they will prove useful and salutary. If the States were all of the size of Connecticut, Maryland, or New Jersey, I should decidedly regard the local Governments as both safe and useful. As the thing now is, however, I acknowledge the most serious apprehensions that the Government of the U States will not be able to maintain itself against their influence. . . .

5

Rising Anger Among the Federalists
Oliver Wolcott, Jr. to Oliver Wolcott, Sr., Philadelphia, February 8, 1793, and Chauncey Goodrich to Oliver Wolcott, Jr., Hartford, February 17, 1793

The two brief letters reprinted here illustrate convictions that had become well established among Federalists by the end of Washington's first term as President: the diabolical demagoguery of the Republican opposition or "Antis" as they continued to be called and the unimpeachable integrity and courage of Hamilton. Partly as political tactic and partly from a belief that where there is smoke there must also be fire, Virginians in the House of Representatives kept up a constant barrage of questions directed at Hamilton, who was suspected of aiding and abetting the speculators either by leaking information to privileged parties or by allowing government funds to be used by syndicates. William B. Giles was the principal watchdog or bloodhound— depending on the point of view—in 1793, a year which also saw the passions of the French Revolution infused into the turmoil of American politics and social life.

Chauncey Goodrich (1759-1815) and the two Wolcotts were well-placed members of the Connecticut establishment. Oliver, the elder (1726-1797), was a perennial public servant—assemblymen, sheriff, signer of the Declaration, general of militia, and governor in the mid-1790's. His son, Oliver Wolcott, Jr. (1760-1833), was Comptroller of the United States Treasury in 1793, a devoted admirer of Hamilton whom he succeeded two years later,

SOURCE. George Gibbs, *Memoirs of the Administrations of Washington and John Adams,* 2 volumes, New York: privately printed, 1846, Volume I, pp. 85-86, 87-88.

and one of the first professional federal civil servants. All three men had Yale and Connecticut Congregationalism in their backgrounds.

OLIVER WOLCOTT, JR. TO WOLCOTT, SR.

I presume Giles' motions and speech have been seen by you, in which he has intimated that the Treasury Department have cabbaged several millions of the public money, for which they cannot account. Though I have no conception that this was seriously believed by any, it became indispensable that a complete disclosure of our pecuniary affairs should be made to Congress and the public; full scope to an enquiry has been, therefore, invited. The labor which this has occasioned has been great, but it will, I presume, answer a good purpose. The effect cannot be indifferent; either the public confidence will be promoted or destroyed. My opinion is sufficiently known when I declare that the scrutiny has given me pleasure. I enclose you the first report of the Secretary on the subject. The statements which are referred to are not yet printed; you will, however, perceive a refutation of the most important of the surmises which was hazarded.

The affairs of this country appear to be verging to some important crisis. The opposition to the measures which have been adopted, conduct as if they were influenced by something more than rivalry and personal ambition. Prejudices are excited and passions enlisted into their party which are alike hostile to every system of government, and such as cannot fail to impede business and render the public service insupportable. The best solution which I can give of this disquiet is the pressure of the foreign debts due from the Virginia planters; these, they imagined, had been thrown off. The effect of the treaty and of the constitution is to make them responsible; at least, this is believed, though no decision of this question has been made by the national judiciary. The prospect of poverty and dependence to the Scotch merchants is what they cannot view with patience. They seem determined to weaken the public force, so as to render the recovery of these debts impossible. On the merits of this question I form no opinion, but a strict, impartial and vigorous exercise of the constitutional authority, I deem indispensable to the repose of the country. No rational attempt to support the existing systems ought to be omitted. The experiment of a union with the southern states ought to be now made conclusively; if it shall prove unsuccessful we ought to part like good friends, but the separation ought to be eternal. The inevitable danger, loss of property, interruption of industry, and painful anxiety, which are inseparable from revolutions, forbid the repetition of another experiment.

The papers printed here contain much insufferable cant about aristocracy—this political vice is supposed to prevail in New England, but especially in Connecticut! Much pains will doubtless be exerted to convince the people that they are unhappy. I wish to be informed whether any impresssion is or can be made upon them—the weak side of that people, if they have any, is to be suspicious that they are cheated. Will it be possible for the Southern people to make the opinion prevail? Of several things they may be confident, viz: that the noisy declaimers are, most of them, unworthy of confidence; that their public affairs never were more honestly conducted; and, lastly, that no people on earth ever realized, equally with themselves, that liberty and equality for which the world is now contending.If they maintain their present manners and character, I have no doubt that the first moment of candid and impartial reflection will attribute to them the first rank in society—that their institutions will serve as models for free nations and themes for philosophical and political discussion. The man who attempts to disturb their tranquillity at this time, is the worst enemy of his country and society.

It has been given out that Jefferson will resign his office next March, since which a *Mirabeau* has addressed him with much adulation, and stated how much the *republican* interests in this country will suffer from his retirement. Time will show whether this is a trick to gain a few compliments.

GOODRICH TO WOLCOTT, JR.

I received your letter of the 8th instant, enclosing the Secretary's Report, with a great deal of satisfaction, for by some means or another, I am become as much interested in the prosperity of that really worthy man, as in the fate of an old friend. Giles' motion and speech made no impression in this quarter, not even on the most ignorant; we had no other anxiety about the business, only that Mr. Hamilton might seasonably administer to him the merited chastisement. He has now for his recompense to feel at least the confusion of detected rascality, whatever he may of remorse. One excellence of the chastisement is that it quickly follows the offence.

It is certainly a sign of the downfall of the party, that they become so impudent and inconsiderate in their attacks, and aim their shafts at so many. Among other instances of their folly, it is not the least to think they can gull people in New England by their noisy clamour. It may do with their untaught back country people at their huskings, but our common folks know their true character, which is bullyism—a Yankee won't be bullied by any body.

We shall attend carefully to your papers, and I have no doubt remain firm. Our greatest danger is from the contagion of levelism; what folly is it that has set the world agog to be all equal to French barbers. It must have its run, and the anti-feds will catch at it to aid their mischievous purposes. I believe it is not best to let it pass without remark, and before long the authors of entire equality will shew the world the danger of their wild rant. We treat their Boston notions with derision, and the name of citizen and citess, are only epithets of fun and joke. Is there any danger of a change of measures from the increased representation? If not, the government is safe, for federal measures will gain strength from opposition; a noisy set of discontented demagogues make a rant, and it seems as if they were about breaking up the foundations, but the great body of men of property move slowly, but move with sure success.

CHAPTER IV
THE FRENCH REVOLUTION
AND INTERNAL SECURITY
1793-1796

1

A Warning Against French Theories
Discourses on Davila, Numbers 11 and 12, by John Adams

*The economic and political programs successfully launched during the first
Washington administration promised results entirely satisfactory to leaders of
national outlook and aspiration. In spite of the disconcerting signs of
opposition evidenced during the elections of 1792, there were good reasons to
believe that the future would see the dimunition of local loyalties, increased
prosperity, and the growth of national power. The realization of these broad
objectives would enable the United States to cope successfully with vexing
problems of western expansion and overseas trade by the application of force to
diplomatic negotiations. British forces still occupied American territory in the*

SOURCE. Charles F. Adams, ed., *Works of John Adams,* 10 vols., Boston: Little,
Brown and Company, 1850-1856, Volume VI, pp. 267, 269-270, 272-273.

Northwest and by so doing blocked any settlement with Indian nations which might unlock vast resources in land, timber, and fur; Spain refused to recognize American rights to transport and trade on the vast Mississippi inland waterway that held the key to western development; and Great Britain continued to thwart the strong American desire for reentry into the West Indian and Far Eastern trade. All of these serious problems were met by negotiations during the second administration but in a manner that exacerbated sectional tensions. Contributing to these tensions and dividing the American people in ways which could not have been predicted in 1789 was the revolution in France which passed through its most violent phase between the time of Washington's second inauguration and the break-up of the first cabinet.

The subject of chapters four and five is the impact of the French Revolution and the European war that sprang from the birth of the radical republic at Paris. The first of these two chapters centers upon the Whiskey Rebellion and the second upon the treaty of 1794 which John Jay negotiated with the British ministry in London. Again, we are examining the Federalist response to these problems and not that of the Jeffersonian opposition or the American people generally. By the end of Washington's term in office, ideological questions had once again become as important as they had been in the early 1780's when the terms "democrat" and "aristocrat" had been freely used as polemic.

At the time that the Vice President of the United States was writing a series of essays for the Philadelphia newspapers against the French Revolution, most Americans—Federalists as well as Jeffersonians—were greeting the news from Paris with enthusiasm. Using a seventeenth-century history of France's civil wars of the Reformation as his backdrop, John Adams, one of the most learned and passionate advocates of the American Revolutionary War era, sketched principles of political science for the edification of his fellow Americans which most of them found scandalous. In English institutions, including a hereditary monarchy and an aristocratic House of Lords, would be found the proper guides to the establishment of liberty, declared Adams, and not in assemblies holding all powers of government in their hands as the French political philosophers advocated. To have the second officer in the new regime appear to repudiate republicanism at its first appearance in France confirmed the worst fears of the Antifederalists, and it was common knowledge that Adams was the author of the Davila essays though published anonymously.

In the selection made here Adams leans heavily upon the theory of moral sentiments and the psychology of politics familiar to Whigs on both sides of the Atlantic. More arresting is his clear prediction of the bloody course which the French Revolution would take, made at a time when constitutional monarchy and bills of rights were the rage at Paris. Unchecked democracy would lead to the same anywhere, Adams insisted. Most Federalist leaders privately agreed.

Emulation, which is imitation and something more—a desire not only to equal or resemble, but to excel, is so natural a movement of the human heart, that, wherever men are to be found, and in whatever manner associated or connected, we see its effects. They are not more affected by it, as individuals, than they are in communities. There are rivalries between every little society in the same city; between families and all the connections by consanguinity and affinity; between trades, faculties, and professions; between congregations, parishes, and churches; between schools, colleges, and universities; between districts, villages, cities, provinces, and nations. . . . But why all this of emulation and rivalry? Because, as the whole history of the civil wars of France, given us by Davila, is no more than a relation of rivalries succeeding each other in a rapid series, the reflections we have made will assist us, both to understand that noble historian, and to form a right judgment of the state of affairs in France at the present moment. They will suggest also to Americans, especially to those who have been unfriendly, and may be now lukewarm to their national constitution, some useful inquiries, such as these, for example: Whether there are not emulations of a serious complexion among ourselves? between cities and universities? between north and south? the middle and the north? the middle and the south? between one state and another? between the government of states and the national government? and between individual patriots and heroes in all these? What is the natural remedy against the inconveniences and dangers of these rivalries? Whether a well-balanced constitution, such as our Union purports to be, ought not to be cordially supported by every good citizen, as our only hope of peace and our ark of safety, till its defects, if it has any, can be corrected? But it must be left to the contemplations of our state physicians to discover the causes and the remedy of that "fever, whereof our power is sick." One question only shall be respectfully insinuated: Whether equal laws, the result only of a balanced government, can ever be obtained and preserved without some sign or other of distinction and degree?

We are told that our friends, the National Assembly of France, have abolished all distinctions. But be not deceived. . .Impossibilities cannot be performed. Have they levelled all fortunes and equally divided all property? Have they made all men and women equally wise, elegant, and beautiful? Have they annihilated the names of Bourbon and Montmorenci, Rochefoucauld and Noailes, Lafayette and La Moignon, Necker and De Calonne, Mirabeau and Bailly? Have they committed to the flames all the records, annals, and histories of the nation? All the copies of Mezerai, Daniel, DeThou, Velly, and a thousands others. . .Have they no record nor memory who are the men who compose the present national assembly? Do they wish to have their distinction forgotten? Have the French officers who served in America melted their eagles and torn their ribbons. . . .

That there is already a scission [schism] in the national assembly, like all others, past, present, and to come, is most certain. There is an aristocratical party, an armed neutrality party, and most probably a monarchical party; besides another division, who must finally prevail, or liberty be lost; I mean a set of members, who are equal friends to monarchy, aristocracy, and democracy, and wish for an equal, independent mixture of all three in their constitution. Each of these parties has its chief, and these chiefs are, or will be, rivals. Religion will be both the object and pretext of some; liberty, of others; submission and obedience of others; and levelling, downright levelling, of not a few. But the attention, consideration, and congratulations of the public will be the object of all. Situation and office will be aimed at by some of all parties. Contests and dissensions will arise between these runners in the same race. The natural and usual progress is, from debate in the assembly to discussions in print; from the search of truth and public utility in both, to sophistry and the spirit of party; evils so greatly dreaded by the ingenuous "Citizen of New Haven" [Condorcet], to whom we have now the honor of paying our first respects. . .the transition is quick and easy to falsehood, imposture, and every species of artificial evolution and criminal intrigue. As unbalanced parties of every description can never tolerate a free injury of any kind, when employed against themselves, the license, and even the most temperate freedom of the press, soon excite resentment and revenge. A writer, unpopular with an opposite party, because he is too formidable in wit or argument, may first be burnt in effigy; or a printer may have his office assaulted. . . .Riots and seditions at length break men's bones, or flay off their skins. Lives are lost; and, when blood is once drawn, men, like other animals, become outrageous. If one party has not a superiority over the other, clear enough to decide everything at its pleasure, a civil war ensues. . . .If this should be the course in France, the poor, deluded, and devoted partisans would soon be fond enough of decorating their leaders with the old titles of dukes, marquises and counts, or doing anything else to increase the power of their commander over themselves, to unite their wills and forces for their own safety and defence, or to give him weight with their enemies.

The men of letters in France are wisely reforming one feudal system; but may they not, unwisely, lay the foundation of another? A legislature in one assembly can have no other termination than in civil dissension, feudal anarchy, or simple monarchy. . . .Pennsylvania and Georgia, who followed her example, have found by experience the necessity of change; and France by the same infallible progress of reasoning will discover the same necessity; happy indeed if the experiment shall not cost her more dear. That the subject is considered in this light by the best friends of liberty in Europe, appears by the words of Dr. [Richard] Price". . .Hereafter when the new constitution, as now formed, has acquired strength by time, the national assembly may find it practicable, as well as expedient, to establish by means of a third estate, such a check as now takes place in the American government and is indispensable in the British government."

French Intrigues in South Carolina

Governor William Moultrie to President George Washington, Columbia, South Carolina, December 7, 1793

It was reports of the kind submitted by Governor Moultrie of South Carolina which preceded as well as followed Genet from Charleston to the capital at Philadelphia and which quickly revealed France's expectations of her official ally. This report of a committee of the South Carolina legislature was specific and left no room for doubt. Others, unofficial and less specific, had been filtering in for seven months, precipitating critical discussions of the posture which the United States should adopt toward the European war. William Moultrie (1730-1805) was a former comrade-in-arms of the President and a respected South Carolina Revolutionary leader on whose word Washington placed reliance.

I have the honor of transmitting to you, the resolves of the Legislature of this State, with a number of affidavits, setting forth that certain persons in this State have been enlisting men for the service of the French public, to go on an expedition against a Power not at war with the United States. The investigation of the whole business is fully expressed in the report of the committee.

P.S. In the message with which the resolves and affidavits were sent to me, I am desired to request, that the names of the several deponents, who have given testimony in the business, may not be made known. The reasons which suggest this secrecy must be obvious. which suggest this secrecy must be obvious.

SOURCE. Walter Lowrie and Matthew S. Clarke, eds., *American State Papers: Documents Legislative and Executive of the Congress of the United States, Class I, Foreign Relations,* Washington: Gales and Seaton, 1833, Volume I, p. 309.

IN THE SOUTH CAROLINA HOUSE OF REPRESENTATIVES, DECEMBER 6, 1793

The committee to whom was referred the business of examining into, and ascertaining the truth of a report, that an armed force is now levying within this State, by persons under a foreign authority without the permission and contrary to the express prohibition of the Government of the United States, report: That they have made diligent inquiry respecting the truth of this report, and have collected such evidence relating thereto as was immediately within their reach; that your committee are perfectly satisfied from the information, on the oaths of divers credible persons, which they have received, that William Tate, Jacob R. Brown, William Urby, Robert Tate, Richard Speke, citizens of this State, and other persons unknown to your committee, also citizens of this State, have received and accepted military commissions from M. Genet, minister plenipotentiary from the republic of France to the United States of America, authorizing them, and instructing them, to raise, organize, train, and conduct troops, within the United States of America; that the avowed purpose for which these troops are now raising, is, to rendezvous in the State of Georgia, and from thence to proceed into the Spanish dominions, with a view to conquest or plunder, as their strength might enable, or opportunity might tempt them; that, in the event of a French fleet approaching the coasts of the Southern States, a junction and cooperation with it is contemplated by the persons above mentioned; but that, though this was the avowed object of these troops and leaders, among themselves; from the injunction to conceal the whole system from persons not initiated, and the subordination established by M. Genet, the author of the plan, and the source of authority to the officers, it is probable that the corps, when raised, must yield to any change of destination which the judgment or inclination of M. Genet may point out to them . . . that the persons above named, in pursuance of the powers vested in them by the said commissions, and in obedience to the instructions of M. Genet and his agents, particularly M. Mangourit, who signed some of the papers, have proceeded by themselves, and by their agents, without any authority from the United States, or from this State, to enroll numbers of the citizens of this State, whom they deluded with the hopes of plunder and the acquisition of riches, in the service of the republic of France, to be subject to the orders of M. Genet, the minister plenipotentiary of France . . . .

That the direct tendency of these measures of the foreign minister is to disturb the internal tranquility of the United States, and to involve them in hostilities with nations with whom they are now at peace, which sound policy requires should be preserved. That, in the opinion of your committee, this attempt is the more dangerous and alarming, as many citizens of the United States have been thereby seduced from their duty by insidious arts practiced on their kindred affections to the French republic; and have been drawn into a scheme, in the execution of which they have usurped the functions of government, and exercised the power of the sword, which the wisdom of the constitution hath vested exclusively in the Congress and President of the United States. . . .

3

The President's Report on the Whiskey Rebellion
Speech to Congress, November 19, 1794

Faced by the two-year breakdown of law and order in western Pennsylvania, Washington turned to military force after his orders to cease and desist had been flaunted. It was a major decision of statecraft for the administration and not the comparatively minor annoyance that on first sight it may appear. The income from the Excise was essential to the functioning of the federal system and to the maintenance of its fiscal integrity; the use of military force against tax-resisters was reminiscent of the Revolution; and the possibility of bloodshed appeared real at the outset. The Confederation had been repeatedly frustrated in its efforts to govern because minorities opposed

SOURCE. Walter Lowrie and Matthew S. Clarke, eds., *American State Papers: Documents Legislative and Executive of the Congress of the United States, Class III, Finance,* Washington: Gales and Seaton, 1832, Volume I, 24-25.

what a majority had agreed upon. Refusal to enforce compliance with the law was judged more hazardous to the life of the republic than the risk of armed confrontation.

Washington's reference to "associations" that had encouraged the rebellion pointed to the many Democratic Societies or Democratic-Republican Societies which had sprung to life following the arrival of Edmund Genet and the pro-French enthusiasms of 1793 and 1794. If, as seems evident, the Republican or Jeffersonian Party benefited in the long run from the outcome of the Whiskey Rebellion, we may doubt the political wisdom of having singled the societies out for public rebuke, Federalists remained convinced that secret cells connected vaguely with the Jacobins at Paris provided a disciplined cadre for the opposition party.

When we call to mind the gracious indulgence of Heaven by which the American People became a nation; when we survey the general prosperity of our country, and look forward to the riches, power, and happiness, to which it seems destined; with the deepest regret do I announce to you that, during your recess, some of the citizens of the United States have been found capable of an insurrection. It is due, however, to the character of our Government, and to its stability, which cannot be shaken by the enemies of order, freely to unfold the course of this event.

During the session of the year one thousand seven hundred and ninety, it was expedient to exercise the legislative power, granted by the constitution of the United States, "to lay and collect excises." In a majority of the States, scarcely an objection was heard to this mode of taxation. In some, indeed alarms were at first conceived, until they were banished by reason and patriotism. In the four western counties of Pennsylvania, a prejudice, fostered and embittered by the artifice of men, who labored for an ascendency over the will of others, by the guidance of their passions, produced symptoms of riot and violence. It is well known, that Congress did not hesitate to examine the complaints which were presented; and to relieve them, as far as justice dictated . . . . The very forbearance to press prosecutions was misinterpreted into a fear of urging the execution of the laws, and associations of men began to denounce threats against the officers employed. From the belief, that, by a more formal concert, their operation might be defeated, certain self-created societies assumed the tone of condemnation. Hence, while the greater part of Pennsylvania itself were conforming themselves to the acts of excise, a few counties were resolved to frustrate them. It is now perceived, that every expectation from the tenderness which had been hitherto pursued was unavailing, and that further delay could only create an opinion of impotency or irresolution in the Government. Legal process was therefore delivered to the marshal against the rioters and delinquent distillers.

No sooner was he understood to be engaged in this duty, than the vengeance of armed men was aimed at his person, and the person and property of the inspector of the revenue. They fired upon the marshal, arrested him, and detained him, for some time, as a prisoner. He was obliged, by the jeopardy of his life, to renounce the service of other process on the west side of the Allegheny mountain; and a deputation was afterwards sent to him to demand a surrender of that which he had served. A numerous body repeatedly attacked the house of the inspector, seized his papers of office, and finally destroyed by fire his buildings and whatsoever they contained. Both of these outrages were to compel the resignation of the inspector; to withstand by force of arms that authority of the United States; and thereby to extort a repeal of the laws of excise, and alteration in the conduct of Government.

Upon the testimony of these facts, an associate justice of the supreme court of the United States notified to me that, "in the counties of Washington, and Allegheny, in Pennsylvania, laws of the United States were opposed, and the execution thereof obstructed, by combinations too powerful to be suppressed by the ordinary course of judicial proceedings, or by the powers vested in the marshal of that district." On this call, momentous in the extreme, I sought and weighed what might best subdue the crisis. On the one hand, the judiciary was pronounced to be stripped of its capacity to enforce the laws; crimes, which reached the very existence of social order, were perpetrated without control; the friends of government were insulted, abused, and overawed into silence, or an apparent acquiescence; and, to yield to the treasonable fury of so small a portion of the United States, would be to violate the fundamental principle of our Constitution, which enjoins that the will of the majority shall prevail. On the other, to array citizen against citizen, to publish the dishonor of such excesses, to encounter the expense, and other embarrassments of so distant an expedition, were steps too delicate, too closely interwoven with many affecting considerations to be lightly adopted. I postponed, therefore, the summoning of the militia immediately into the field; but I required them to be held in readiness, that, if my anxious endeavors to reclaim the deluded, and to convinece the malignant of their danger, should be fruitless, military force might be prepared to act, before the season should be too far advanced.

My proclamation of the 7th of August last was accordingly issued, and accompanied by the appointment of commissioners, who were charged to repair to the scene of insurrection. They were authorized to confer with any bodies of men or individuals. They were instructed to be candid and explicit in stating the sensations which had been excited in the Executive, and his earnest wish to avoid a resort to coercion; to represent, however, that, without submission, coercion *must* be the resort; but to invite them at the same time to return to the demeanor of faithful citizens, by such accommodations as lay within the sphere of Executive power. Pardon, too, was tendered to them by the Government of the United States, and that of Pennsylvania, upon no other condition than a satisfactory assurance of obedience to the laws.

Although the report of the commissioners marks their firmness and abilities, and must unite all virtuous men, by shewing that the means of conciliation have been exhausted, all of those who had committed or abetted the tumults did not subscribe the mild form which was proposed as the atonement; and the indications of a peaceable temper were neither sufficiently general nor conclusive to recommend or warrant the farther suspension of the march of the militia.

Thus the painful alternative could not be discarded. I ordered the militia to march, after once more admonishing the insurgents, in my proclamation of the 25th of September last.

It was a task too difficult to ascertain with precision the lowest degree of force competent to the quelling of the insurrection. From a respect, indeed, to economy, and the ease of my fellow-citizens belonging to the militia, it would have gratified me to accomplish such an estimate. My very reluctance to ascribe too much importance to the opposition, had its extent been accurately seen, would have been a decided inducement to the smallest efficient numbers. In this uncertainty, therefore, I put into motion fifteen thousand men, as being an army which, according to all human calculation, would be prompt and adequate in every view, and might by rendering resistance desperate, prevent the effusion of blood. Quotas had been assigned to the States of New Jersey, Pennsylvania, Maryland, and Virginia; the Governor of Pennsylvania having declared, on this occasion, an opinion which justified a requisition to the other states.

As commander in chief of the militia, when called into the actual service of the United States, I have visited the places of general rendezvous, to obtain more exact information, and to direct a plan for ulterior movements. Had there been room for persuasion, that the laws were secure from obstruction; that the civil magistrate was able to bring to justice such of the most culpable as have not embraced the proffered terms of amnesty, and may be deemed fit objects of example; that the friends to peace and good government were not in need of that aid and countenance which they ought always to receive, and, I trust, ever will receive, against the vicious and turbulent; I should have caught with avidity the opportunity of restoring the militia to their families and homes. But succeeding intelligence has tended to manifest the necessity of what has been done; it being now confessed by those, who were not inclined to exaggerate the ill conduct of the insurgents, that their malevolence was not pointed merely to a particular law, but that a spirit inimical to all order, has actuated many of the offenders. If the state of things had afforded reason for the continuance of my presence with the Army, it would not have been witholden. But every appearance assuring such an issue as will redound to the reputation and strength of the United States, I have judged it most proper to resume my duties at the seat of government, leaving the command with the Governor of Virginia. . . .

In the arrangements to which the possibility of a similar contingency will naturally draw your attention, it ought not to be forgotten that the militia laws have exhibited such striking defects as could not have been supplied but by the zeal of our citizens. Besides the extraordinary expense and waste, which are not the least of the defects, every appeal to those laws is attended with a doubt of its success.

The devising and establishing of a well regulated militia would be a genuine source of legislative honor, and a perfect title to public gratitude. I, therefore, entertain a hope, that the present session will not pass, without carrying, to its full energy, the power of organizing, arming, and disciplining the militia; and thus providing, in the language of the Constitution, for calling them forth to execute the laws of the Union, suppress insurrections, and repeal invasions. . . .

4

Private Reactions to the Whiskey Rebellion
Fisher Ames to Christopher Gore, Philadelphia,
December 17, 1794

In the private letters of Federalist leaders a new note of fear and disdain begins to sound. The concurrence of armed rebellion and feverish excitement over the French Revolution produced in administration supporters a conviction that they stood at the beginning of a dangerous social and political revolution in America. The public generally had not grasped the meaning of The Terror or comprehended the degree of violence unleashed by Robespierre's rise to dominance. Those who were in contact with European developments and who disapproved the levelling or democratic thrust of the French Revolution found it increasingly difficult to understand those who continued to defend it. The phenomenon has become familiar in the twentieth century. Here Fisher Ames, the best of good candidates, points not to opposition but to disloyalty to government. By the end of 1794 polarization was clearly evident.

Your and Mrs. G's approbation of my speech is very flattering, even if your friendly partiality should have augmented it; for that

SOURCE. Seth Ames, ed., *Works of Fisher Ames,* 2 volumes, Boston: Little, Brown and Company, 1854, Volume I, pp. 156-157.

partiality is worth as much as the praise of more partial critics. Indeed, the resources of private friendship are peculiarly necessary to a man in such a government as ours. Bright as the prospect now is, I am decided one thing will make it answer: to speak [in the manner of the] French, a revolutionary effort, a rising, in mass, at the elections, to purify Congress from the sour leaven of antifederalism. So much faction as now exists in it will kill. Good men must not be duped. I stake my credit on it. The disease may and will produce many deaths. I know but one cure—the real federalism of the body of the electors. The lottery was three blanks to one prize in August last; and had Harry Lee been Governor of Virginia, probably that region would have *whiskeyed* This state for a long time acted a whiskey part, till, by the zeal of New Jersey, the talents of the little Secretary [Hamilton], the weight of the President's name, and bad management among the rioters, the tide turned in favor of government. Disaffection enough to begin, if not to complete, a revolution actually existed. The talk of all rascals, that they are in favor of supporting government, ought to deceive only blockheads. . . .

Excuse my croaking. I feel sure of turbulent times, unless more changes take place than I see any cause to expect. Time, I begin to think, is against us. State factions get better organized and more diffused. The best men are weary, and in danger of being driven out. The President, with whom his country lives, will quit in disgust, or be in a few years with Timoleon and Epaminondas. As our system is now constituted, the reaction of party will be, in ordinary times, infinitely stronger than the action of the constituted authorities. . . .

A storm will rise on the plan for sinking the debt. It is proposed to pay off the redeemable part yearly; but it will be necessary to prolong or render perpetual the revenue acts of the last session. That will be opposed, under the old pretext of a land tax in lieu of them but really with a view of having no tax. Keep your eye on the progress of this business, for as the faction [the Republicans] will labor hard to take away, or at least to lessen, the purse of the government, they will be obliged to run on the shoals of a land tax to hide their design. To dismiss the troops, will be another object. No purse, no sword, on the part of authority; clubs, mobs, French influence on the side of faction. A very intelligible arrangement. . . .

5

Continued French Activity in the Back Country Memorandum of Oliver Wolcott, Jr. to the President, May 19-21, 1796

The extent of French ambitions in the New World was far greater than even the most suspicious Federalist realized at the time. Genet's hopes of fomenting rebellion in Canada and of launching expeditions against Spanish Louisiana came to nought when his own government recalled him upon the demand of the United States. He chose not to risk trial at the hands of the Paris Jacobins and was granted asylum in the United States. His more circumspect successor, Joseph Fauchet, put a stop to the most flagrant of these filibustering activities but was implicated along with Secretary of State Edmund Randolph in the Whiskey Rebellion and in the last days of his mission openly courted the Philadelphia populace in good revolutionary style. The third and last of France's ministers before the open break in the relations of the two countries, Pierre Adet, ended his official activities in the United States by publishing broadsides against the government in an attempt to influence a national election in favor of the Republican Party.

France's great dream, regardless of factional fortunes and the recurrent Coup d'etat at Paris, was the re-creation of her North American empire. It was not abandoned until the Louisiana Purchase of 1803. Reports of the kind written by Wolcott in 1796 were substantially accurate. It only added to the bitterness of political division in the United States that the Antifederalists or Republicans either justified French intrigues or doubted that they existed.

In the latter part of March last, a gentleman in whose honour and veracity I have entire confidence, called upon me at my office and informed me that M. Collot and M. Warin, with another Frenchman, whose name he did not know, were shortly to proceed

SOURCE. George Gibbs, *Memoirs of the Administrations of Washington and John Adams,* 2 volumes, New York: privately printed, 1846, Volume I, pp. 350-352.

on a tour through the western parts of the United States; that they were to visit the western parts of Pennsylvania, the northwestern territory, Kentucky and the southwestern territory, and that they were to be furnished with maps and drafts of those countries.

They were instructed by M. Adet, the French minister, to observe the posts of the United States on the lakes and elsewhere, and to note all places possessing remarkable natural advantages, either for defence or commerce; that they were to proceed down the Mississippi to New Orleans, and were there in concert with officers of the Spanish government, to ascertain the proper place for a depot; that in their travels they were to ascertain and note the names of the persons of most influence, in every town and village, and were to avail themselves of proper opportunities of observing the temper of the country in respect to a political connection with France; that they were to cherish sentiments favourable to such a connection, observing that the interests of the eastern and western parts of the United States were in collision, that the period was not distant when a separation must take place, and the range of mountains on this side the Ohio, was the natural boundary of the new government, and that in the event of a separation the western people ought to look to France as their natural ally and protector.

The Frenchmen before mentioned were moreover instructed to use all means in their power to promote the election of Mr. Jefferson as President of the United states.

The gentleman who gave me the information before related, said that I might rest satisfied with its truth, as he had seen the instructions in writing from M. Adet, the French minister. He moreover said the expenses of the mission to the western country were to be borne by the French government.

It is not to be understood that what is herein said of the instructions is literally exact, as the gentleman relied upon his memory. He said, however, that he had seen and read the instructions but two days before he informed me of their purport as above stated.

I communicated the information immediately to the President, with the name of the gentleman from whom I received it, and took measures for observing the conduct of the Frenchmen, particularly Collot, and am well assured that they left Philadelphia for the westward about the latter part of April. I have reason to believe that they carried letters from Messrs. Gallatin and Findley [Pennsylvania Republican congressmen].

Having conferred this day with the gentleman who gave me the information before stated, he admitted it to be correctly related in this paper.

CHAPTER V
FEDERALIST FOREIGN
POLICY UNDER WASHINGTON
1794-1796

1

Settling the Mississippi Navigation Problem with Spain
Thomas Pinckney to Secretary of State Edmund Randolph,
San Lorenzo, Spain, October 28, 1795

Officially, the foreign policy of the United States during the Federalist era
was one of neutrality. Washington proclaimed it, and his successor labored to
maintain it. Yet the persistent charge of administration critics throughout the
decade of the nineties was that the orientation of American diplomacy was
pro-British and anti-French. Astute Republican leaders pointed to the dangers
of too great a dependence upon Great Britain and made a strong case for
deliberately shifting avenues of trade to the continent of Europe and especially
toward France. With the outbreak of war in 1793 a great share of the

SOURCE. Walter Lowrie and Matthew S. Clarke, eds., *American State Papers:*
Documents Legislative and Executive of the Congress of the United States, Class I, Foreign
Relations, Volume I, Washington: Gales and Seaton, 1832, pp. 546-549.

carrying trade of Europe fell to the United States, and, although harrassment of American ·shipping sharply increased from both sides, potential profits made the risks worth taking. Federalists, guided by Hamilton, placed a high premium upon enlarging these profits and correctly decided that British sea power was unavoidably the key factor in the commercial equation. Differences with Great Britain were adjusted even at the cost of considerable humiliation; differences with France were also adjusted by means of diplomacy but only after armed defiance. By custom, language, and history—despite the Revolution—Americans were linked with Britain, but the rapprochement with Great Britain that developed in the wake of the Jay Treaty of 1794 rested upon considerations of self-interest as interpreted by a largely northern, commerical elite. The documents in Chapter Five illustrate the manner in which problems which the Confederation had failed to solve were met and overcome.

Spanish policy in the Southwest was similar to that which Great Britain had followed in the Northwest in the period following the Revolutionary War. The Spanish crown refused to recognize either the boundaries or the Mississippi navigation rights established by the peace treaty. It had been one of the striking weaknesses of the Confederation that the rights of Americans to use the great inland water system and to trade their produce at New Orleans could not be wrenched from a second-rate European power. John Jay had negotiated these rights away in 1785 in exchange for a commercial treaty which southerners in particular protested as sectional favoritism at its worst. Jay's agreement was repudiated, but ten years passed before the prize was won after the victory of Anthony Wayne's army over the Indians and their British allies in the Battle of Fallen Timbers in August 1794. Without these rights dreams of wealth from the exploitation of the Southwest were stillborn; for even products of the upper Ohio country could find markets only by river navigation.

The official transmittal letter of the minister plenipotentiary who negotiated a settlement, Thomas Pinckney (1750-1828), is presented here together with key articles from the Treaty of San Lorenzo because they serve to remind us of the successful frontier policy of the Federalists and of the possibilities which existed for the administration to build a strong western and southern following. Pinckney, a South Carolina patrician and lawyer, had served as an officer during the Revolution, as governor of his state, and as minister to Great Britain prior to his Spanish mission. The Pinckney Treaty stood in marked contrast to Jay's more famous treaty of the same historical moment.

I herewith send to you a treaty which I have just signed with the Prince de la Paz, His Catholic Majesty's first minister, and plenipotentiary for negotiating this business. The stipulations which it contains have been formed to the best of my judgement, in conformity to my instructions, and, where they left a latitude to the negotiator, according to what I conceived the interest of our country; and I sincerely believe them to be placed on the most advantageous footing which we could, at this time, obtain, by friendly negotiation. I enclose copies of the written correspondence which passed between the minister and myself, since my letter of the 30th of September, which covered our written negotiation to that time. These will throw some light on points in the treaty which may require it, and render it unnecessary for me to give you a long detail of the oral part of the negotiation, which was frequent, diffuse, and extensive. I, however, took care to bring forward the written documents herewith, which relate to the most material points. I can safely say that, if the treaty be defective, it has not originated in want of assiduity. You will observe by my note of the 24th of October, that I found the difficulties of such an accomodation as I could accede to were so insuperable that I had asked for my passports to return. This may illustrate the difficulties I had to encounter, and the prejudices to be removed, which it requires some knowledge of the national character fully to conceive. The peace concluded between this country and France, and the pacific disposition (at least exteriorly) exhibited to Spain by the British cabinet, added to our critical situation with the last Power, render this negotiation more difficult than it might otherwise have been. With respect to commerical arrangements, you will find the minister completely made up on this point, and that he advanced reasons for delaying arrangements of this nature, which appeared to me to be founded on the true interests of Spain, connected with views to other nations at this juncture, I have lately ceased to insist on this subject; besides which, I believe they wish to reserve the commercial advantages they can offer as the equivalent for a guarantee of their American possessions. . . .

Article 2. To prevent all disputes on the subject of the boundaries which separate the territories of the two high contracting parties, it is hereby declared and agreed as follows, to wit: the southern boundary of the United States, which divides their territory from the Spanish colonies of East and West Florida, shall be designated by a line beginning on the river Mississippi at the northernmost part of the thirty-first degree of latitude north of the equator, which from thence shall be drawn due east to the middle of the river Apalachicola, or Chatahoochee; thence along the middle thereof to the Atlantic Ocean. . . .

Article 4. It is likewise agreed that the western boundary of the United States, which separates them from the Spanish colony of Louisiana, is in the middle of the channel or bed of the river Mississippi, from the northern boundary of the said States to the completion of the thirty-first degree of latitude north of the equator. And His Catholic Majesty has likewise agreed that the navigation of the said river, in its whole breadth, from its source to the ocean, shall be free only to his subjects and the citizens of the United States, unless he shall extend this privilege to the subjects of other Powers by special convention. . . .

Article 22. . . . And in consequence of the stipulations contained in the fourth article, His Catholic Majesty will permit the citizens of the United States, for the space of three years from this time, to deposit their merchandises and effects in the port of New Orleans, and to export them from thence, without paying any other duty than a fair price for the hire of the stores; and His Majesty promises, either to continue this permission, if he finds, during that time, that it is not prejudicial to the interests of Spain, or, if he should not agree to continue it there, he will assign to them, on another part of the banks of the Mississippi, an equivalent establishment. . . . another part of the banks of the Mississippi, and equivalent establishment . . . .

2

Jay's Unofficial Instructions
Alexander Hamilton to John Jay, Philadelphia, May 6, 1794

Britain's declaration of war against France in 1783 and her successful attacks upon French shipping in the months that followed promised immense commercial opportunities to American merchants; for France was forced to immediately open her West Indian islands to neutrals. Completely brushing aside the liberal American principle of free ships-free goods, the British ministry, without sufficient prior notice, began a relentless campaign of attrition. Her maritime rule that trade closed in peacetime could not be opened in wartime was vigorously applied, and in June 1793 grain and flour, important products of the middle states, were added to the list of contraband subject to seizure. So began the process of attack and impressment that plagued relations between the two nations throughout the period of the French Revolution and Napoleon. In 1794 the two stood on the brink of a war which Washington and his advisors believed potentially disastrous.

John Jay, Chief Justice of the United States, was selected to carry out an extremely delicate mission whose aims were set forth officially in Secretary of State Randolph's instructions and influentially, though unofficially, by his friend Hamilton.

I send you herewith sundry papers and documents which contain information that may not be useless to you in your mission. I had wished to have found leisure to say many things to you, but my occupations permit me to offer only a few loose observations.

We are both impressed equally strongly with the great importance of a right adjustment of all matters of past controversy and future good understanding with Great Britain. Yet, important as

SOURCE. Henry C. Lodge, ed., *The Works of Alexander Hamilton*, 12 volumes, New York: G.P. Putnam's Sons, 1904, ZVolume V, pp. 123-128.

this object is, it will be better to do nothing, than to do any thing that will not stand the test of the severest scrutiny—and especially, which may be construed into the relinquishment of substantial right or interest.

The object of indemnification for the depredations committed on our trade, in consequence of the instructions of the 6th of November, is very near the hearts and feelings of the people of this country. The proceeding was an atrocious one. It would not answer in this particular to make any arrangement on the *mere appearance* of indemnification. If nothing substantial can be *agreed upon*, it will be best to content yourself with endeavoring to dispose the British Cabinet, of their own accord, to go as far as they think fit in reparation, leaving the United States at full liberty to act afterwards as they deem proper. . . .

What I have said goes upon the idea of the affair of indemnification standing alone. If you can effect solid arrangements with regard to the points unexecuted of the treaty of peace, the question of indemnification may be managed with less rigor, and may be still more laxly dealt with, if a truly beneficial treaty of commerce, embracing privileges in the West India Islands, can be established. It will be worth the while of the government of this country, in such case, to satisfy, itself, its own citizens who have suffered.

The principle of Great Britain is that a neutral nation ought not to be permitted to carry on, in time of war, a commerce with a nation at war, which it could not carry on with that nation in time of peace. It is not without importance in this question, that the peace system of France allowed our vessels access to her islands with a variety of our principal staples, and allowed us to take from thence some of their products; and that, by frequent colonial regulations, this privilege extended to almost all other articles.

The great political and commercial considerations which ought to influence the conduct of Great Britain towards this country are familiar to you. They are strengthened by their increasing acquisitions in the West Indies, if these shall be ultimately confirmed, which seems to create an absolute dependence on us for supply.

I see not how it can be disputed with you, that this country, in a commerical sense, is more important to Great Britain than any other. The articles she takes from us are certainly precious to her; important, perhaps essential, to the ordinary subsistence of her islands; not unimportant to her own subsistence *occasionally;* always very important to her manufactures, and of real consequence to her revenue. As a consumer, the paper will show that we stand unrivalled. We now consume of her exports from a million to a million and a half sterling more in value than any other foreign country; and while the consumption of other countries, from obvious causes, is likely to be stationary, that of this country is increasing, and for a long series of years will increase rapidly. Our manufactures are no doubt progressive. But our population and means progress so much faster, that our demand for manufactured supply far outgoes the progress of our faculty to manufacture. Nor can this cease to be the case for any calculable period of time.

How unwise then in Great Britain, to suffer such a state of affairs to remain exposed to the hazard of constant interruption and derangement, by not fixing on the basis of a good treaty the principles on which it should continue.

Among the considerations which ought to lead her to a treaty, is the obtaining a renunciation of all pretension of right to sequester or confiscate debts by way of reprisal, etc., though I have no doubt this is modern law of nations. Yet the point of right cannot be considered so absolutely settled as not to make it interesting to fix it by treaty.

There is a fact which has escaped observation in this country, and which, as there has existed too much dispostion to convulse our trade, I have not thought it prudent to bring into view, which it is interesting you should be apprised of. An act of Parliament (27 Geo. III, chap. 27) allows *foreign European vessels,* single decked and not exceeding seventy tons burthen, to carry to certain ports in the British West Indies, particular articles therein enumerated, and also to take from thence certain articles.

This consequently puts an end to the question of precedent, which is so strongly urged against a departure from the British navigation act in our favor, since it gives the precedent of such a departure in favor of others, and to our *exclusion*—a circumstance worthy of particular notice. Our relative situation gives us a stronger plea for an exception in our favor, than any other nation can urge. In paper B [enclosed] the idea of a treaty of commerce on the footing of a *status quo,* for a short period (say five years), is brought into view. I should understand this as admissible *only* in the event of a satisfactory arrangement with regard to the points unexecuted of the treaty of peace.

But you will discover from your instructions, that the opinion which has prevailed is, that such a treaty of commerce ought not to be *concluded* without previous reference here for further instruction. It is desirable, however, to push the British ministry in this respect to a result, that the extent of their views may be ascertained.

The navigation of the Mississippi is to us an object of immense consequence. Besides other considerations connected with it, if the Government of the United States can procure and secure the enjoyment of it to our Western country, it will be an infinitely strong link of union between that country and the Atlantic States. As its preservation will depend on the naval resources of the Atlantic States, the Western country cannot but feel that this essential interest depends on its remaining firmly united with them.

If any thing could be done with Great Britain to increase our chances for the speedy enjoyment of this right, it would be, in my judgement, a very valuable ingredient in any arrangement you could make. Nor is Great Britain without a great interest in the question, if the arrangment shall give to her a participation in that navigation, and a treaty of commerce shall admit her advantageously into this large field of commercial adventure. May it not be possible to obtain a guaranty of our right in this particular from Great Britain, on the condition of mutual enjoyment and a trade on the same terms as to our Atlantic ports. . . . I throw out the subject merely that you may comtemplate it.

3

Hamilton's Opinion of a League of Neutrals
Alexander Hamilton to Secretary of State Edmund Randolph, Philadelphia, July 8, 1794

What power could the United States apply to the problems Jay was instructed to settle? Wayne's military victory had been helpful but only to one area of disagreement. The great prizes of negotiation would be entrance into the British West Indians trade and the avoidance of war. The only trump mentioned in Jay's instructions was the possibility of seeking joint action with other neutrals. In Federalist eyes the great gain of the new regime was the establishment of a financial program which was providing capital and incentive for the building of a strong mercantile and agricultural nation. This edifice rested upon a continuous and growing overseas trade, and British credit as well as markets and goods were the cornerstone. Hamilton, the dominant figure on the administration side of the Jay Treaty struggle, allowed his poor opinion of a flirtation with comparatively weak neutrals to be known to the British minister at Philadelphia. Clearly, he would not allow all that had been built to be jeopardized by an attempted finesse.

The Secretary of the Treasury presents his compliments to the Secretary of State; begs leave to inform him that his opinion on the question lately proposed, respecting the instruction of Mr. Jay, eventually to establish *by treaty* a concert with Sweden and Denmark, is against the measure. The United States have peculiar advantages from situation, which would thereby be thrown into common stock without an equivalent. Denmark and Sweden are too weak and too remote to render a cooperation useful; and the entanglements of a treaty with them might be found very inconvenient. The United States had better stand upon their own ground.

SOURCE. Henry C. Lodge, ed., *The Works of Alexander Hamilton*, 12 volumes, New York: G.P. Putnam's Sons, 1904, Volume V, pp. 135-136.

If a war, on the question of neutral rights, should take place, common interest would be likely to secure all the co-operation which is practicable, and occasional arrangments can be made. What has been already done in this respect appears, therefore, to be sufficient. The subject was varied in the impression entertained of it; but the foregoing is the final result of full reflection.

4

Hamilton's Defense of the British Treaty
"Camillus" Essay Number I, July 22, 1795

The uproar against Jay's treaty called forth all of Hamilton's skill as a pamphleteer which had been recognized since his undergraduate days. Jefferson so feared and respected his talents for persuasion that he pleaded with Madison to enter the lists with him when in the summer of 1795 the Federalist Leader began his "Camillus" series in the New York Argus. In Lodge's edition of Hamilton's writings, these essays, 38 in number, fill three-hundred pages, an indication of the tremendous energy as well as skill which Hamilton could concentrate upon an object of his will. He had been hit by a stone when he tried to address an open-air meeting in New York and took to the newspapers instead. This selection from the first effort by "Camillus" summarizes the line of argument which Hamilton set out for himself in the entire series. His task was not easy; for, despite the gains of entry into Britain's East Indian trade and agreement to evacuate the American Northwest, the treaty was humiliating in many respects. Economic reprisal was given up by the United States in return for very limited trade with the West Indies, American principles of trade were overlooked, and southerners received no compensation for slaves seized during the Revolutionary War.

It was to have been foreseen, that the treaty which Mr. Jay was

SOURCE. Henry C. Lodge, ed., *The Works of Alexander Hamilton,* 12 volumes, G.P. Putnam's Sons, 1904, Volume V, pp. 189-199.

charged to negotiate with Great Britain, whenever it should appear, would have to contend with many perverse dispositions and some honest prejudices; that there was no measure in which the government could engage, so little likely to be viewed according to its intrinsic merits—so very likely to encounter misconception, jealousy, and unreasonable dislike. For this, many reasons may be assigned. . . .

It was known, that the resentment produced by our revolution war with Great Britain had never been entirely extinguished, and that recent injuries had rekindled the flame with additional violence. It was a natural consequence of this, that many should be disinclined to any amicable arrangement with Great Britain, and that many others should be prepared to acquiesce only in a treaty which should present advantages of so striking and preponderant a kind as it was not reasonable to expect could be obtained, unless the United States were in a condition to give the law to Great Britain, and as, if obtained under the coercion of such a situation, could only have been the short-lived prelude of a speedy rupture to get rid of them. . . .

It was not to be mistaken, that an enthusiasm for France and her revolution, throughout all its wonderful vicissitudes, has continued to possess the minds of the great body of the people of this country; and it was to be inferred, that this sentiment would predispose to a jealousy of any agreement or treaty with her most persevering competitor—a jealousy so excessive, as would give the fullest scope to insidious arts to perplex and mislead the public opinion. It was well understood, that a numerous party among us, though disavowing the design, because the avowal would defeat it, have been steadily endeavoring to make the United States a party in the present European war, by advocating all those measures which would widen the breach between us and Great Britain, and by resisting all those which would tend to close it; and it was morally certain, that this party would eagerly improve every circumstance which would serve to render the treaty odious, and to frustrate it, as the most effectual road to their favorite goal.

It was also known beforehand, that personal and party rivalships, of the most active kind, would assail whatever treaty might be made, to disgrace, if possible, its organ. There are three persons prominent in the public eye, as the successor of the actual President of the United States—Mr. Adams, Mr. Jay, and Mr.

Jefferson. No one has forgotten the systematic pains which have been taken to impair the well-earned popularity of the first gentleman. Mr. Jay, too, has been repeatedly the object of attacks with the same view. . . .

Before the treaty was known, attempts were made to prepossess the public mind against it. It was absurdly asserted, that it was not expected by the people that Mr. Jay was to make any treaty; as if he had been sent, not to accomodate differences by negotiation and agreement, but to dictate to Great Britain the terms of an unconditional submission.

Before it was published at large, a sketch, calculated to produce false impressions, was handed out to the public, through a medium noted for hostility to the administration of the government. Emissaries flew through the country, spreading alarm and discontent; the leaders of clubs were everywhere active to seize the passions of the people, and preoccupy their judgments against the treaty. At Boston it was published one day, and the next a town-meeting was convened to condemn it; without ever being read, without any serious discussion, sentence was pronounced against it. . . The intelligence of this event had no sooner reached New York than the leaders of the clubs were seen haranguing in every corner of the city, to stir up our citizens into an imitation of the example of the meeting at Boston. An invitation to meet at the City Hall quickly followed, not to consider or discuss the merits of the treaty, but to unite with the meeting at Boston to address the President against its ratification. This was immediately succeeded by a handbill, full of invectives against the treaty. . .In vain did a respectable meeting of the merchants endeavor, by their advice, to moderate the violence of these views. . .

To every man who is not an enemy to the national government, who is not a prejudiced partisan, who is capable of comprehending the argument, and dispassionate enough to attend to it with impartiality, I flatter myself I shall be able to demonstrate satisfactorily in course of some succeeding papers: 1. That the treaty adjusts, in a reasonable manner, the points in controversy between the United States and Great Britain, as well those depending on the inexecution of the treaty of peace, as those growing out of the present war. 2. That it makes no improper concessions to Great Britain, no sacrifices on the part of the United States. 3. That it secures to the United States equivalents for what they grant. 4. That it lays upon them no restrictions which are incompatible with their honor or their interest. 5. That in the articles which respect war, it conforms to the laws of nations. 6. That it violates no treaty with, nor duty towards, any foreign power. 7. That compared with our other commercial treaties, it is, upon the whole, entitled to a preference. 8. That it contains concessions of advantages by Great Britain to the United States, which no other nation has obtained from the same power. 9. That it gives her no superiority of advantages over other nations with whom we have treaties. 10. That the interests of primary importance to our general welfare are promoted by it. 11. That the too probable result of a refusal to ratify is war, or, what would be still worse, a disgraceful passiveness under violations of our rights, unredressed, and unadjusted; and consequently that it is the true interest of the United States that the treaty should go into effect.

It will be understood that I speak of the treaty as advised to be ratified by the Senate—for this is the true question before the public.

5

Fisher Ames's Speech in the House of Representatives, April 28, 1796

The Senate, after eliminating the article covering West Indian trade, ratified Jay's treaty in June 1795, and President Washington without enthusiasm signed it to complete the American ratification process. The battle was by no means over, however; for money bills originate in the House, and without appropriations to underwrite the costs of the joint Angle-American claims commission proposed by the treaty it was a dead letter. Against Federalist insistence that ratification demanded support from the lower chamber, Republicans fell back upon Virginia theories of republicanism which emphasized popular sovereignty. As maneuvering began in the House,

SOURCE. Seth Ames, ed., *Works of Fisher Ames,* 2 volumes, Boston: Little, Brown and Co., 1854, Volume II, pp. 45-71.

opponents of the treaty—not all of them bona fide *Republicans—were in a clear majority which was gradually reduced by administration and party strategem. Crucial to the outcome was the confusion in the public mind, deliberately created by the Federalists, over the relationship of the British and Spanish treaties; they claimed that one was inoperative without the other. The final vote was a 49 to 49 deadlock broken by the unfortunate presiding officer, Frederick Muhlenburg, in favor of appropriation. It followed immediately after what contemporaries regarded as one of the two or three great speeches of the Federalist era, and selections from it—about one-tenth of the whole—given here suggest its power as the main argument is followed. Ames, sickly and rumored to be near death, speaks in favor of a resolution to appropriate against Representative Blount's resolution that it was inexpedient to appropriate.*

The treaty is bad, fatally bad, is the cry. It sacrifices the interst, the honor, the independence of the United States, and the faith of our engagements to France. If we listen to the clamor of party intemperance, the evils are of a number not to be counted, and of a nature not to be borne, even in idea. The language of passion and exaggeration may silence that of sober reason in other places; it has not done it here. The question here, is whether the treaty is really so very fatal as to oblige the nation to break its faith. I admit that self-preservation is the first law of society, as well as of individuals. It would, perhaps, be deemed an abuse of terms to call that a treaty which violates such a principle. I waive, also, for the present, any inquiry what department shall represent the nation, and annul the stipulations of a treaty. I content myself with pursuing the inquiry whether the nature of the compact can be such as to justify our refusal to carry it into effect. A treaty is the promise of a nation. Now, promises do not always bind him that makes them. . . .

The undecided point is, shall we break faith? And while our country, and enlightened Europe, await the issue with more than curiosity, we are employed to gather, piece-meal, and article by article, from the instrument, a jusitfication for the deed by trivial calculations of commercial profit and loss. This is little worthy of the subject, of this body, or of the nation. If the treaty is bad, it will appear to be so in its mass. Evil to a fatal extreme, if that be its tendency, requires no proof: it brings it. . . .

No government, not even a despotism, will break its faith without some pretext; and it must be plausible, it must be such as will carry the public opinion along with it. Reasons of policy, if not of morality, dissuade even Turkey and Algiers from breaches of treaty in mere wantonness of perfidy, in open contempt of the reproaches of their subjects. Surely a popular government will not proceed more arbitrarily as it is more free; nor with less shame or scruple in proportion as it has better morals. It will not proceed against the faith of treaties at all unless the strong and decided sense of the nation shall pronounce, not simply that the treaty is not advantageous, but that it ought to be broken and annulled. . . .

And who, I would inquire, is hardy enough to pretend that the public voice demands the violation of the treaty? The evidence of the sense of the great mass of the nation is often equivocal; but when was it ever manifested with more energy and precision than at the present moment? The voice of the people is raised against the measure of refusing the appropriations. If gentlemen should urge, nevertheless, that all this sound of alarm is a counterfeit expression of the sense of the public, I will proceed to other proofs. Is the treaty ruinous to our commerce? What has blinded the eyes of the merchants and traders? Surely they are not enemies to trade, nor ignorant of their own interests. Their sense is not so liable to be mistaken as that of a nation, and they are almost unanimous. The articles stipulating the redress of our injuries by captures on the sea are said to be delusive. By whom is this said? The very men whose fortunes are staked upon the competency of that redress say no such thing. They wait with anxious fear, lest you should annul that compact, on which all their hopes are rested. . . . Every treaty is as sure to disappoint extravagant expectations as to disarm extravagant passions. Of the latter, hatred is one that takes no bribes. They who are animated by the spirit of revenge will not be quieted by the possibility of profit.

Why do they complain that the West Indies are not laid open? Why do they lament that any restriction is stipulated on the commerce of the East Indies? Why do they pretend that if they reject this and insist upon more, more will be accomplished? Let us be explicit—more would not satisfy. If all was granted, would not a treaty of amity with Britain still be obnoxious? Have we not this instant heard it urged against our envoy, that he was not ardent enough in his hatred of Great Britain? A treaty of amity is condemned because it was not made by a foe, and in the spirit of one. . . .

I like this, sir, because it is sincerity. With feelings such as these we do not pant for treaties; such passions seek nothing, and will be content with nothing but the destruction of their object. If a treaty left King George his island, it would not answer, not if he stipulated to pay rent for it. It has been said the world ought to rejoice if Britain was sunk in the sea; if, where there are now men, and wealth, and laws, and liberty, there was no more than a sand bank for the sea monsters to fatten on, a space for the storms of the ocean to mingle in conflict. . . .

I can scarcely persuade myself to believe, that the consideration I have suggested requires the aid of any auxiliary; but, unfortunately, auxiliary arguments are at hand. Five millions of dollars, and probably more, on the score of spoliations committed on our commerce, depend upon the treaty; the treaty offers the only prospect of indemnity. Such redress is promised as the merchants place some confidence in. Will you interpose and frustrate that hope, leaving to many families nothing but beggary and despair? It is a smooth proceeding to take a vote in this body; it takes less than half an hour to call the yeas and nays, and reject the treaty. But what is the effect of it? What but this: the very men, formerly so loud for redress, such fierce champions, that even to ask for justice was too mean and too slow, now turn thair capricious fury upon the sufferers, and say by their vote, to them and their families, no longer eat bread; petitioners, go home and starve; we cannot satisfy your wrongs, and our resentments.

Will you pay the sufferers out of the treasury? No. The answer was given two years ago, and appears on our journals. Will you give them letters of marque and reprisal, to pay themselves by force? No. That is war. Besides, it would be an opportunity for those who have already lost much, to lose more. Will you go to war to avenge their injury? If you do, the war will leave you no money to indemnify them. If it should be unsuccessful, you will aggravate existing evils; if successful, your enemy will have no treasure left to give our merchants; the first losses will be confounded with much greater, and be forgotten. . . .

The refusal of the [frontier] posts, inevitable if we reject the treaty, is a measure too decisive in its nature to be neutral in its consequences. From great losses we are to look for great effects. A plain and obvious one will be, the price of the Western lands will fall; settlers will not choose to fix their habitation on a field of battle. Those who talk so much of the interest of the United States, should calculate how deeply it will be affected by rejecting the treaty; how vast a tract of wild land will almost cease to be property. This loss, let it be observed, will fall upon a fund expressly devoted to sink the national debt. What, then, are we called upon to do? However the form of the vote, and protestations of many, may disguise the proceeding, our resolution [not to appropriate] is in substance, and it deserves to wear the title of a resolution, to prevent the sale of Western lands, and the discharge of the public debt.

Will the tendency to Indian hostilities be contested by any one? Experience gives the answer. The frontiers were scourged with war, until the negotiation with Great Britain was far advanced; and then the state of hostility ceased. Perhaps the public agents of both nations are innocent of fomenting Indian war, and perhaps they are not. We ought not, however, to expect that neighboring nations, highly irritated against each other, will neglect the friendship of the savages. . . .

By rejecting the posts, we light the savage fires, we bind the victims. This day we undertake to render account to the widows and orphans whom our decision will make; to the wretches that will be roasted at the stake; to our country; and I do not deem it too serious to say, to conscience and to God. We are answerable; and if duty be any thing more than a word of imposture, if conscience be not a bugbear, we are preparing to make ourselves as wretched as our country. . . .

Let us not hesitate, then, to agree to the appropriation to carry it into faithful execution. Thus we shall save the faith of our nation, secure its peace, and diffuse the spirit of confidence and enterprise that will augment its prosperity. The progress of wealth and improvement is wonderful, and some will think, too rapid. The field for exertion is fruitful and vast, and if peace and good government should be preserved, the acquisitions of our citizens are not so pleasing as the proofs of their industry, as the instruments of their future success. The rewards of exertion go to augment its power. Profit is every hour becoming capital. The vast crop of our neutrality is all seed wheat, and is sown again, to swell beyond calculation, the future harvest of prosperity. In this progress what seems to be fiction is found to fall short of experience. . . .

6

Joseph Charles
The Political Consequences of the Jay Treaty

In a series of superbly constructed essays published posthumously in The William and Mary Quarterly during the year 1955, Joseph Charles (1906-1952) explored the origins of the first American political party system. He clearly presented the evidence that the great furor over the Jay Treaty represented a political watershed. Sectional and economic considerations as well as ideological differences were brought to the surface of American life in an atmosphere of passionate debate which solidified party lines as no other measure or series of measures had done. If the Federalists were ultimately victorious in this struggle, they were nonetheless damaged beyond repair in Charles's view. They would not again be able to decry partisanship or effectively appeal for the kind of broad consensus that Washington had sought for and believed essential to a well ordered republic. Later his successor, John Adams, attempted to re-create it but only to sharpen differences still further. After the Jay Treaty struggle and after the election of 1796 with which it became intimately connected, men in political life found it increasingly impossible to escape the discipline of party loyalty and caucus. In reviewing Charles's work in the October 1957 American Historical Review, *pp.*

SOURCE. Joseph Charles, *The Jay Treaty: Origins of the American Party System,* New York: Harper Torchbooks 1961, pp. 103-118, copyright (c) 1956 by the Institute of Early American History and Culture; originally appeared in *William and Mary Quarterly,* 3rd Ser., Vol. XII (October 1955), pp. 593-608. Reprinted by permission of Mary Louise Charles.

136-137, Richard B. Morris pointed to the author's heavy bias against Hamilton and the Federalists and his tendency to portray Washington as a passive and dispirited observer of the events described here. Nonetheless, as an analysis of the party development occasioned by the Jay Treaty this essay holds up well in the light of later study.

As we have seen, Jay was sent to Great Britain not only because of the strained relations between that country and the United States, which is the reason usually given for his mission, but also because of the party struggle and the condition of public opinion in this country. In order to understand the prolonged and bitter fight over the adoption of the Jay Treaty, it is necessary to keep in mind each of these factors in its immediate background: the one which grew out of the international situation and the one which sprang from domestic politics. Viewing only the relative situations of the two countries, the terms which Jay brought back may have been as good as we could have expected, as defenders of the Treaty have always maintained. The opposition, however, as well as many who had previously been strong Federalists, did not believe them to be, and the conditions of the Treaty put more powerful weapons into the hands of the Republicans for the struggle against it than any of them had expected beforehand. The party struggle had gone far enough that there would probably have been at least a perfunctory opposition to almost any treaty that could have been drawn up between the two countries in 1794, but only the conditions of the Jay Treaty itself could have brought about such widespread popular opposition as occurred. We must then, before plunging into the fight over the Treaty, examine its terms briefly.

Since Madison's proposal of the commercial resolutions directed against Great Britain had been of importance in bringing about the Treaty, it is interesting to note that all such regulation of British commerce and shipping to our shores as his resolutions proposed was barred under the Treaty. Although Jay obtained no commercial privileges except trade with the West Indies, and that on conditions so stringent that we refused to accept that part of the Treaty, we gave up for ten years the right to impose any tonnage or tariff discrimination upon British ships or goods. Thus such questions as those raised by Madison's resolutions, which had afforded a strategic rallying point for Republicans, could no longer vex the Federalists once the Treaty was ratified. As far as trade with Great Britain was concerned, we were left in the same position that we had thought so intolerable under the Confederation. Other weaknesses of the Treaty, as evaluated by Samuel Flagg Bemis, include Jay's failure to maintain the honor of the Federal courts in the matter of debts owed to British citizens, which were now to be determined by a mixed commission; the lack of a provision to secure recognition of our adopted principles of international maritime law; the absence of an article protecting our seamen from impressment; and, finally, the failure to secure a mutual hands-off policy with regard to Indians in each other's territory.

It would appear that this treaty could be defended, from the American point of view, only upon the assumptions which underlie "Admiral Mahan's statement that the signature by England of any treaty at all with the United States at that time was an event of 'epochal significance,' a recognition of the existence of American nationality of far greater import than the technical recognition of independence forced from George III in 1783." This was not, however, the view which most Americans of that time took of the matter. They were not asking for recognition of the existence of American nationality. They were asking for a removal of grievances, some of which impaired our sovereignty, and for a basis of commercial and diplomatic relationship which would enable us to remain at peace with her without becoming a British satellite.

A deep and general aversion to the terms of the Jay Treaty is apparent throughout the whole effort to get it approved. As Gaillard Hunt says, "Washington did not pretend to like the treaty. After Jay had delivered it he kept it for four months before he could bring himself to submit it to the Senate." When it was finally submitted, it was passed, after prolonged discussion, on June 24, 1795, by the minimum number of votes necessary. Senator Mason of Virginia, in violation of the resolution of complete secrecy passed by the Senate when consideration of the Treaty began, gave a copy of it to Benjamin Franklin Bache, editor of the *Aurora*, who printed it on June 29 and personally carried the news to Boston, scattering copies of the Treaty at all his stops along the way. Washington had expected to sign the Treaty if the Senate recommended it, but hesitated as the feeling against it began to mount. At the same time the Administration learned that the British had issued a new order for the seizure of our ships carrying provisions to France, an order mistakenly regarded at that time as a renewal of their provision order of June, 1793. Britain continued to retain our posts, the surrender of which was to be our one tangible benefit from the Treaty, until we should ratify, and the new order for the seizure of our ships was regarded as a further attempt at coercion on her part. According to Randolph, Washington told him on July 13 that he "might have informed Mr. Hammond that he [Washington] would never ratify if the provision-order was not removed out of the way." Of Washington's Cabinet, Randolph alone opposed ratification before the order should be rescinded, though Wolcott wished us to ratify without communicating the fact that we had done so until the order was removed.

While the question was in this state, Washington left for Mount Vernon to deliberate further on the matter. Fearful that if the Treaty were ratified, it would so divide the country as to give the French every opportunity to cause embarrassment to our government, he considered that there was more to be apprehended, whether the Treaty was signed or not "than from any other crisis since the beginning of the government." The inner circle of the Federalist party fairly held its breath, awaiting Washington's decision. Oliver Ellsworth wrote cryptically, "If the President decides wrong, or does not decide *soon, his good fortune will forsake him.*" Noah Webster wrote to Oliver Wolcott, "The peace of our Country stands almost committed in either event. . . . A rejection sacrifices Mr. Jay & perhaps many of his friends, a ratification threatens the popularity of the President, whose personal influence is now more essential than ever to our Union." Christopher Gore wrote to King that Washington's delay in signing the Treaty was doing the government incalculable harm in New England:

"Of all the critical situations in which the government has been placed, this is the most extreme. . . . I know of but one step that can arrest this mania, that affords any hope of supporting the government. An address from the President to the people of the United States, stating that he had ratified the treaty. . . ."

When in 1791 Washington had hesitated and taken his full ten days before signing the Bank Bill, the Republicans claimed that the Federalists became very impatient and even threatening. In 1795 Federalist sources show that there would probably have been a split in the party had Washington failed them. Stephen Higginson wrote that if the Treaty were not ratified, "The President and Senate will be at open points, with Jay & Hamilton &c on the side of the latter." We have no evidence that intimations of this sort reached Washington, and that they did seems highly improbable. Such threats would not have influenced him. What is significant is that during this period when the Republicans were most active in stirring up public opinion, the Federalists were comparatively quiet. Until they had obtained Washington's approval, they had little basis for an appeal to the public.

While the country was completely absorbed in the question of what Washington would do, Hammond, the British minister, showed Wolcott a dispatch written by Fauchet, the former French minister to the United States, which had been taken in March of that year when the corvette *Jean Bart* was captured by the British man-of-war *Cerberus* The dispatch contained an account dated October 24, 1794, which stated that Randolph, the Secretary of State, had approached Fauchet at that time and had asked him for a sum of money with which he could insure the loyalty of three or four men whose conduct was believed to be of vital importance to the Republicans and hence to France. Upon news that a very urgent matter required his immediate presence, Washington left Mount Vernon and returned to Philadelphia on August 11. On the following day he saw the dispatch and said that he would ratify the Treaty. Randolph, from whom all news of this had been kept, was sent to tell Hammond, with whom he was not on good terms, that we would ratify the Treaty. When the dispatch was shown to Randolph in the presence of the Cabinet, he resigned and the Treaty was ratified. In the controversy which followed Randolph's attempt at self-vindication, he and those Republicans who embraced his cause sought to prove that the accusations against him were merely part of a maneuver to get the Treaty accepted and that Randolph had been disgraced because he was the one Cabinet member who was not in favor of immediate and unqualified acceptance of the Treaty as passed by the Senate. In answer, Washington maintained that the charges against Randolph had had nothing to do with his decision to sign the Treaty.

It seems probable that the Republicans weakened their hold

upon the public and their position with regard to the Treaty to the extent that they embraced Randolph's side of the dispute. Many Republicans thought that Washington had lost all his influence and popularity by signing the Treaty, but no matter how great his losses in this respect, few people were willing to hear him attacked in the terms which Randolph and his adherents used. In one letter Randolph said that Washington had shown toward him "treachery unexampled since Tiberius," and such charges as this only placed Randolph in a worse light than before. It seems clear that whatever motives lay behind his "exposure" and disgrace, the incident was highly effective in diverting attention from questions relating directly to the Treaty, where the Republicans stood on comparatively firm ground with regard to the public opinion of the time, to a contest largely personal in nature.

While the events related above were taking place, the attention of the American people from Georgia to New Hampshire was engrossed as never before in a practical decision of government. Should we or should we not ratify the Treaty? The Republicans had taken the initiative with petitions, incendiary pamphlets, and a series of public meetings held in the larger cities, each of which addressed a memorial to the President. The Federalists denounced those who attended these meetings as the scum of society; but if it was the scum of society which showed this degree of interest—for some of the meetings were large—Jay's treaty is all the more noteworthy as a lesson in the political education of the public during this decade. John Beckley, who had taken a leading part in the planning of these meetings all over the country, wrote of the one in Philadelphia:

"On Saturday, a memorial to the President will be presented, which if adopted will be carried through the different wards of the city and offered for the signature of the individual citizens, by which means we shall discover the names and numbers of the British adherents, old Tories and Aristocrats who modestly assume the title of Federalists, and stile themselves *the best* friends of our beloved President. At the same time it will effectually show the major and decided sense of the great commercial city of Philadelphia. Is it not a painful reflection, my friend, that the machinations and intrigues of a British faction in our country, should place our good old President in the distressing situation of singly opposing himself to the almost unanimous voice of his fellow citizens, and endangering the peace, happiness, and union of America, as well as destroying his own tranquility, peace of mind, good name, and fame. But I trust in heaven to enlighten his mind and give him wisdon and firmness to turn away the evil cup so insidiously prepared for him."

Once the President had signed the Treaty, the real contest over it began, as the Republicans were determined to block the appropriation which the House of Representatives had to make in order to carry into effect certain provisions of the Treaty. After the President's signature, Beckley and his associates made a second attempt to whip up general public feeling, or at least to prevent its decline. To DeWitt Clinton, Beckley wrote:

"We perfectly accord with you in sentiment, and are adopting measures on our part in furtherance of your ideas. A change in the public sentiment now so universally manifested against the treaty, is the great desideratum of our opponents, as they mean to influence a majority of the Representatives in its favor at the coming meeting of Congress;—to this object all their efforts will be pointed, and to frustrate them we have concluded an address to the people of the United States to be printed and dispersed in handbills in the same mode and subject to the same rules of secrecy that we observed in the case of the petition, respecting which not a suspicion is yet excited here—By this means, we hope to give the first effectual blow and to make it as impressive as possible, we shall incorporate in it . . . a history of the late intrigues in the Cabinet, connected with the causes of Mr. Randolph's resignation, which produced the President's ratification of the treaty, and a revocation of his first determination officially made known to Hammonds *sic* not to ratify. . . . Rely on every effort and cooperation here in pursuit of what we religiously think our country's political salvation rests on—the defeat of the treaty."

Although public interest in the Treaty did not remain during the winter of 1795-96 at the level it had reached during the previous summer and fall, it soon revived. In March the question

was brought beofe the House of Representatives for an appropriation to put the Treaty into effect. The parties fought now not only
over the merits of the Treaty, but also over the question whether
the House had the power under the Constitution to refuse to
appropriate the money necessary for a treaty already ratified by
the President and the Senate. Thus the passing of the Treaty had
again come to depend largely upon extraneous factors. The
Constitutional issue presented a true dilemma. Either the Senate
did not have complete power as to treaties, or the House complete
power to initiate financial measures, both of which powers had
been generally assumed supreme.

The immediate effect of this apparent conflict of jurisdication
was to win some support for the Federalists from those who
thought that the House was moved by jealousy of its powers or by
mere political obstructionism, and who regarded its conduct as
another example of the viciousness of party spirit. To many
Republican representatives it must have appeared that the practical question for them to decide was whether it was best to defeat
the Treaty and destroy the prestige of the House, or to pass the
Treaty, vindicate their party and body as moderate and magnanimous, and hope thereby to prevent disaster to Republicanism
later. Aaron Kitchell, a Republican representative from New
Jersey who regarded the Jay Treaty as part of an effort to prepare
the minds of the people for a rupture with France, nevertheless
voted for it so that whatever evils followed could not then be laid
on the House of Representatives. "Should this be the case it would
exactly answer the wish of those who are wishing to destroy the
check which the House of Representatives have in the government."

When the House voted to ask Washington for the papers which
would explain the negotiations on the Treaty, his negative reply,
instructing the House to limit its concern with treaties to appropriations, must have been very galling to Madison and other
Republicans who knew at least as much as Washington of the
view which the Federal Convention took on this and other
matters. On the other hand, it seems to have strengthened the
Federalist position in the country at large.

After the necessary funds were appropriated by the House,
Washington spoke of the public mind as having been agitated at
this time "in a higher degree than it has been at any period since

the Revolution." The agitation was stirred up by both parties and there are letters extant from those who were in a position to know, showing how the public excitement was induced. Beckley wrote to DeWitt Clinton in April concerning three Republican congressmen he considered unreliable on the coming vote for appropriations to implement the Treaty:

"Elected by small majorities, and doubtful from the present circumstance of your state how the political scale will preponderate at another Election, they perhaps wish to steer that course which will best ensure their reelection. So often and so fatally, my friend, do personal supersede public considerations. You can best judge of and will I am sure pursue, *the most prudent* means to keep our three friends in the true course—If *they* go right, the British treaty will infallibly be rejected. But remember whatever is done, *must be done quickly.* You possibly know their political connections, and from *whence* they can be best encouraged and supported."

The development of party machinery had gone a long way when party leaders began to put pressure in this fashion on representatives through their constituents. The Republicans were not the only ones who employed these tactics, however. At about the same time, Rufus King wrote to Hamilton of one of the men Beckley mentions:

"Van Cortlandt will leave this place on Wednesday. Would it not be well to prepare a reception for him which may return him in favor of the Treaty—His friends may be induced to act upon his mind, which balances, as to decide it."

Hamilton was at the same time writing to King, reporting on the situation in New York and giving instructions for the final effort so to arouse public opinion that the recalcitrant representatives should be forced to grant the appropriation for the Treaty. On April 16 he wrote:

"Our merchants here are not less alarmed than those of Philadelphia & will do all they can. All the insurance people meet today— The merchants and traders will meet tomorrow or the next day. A petition will be prepared and circulated among the other citizens."

On April 18 he stated the steps which must be taken in Philadelphia. First the President must rebuke the House of Representatives:

". . .then have the merchants meet in the. . .cities & second by their resolutions the measures of the President & Senate and further address their fellow citizens to cooperate with them, petitions afterward to be handed throughout the United States. The Senate to hold fast and consent to no adjournment till the expiration of the term of service of the present house unless provision made. The President to cause a confidential communication to be made to the British stating candidly what has happened, his regrets, his adherence, nevertheless to the treaty, his resolution to persist in the execution as far as depends on the Executive & his hope that the faith of the country will be eventually preserved. But all this must begin with the President. P. S. If the Treaty is not executed the President will be called on in regard to his character & the public good to *keep the post* till another House of Representatives has pronounced."

These are the concrete suggestions, in a time of crisis, of the man who professed to believe in majority rule.

The appropriations for the Treaty were passed because Republican members from New York, New Jersey, and Pennsylvania who had been opposed to the Treaty and who had not intended to vote the money to put it into effect were finally brought to do so. Washington thought that it was passed because of the "the torrent of Petitions, and remonstrances which were pouring in from all the Eastern and middle States, and were beginning to come pretty strongly from that of Virginia. . ." but it does not seem to have been the pressure of public opinion, stirred up as we have seen by both sides, which changed the views of these men. The vote of the doubtful members was changed by two means: by the threat that the Senate would not ratify Pinckney's treaty with Spain which gave us the use of the Mississippi, and by talk of breaking up the Union such as was used at the time the passing of Assumption was delayed. Chauncey Goodrich wrote to Oliver Wolcott, Sr., in April:

". . .'tis well known that the Senate will, as soon as a vote shall be

had on the resolution before us, if unfortunate, tack an amendment providing for the British treaty, to the Spanish treaty bill,
and inflexibly adhere for all or none. I am not warranted to assert,
but I trust they also will arrest the federal city loan bill, land
office, perhaps appropriation for the army, refuse to rise; in short,
arrest the whole government, and let the people decide."

The way in which these threats affected Republicans may be
seen in the letters of Aaron Kitchell, the center of resistance to the
Treaty among the representatives from New Jersey, who wrote to
Ebenezer Elmer late in March, ". . .my mind recoils from the
issue. I must confess I have heard so many hints lately thrown out
Seeming to espouse a wish for Separation of the union that I fear
it is more than thought of." A little earlier Kitchell had warned
his friend Elmer against resolutions from the New Jersey legislature approving or disapproving the Treaty, lest their state offend
some of the larger ones. He had heard, furthermore, that Judge
Paterson of the Supreme Court had said that Jersey wished to
break off from the Southern states and was ready to do so:

"I fear a Separation may take place Sooner than wee would wish.
In Such a case whether wee are joined to the Eastern or Southern
states we are sure to be the Sufferers. I take it for Granted Mr.
Patterson had no authority for what he said and he must have
been drunk or a fool to make such a declaration."

It was not Kitchell alone who heard rumors that there would be
a separation of the Union if the appropriation were not granted.
The British consul in Philadelphia, Phineas Bond, relied on the
threat of dissolution ". . .for which the leaders of the democratic
party, with all that spirit of Disunion and Discontent, which
marks their conduct are not yet ripe," for the granting of the
money. Early in March Sedgwick wrote "If Disorganization
[meaning a refusal to vote the appropriation] prevails I see not but
that it will then be demonstrated that We cannot live in the same
family." A month later he stated that the anxiety in the city of
Philadelphia was the greatest he had ever seen. "The conversation
of a separation is taking place in almost every company and even I
am obliged to moderate the zeal and cool the passions of more cool
and temperate men."

There had long been a close connection between Sedgwick and

Jonathan Dayton, a representative from New Jersey; and when the House met in December, 1795, Sedgwick had the bulk of the Federalist votes for Speaker, which had been cast unanimously for him in caucus, transferred to Dayton, "whom we carried in triumphantly." During the last of March, Dayton, who had been expected by the Republicans to join them in the Treaty fight, told Sedgwick that he would no longer remain indifferent but would take a decided part for the Treaty. A few days later Sedgwick applied to him for aid on the bill, and Dayton then asked "'what to do to be saved?'" Sedgwick told him to go to Findley, who was from Western Pennsylvania, and tell him that "he alone could save his country from anarchy & probably civil war." If he found Findley malleable, he was to suggest that the latter make the motion "that provision ought to be made for carrying into effect the several late treaties." Sedgwick then suggested to Dayton an outline of the speech Dayton should make at that time, and Dayton said he would "follow my directions explicity." Sedgwick prided himself that he did not rely upon the patriotism of these men but the reverse:

"Dayton is ambitious, bold, and vindictive. Because Jay has prevented the sequestration of debts he has incurred his mortal enmity. But New Jersey is alarmed and Dayton must regain her confidence or he is finished politically. . . . Findley knows that the Spanish treaty will meet the same fate as the British—the Senate will provide for the whole or none. The Spanish treaty is necessary to Findley's constituents and the opposition of the representative has already created prodigious sensibility. How disgusting it is, my friend, that on the weakness & wickedness of unprincipled men in a popular government the happiness of millions may frequently depend."

Sedgwick's last letter on these maneuvers stated that the vote had been delayed until Monday because Dayton thought his influence would get the necessary votes by then. "New Jersey is perfectly electrified and Dayton is anxious to retrieve his character as are Kitchell, Samuel Smith and we hope even Findley and Gallatin. . .it seems impossible to live long in the same family with these scoundrels."

If Sedgwick did not exaggerate his part in getting the appropriation for the Jay Treaty passed and did not misrepresent the considerations which caused several Republicsans to change their votes, the effect of the famous "tomahawk speech" of Fisher Ames, which is frequently credited with passing the bill, has been greatly overestimated. Ames's tone throughout the speech was one warning of the dire effects which would follow refusal to appropriate the money. Without the treaty, he stated, the Union would be endangered and Indian warfare would be brought to the frontiers. The concern of the frontiersmen for our commercial rights is well known; we see here the invalid recluse of Dedham pleading with frontier representatives for the lives of their wives and children. Gallatin remarked in his answer to this famous speech:

"I cannot help considering the cry of war, the threats of a dissolution of government, and the present alarm, as designed for the same purpose, that of making an impression on the fears of this house. It was through the fear of being involved in a war that the negotiation with Great Britain originated; under the impression of fear the treaty has been negotiated and signed; a fear of the same danger, that of war, promoted its ratification; and now every imaginary mischief which can alarm our fears is conjured up, in order to deprive us of that discretion which this House thinks it has a right to exercise, and in order to force us to carry the treaty into effect."

The means by which support for the appropriation was won should be kept in mind when we read such statements as the following:

". . .he [Hamilton] cemented the Federalist group in Congress, and gave it such a pointed efficiency that even when the majority was in fact made up of Jeffersonians, he was able to dominate it and manoeuver it, as is proved by the long discussions and final votes on the Jay treaty."

The above statement was made to prove the contention that Hamilton was a more able party leader than Jefferson; and if use of influence and coercion be the test of party leadership, he unquestionably was. An American counterpart of the scene so frequent in eighteenth-century London, the mob rioting outside a subservient House of Commons, apparently had no terrors for Hamilton. The question of Jefferson's party leadership at the time can hardly be discussed. As we have seen, it was the Jay Treaty more than anything else which made a party leader of him. In addition to this circumstance we must remember that Hamilton and Jefferson were party leaders of such different types that it is very difficult to compare them profitably, in spite of the common tendency to do so. Hamilton must be admitted to have had an undisputed supremacy in the use of the sort of management and pressure which we have seen exhibited in the struggle over the Treaty, but it ought always to be noted that the technique exhibited here is not, under a representative government, the whole story of party leadership. There is no indication that Hamilton ever realized how expensive this Federalist victory was to prove.

The immediate political results of the Jay Treaty may be seen in the changes of party affiliation which it brought about and in the way in which approval or disapproval of it became an issue in the elections of 1796. It altered party alignments and caused each group to close ranks. Because of the stand of the two parties on the Jay Treaty, such men as John Dickinson, Charles Pinckney, and John Langdon became active Republicans, although each was essentially conservative and each came from a state still dominated by the Federalists. Only one of these men, Pinckney, carried his own state for Jefferson in 1800, but each of them was a source of great strength to the Republicans through the country as a whole from 1796 to 1800.

Probably more important in the eventual Federalist defeat than the open defection of such leaders as these was the Federalist loss at this time of many less prominent men who had nevertheless been the backbone of the party. The disastrous effect of the Jay Treaty upon the Federalist party in the South may be estimated by the statement of Judge Iredell, who wrote, ". . .the sentiments *publicly* expressed by Mr. John Rutledge [who had attacked the Treaty], which procured his rejection by the Senate as Chief Justice, although nominated by General Washington, were shared by almost every other man south of the Potomac, even by those personally friendly to Mr. Jay and stanch Federalists."

One of the immediate effects of the Treaty upon party organization was that it occasioned the first of the two Republican caucuses of the decade, thus taking the development of party machinery a step further. In the Republican campaign to elect members of the House in 1796, attacks upon those who had voted for the Treaty were more prominent than any other form of appeal. In Pennsylvania, Republicans were rallied with the call to throw out "Gregg the Trimmer," and to substitute for Federick Muhlenberg, Blair McClenachan, who had recommended "kicking the treaty to hell." The Republicans relied on this type of appeal almost as much in New York, where they were unsuccessful, as in Pennsylvania, which they carried.

It was not only the Republicans who made an issue of the Treaty in the election of 1796. Hugh Williamson wrote in October, 1796, "Yesterday I returned from the Eastern States, having been about 200 miles beyond Boston. Nothing was talked of six weeks ago, but the measures of placing federal Members in the Place of those who voted against supporting the Treaty." A little later William Vans Murray wrote from the Eastern Shore of Maryland that he "never knew an election so much of *principles*," that although the Federalists had a candidate who was very unpopular personally, ". . .yet the language is, our choice is a party question, not a personal matter. . . ." William Bentley, the Unitarian minister of Salem, Massachusetts, noted that a new element appeared to have entered politics. "Electioneering goes on in our own state & in New Hampshire. It extends itself in Boston for the petty officers of the Town. This is the commencement of a new career." Jefferson wrote later of the period following the struggle over the Jay Treaty:

"One source of great change in social intercourse arose. . .tho' its effects were as yet scarcely sensible on society or government. I mean the British treaty, which produced a schism that went on widening and rankling till the years '98, '99, when a final dissolution of all bonds, civil & social, appeared imminent."

CHAPTER VI
THE ADAMS
ADMINISTRATION, 1797-1801

1

Adams Calls for Defense Measures
Message to Congress, Philadelphia, May 16, 1797

For the vast majority of the three and one-half million people who lived in the United States during the late 1790's the fact that political parties skirmished for votes in an atmosphere of increasing ideological tensions or that Federalists retained a hold on the presidency by the slim margin of three electoral votes were not of crucial significance; what mattered to most was the generally prevailing prosperity despite a European war, the state of their crops, and local conditions that touched their immediate well-being. In states such as Pennsylvania and Massachusetts where presidential electors were chosen by popular ballot there was greater interest in politicking than in states where legislatures chose electors, but it was widely assumed that

SOURCE. Walter Lowrie and Matthew S. Clarke, eds., *American State Papers: Documents Legislative and Executive of the Congress of the United States, Class I, Foreign Relations,* Volume I, Washington: Gales and Seaton, 1832, pp. 40-42.

Washington would be reelected until late in the fall, and neither Adams nor Jefferson made any attempt to excite popular interest or solicit support. Problems that worried the political managers and their lieutenants, then, were not those that most men and women knew much about.

The administration that assumed office on March 4, 1797 was, nonetheless, significantly different from either of those over which Washington had presided: the Vice-President was an outsider and a foe to all Federalists except the President, who for a few weeks had hopes of overlooking parties whose existence he despised and of working in harmony with his Revolutionary colleague and formerly close friend, Jefferson; the President's advisers were Washington appointees and, in the main, closer to Hamilton than to Adams; and the party itself reflected the animosity of those two leaders, neither one of whom trusted the other. Perhaps all of these sources of disruption could have been overlooked or glossed over in an atmosphere of peace, but, as the documents in this chapter reveal, decisions which further divided Americans and which divided Federalists against themselves were made in Paris as well as in Philadelphia or in Washington where the federal capitol was moved in 1800. France viewed the Jay Treaty as little more than a thinly disguised alliance and, acting upon this conclusion, pursued policies which turned the Adams administration into a wartime administration subject to pressures which revealed deep cracks in the Federalist edifice.

The second President had devoted a considerable portion of his inaugural address to a testimonial of his impartiality toward European powers and had particularly expressed his liking for the French people among whom he had lived for five years. It was obvious even as he attempted to allay suspicions of his pro-British sympathies that he would inherit serious problems arising from the response of the French Directory to American policies. France, as well as Britain, had seized many American ships and their crews and, in American eyes, without good cause. Charles Cotesworth Pinckney, United States Minister to France, had been ordered out of the French Republic, and five weeks after taking office Adams learned of a new decree from Paris which amounted to a declaration of limited maritime war against the United States—free ships-free goods was repudiated, neutrals carrying British goods would be forced to land in French ports to face condemnation, and American ships not carrying a detailed roster of officers and crewmen, a role d'equipage, were to be considered lawful prizes. Worst, perhaps, Americans serving on foreign vessels flying an enemy flag would be treated as pirates.

Adams ordered Congress into extra sessions and turned to his department heads for advice. Three of them—Pickering, Wolcott, and McHenry—asked Hamilton for suggestions amidst talk of a war which some Federalists openly advocated. Not so Hamilton or Adams. To lead into hostilities a nation whose sympathies had been running so strongly in favor of revolutionary France they both recognized as folly. Adams's recommendation that a new negotiation be attempted while simultaneously arming ships and coastal cities met with enthusiastic approbation from Federalists and marked the beginning of his ascent to unexpected popularity. For Jefferson and his party cohorts, the message was uncalled for and hysterical. They believed the worst about the administration and regarded the "war program" as proof positive of the administration's British bias.

The personal inconveniences to the members of the Senate and of the House of Representatives, in leaving their families and private affairs at this season of the year, are so obvious, that I the more regret the extraordinary occasion which has rendered the convention of Congress indispensable.

It would have afforded me the highest satisfaction to have been able to congratulate you on a restoration of peace to the nations of Europe, whose animosities have endangered our tranquility- . . .While other States are desolated with foreign war or convulsed with intestine divisions, the United States present the pleasing prospect of a nation governed by mild and equal laws, generally satisfied with the possession of their rights. . .yielding a ready and general odedience to laws flowing from the reason, and resting on the only solid foundation, the affections of the people.

It is with extreme regret that I shall be obliged to turn your thoughts to other circumstances, which admonish us that some of these felicities may not be long lasting; but if the tide of our prosperity is full, and a reflux commencing, a vigilant circumspection becomes us, that we may meet our reverses with fortitude, and extricate ourselves from their consequences with all the skill we possess, and all the efforts in our power.

In giving to Congress information of the state of the Union, and recommending to their consideration such measures as appear to me to be necessary or expedient, according to my constitutional duty, the causes and objects of the present extraordinary session will be explained.

After the President of the United States received information that the French government had expressed serious discontents at some proceedings of the government of these States, said to affect the interests of France, he thought it expedient to send that country a new minister, fully instructed to enter on such amicable discussions, and to give such candid explanations, as might happily remove the discontents and suspicions of the French government, and vindicate the conduct of the United States. For this purpose he selected from among his fellow-citizens a character, whose integrity, talents, experience, and services, had placed him in the rank of the most esteemed and respected in the nation. The direct object of his mission was expressed in his letter of credence to the French republic; being "to maintain that good understanding, which, from the commencement of the alliance, had subsisted between the two nations; and to efface unfavorable impressions, banish suspicions, and restore that cordiality which was at once the evidence and the pledge of a friendly union;" and his instructions were to the same effect. . .

A minister thus specially commissioned, it was expected, would have proved the instrument of restoring mutual confidence between the two republics. The first step of the French government corresponded with that expectation.

A few days before his arrival at Paris, the French minister of foreign relations informed the American minister then resident at Paris, of the formalities to be observed by himself in taking leave, and by his successor preparatory to his reception. These formalities they observed, and on the 9th of December, presented officially to the minister of foreign relations, the one, a copy of his letters of recall, the other, a copy of his letters of credence. These were laid before the executive directory. Two days afterwards, the minister of foreign relations informed the recalled American minister, that the executive directory had determined not to receive another minister plenipotentiary from the United States until after the redress of grievances demanded of the American government, and which the French republic had a right to expect from it. The American minister immediately endeavored to ascertain whether, by refusing to receive him, it was intended that he should retire from the territories of the French republic; and verbal answers were given that such was the intention of the directory. For his own justification he desired a written answer, but obtained none until towards the last of January, when, receiving notice in writing, to quit the territories of the republic, he proceeded to Amsterdam, where he proposed to wait for instructions from his government. During his residence in Paris, cards of hospitality were refused him, and he was threatened with being subjected to the jurisdiction of the minister of police. . .

As it is often necessary that nations should treat for the mutual advantage of their affairs, and especially to accommodate and terminate differences, and as they can treat only by ministers, the right of embassy is well known and established by the law and usage of nations. The refusal on the part of France to receive our minister, is then the denial of a right; but the refusal to receive him until we have acceded to their demands without discussion and without investigation, is to treat us neither as allies, nor as friends, nor as a sovereign State.

With this conduct of the French government, it will be proper to take into view the public audience given to the late minister of the United States on his taking leave of the executive directory. The speech of the President discloses sentiments more alarming than the refusal of a minister, because more dangerous to our independence and union, and at the same time studiously marked with indignities towards the government of the United States. It evinces a disposition to separate the people of the United States from the government. . .

I should have been happy to have thrown a veil over these transactions, if it had been possible to conceal them; but they have passed on the great theatre of the world, in the face of all Europe and America, and with such circumstances of publicity and solemnity that they cannot be disguised and will not be soon forgotten. They have inflicted a wound in the American breast. It is my sincere desire, however, that it may be healed. It is my desire, and in this I presume I concur with you and with our constituents, to preserve peace and friendship with all nations; and believing that neither the honor nor the interest of the United States absolutely forbids the repetition of advances for securing these desirable objects with France, I shall institute a fresh attempt at negotiation, and shall not fail to promote and accelerate an accommodation on terms compatible with the rights, duties, interests, and honor of the nation. . . .

The diplomatic intercourse between the United States and France being at present suspended, the government has no means of obtaining official information from that country; nevertheless there is reason to believe that the executive directory passed a decree, on the 2nd of March last, contravening, in part, the treaty of amity and commerce of one thousand seven hundred and seventy-eight, injurious to our lawful commerce, and endangering the lives of our citizens. A copy of this decree will be laid before you. . . .

The naval establishment must occur to every man who considers the injuries committed on our commerce, the insults offered to our citizens, and the description of the vessels by which these abuses have been practised. As the sufferings of our mercantile and seafaring citizens cannot be ascribed to the omission of duties demandable, considering the neutral situation of our country, they are to be attributed to the hope of impunity, arising from a supposed inability on our part to afford protection. To resist the consequences of such impressions. . .is an important duty of government.

A naval power, next to the militia, is the natural defence of the United States. The experience of the last war would be sufficient to show, that a moderate naval force, such as would be easily within the present abilities of the Union, would have been sufficient to have baffled many formidable transportations of troops from one State to another, which were then practised. Our sea-coasts, from their extent, are more easily annoyed, and more easily defended, by a naval force, than any other. With all the materials our country abounds; in skill our naval architects and navigators are equal to any; and commander and seamen will not be wanting.

But although the establishment of a permanent system of naval defence appears to be requisite, I am sensible it cannot be formed so speedily and extensively as the present crisis demands. . . . It remains for Congress to prescribe such regulations as will enable our seafaring citizens to defend themselves against violations of the law of nations; and at the same time restrain them from committing acts of hostility against the powers at war. In addition to this voluntary provision for defence, by individual citizens, it appears to me necessary to equip the frigates, and provide other vessels of inferior force to take under convoy such merchant vessels as shall remain unarmed. . . .

But besides a protection of our commerce on the seas, I think it highly necessary to protect it at home, where it is collected in our most important ports. The distance of the United States from Europe, and the well known promptitude, ardor, and courage of the people in defence of their country, happily diminish the probability of invasion. Nevertheless, to guard against sudden and predatory incursions, the situation of some of our principal seaports demands your consideration; and as our country is vulnerable in other interests besides those of its commerce, you will seriously deliberate whether the means of general defence ought not to be increased by an addition to the regular artillery and cavalry, and by arrangements for forming a provisional army.

With the same view, and as a measure which, even in a time of universal peace, ought not to be neglected, I recommend to your consideration a revision of the laws for organizing, arming, and disciplining the militia, to render that natural and safe defence of the country efficacious. . . .

However we may consider ourselves, the maritime and commercial powers of the world will consider the United States of America as forming a weight in the balance of power in Europe, which never can be forgotten or neglected. It would not only be against our interst, but it would be doing wrong to one half of Europe at least, if we should voluntarily throw ourselves into either scale. It is a natural policy for a nation that studies to be neutral, to consult with other nations engaged in the same studies and pursuits; at the same time that measures ought to be pursued with this view, our treaties with Prussia and Sweden, one of which is expired, and the other near expiring, might be renewed.

2

A Summary Statement of American Grievances
Pinckney, Marshall, and Gerry to Talleyrand, Paris, April 3, 1798

The President followed up his call for defense measures by dispatching John Marshall and Elbridge Gerry to France where as special envoys they joined Pinckney in attempting to adjust differences. After six months of being rebuffed, eluded and divided, the ministers plenipotentiary of the United States prepared a lengthy summary of the American position before Pinckney and Marshall demanded their passports and headed home to heroes' welcomes. Talleyrand, in what was apparently an attempt to play for time, took advantage of Gerry's political sensibilities—or what Marshall and Pinckney angrily regarded as his gullibility—by offering to treat only with him. Talleyrand was able to convince the Massachusetts merchant that he alone represented the last remaining hope for peace between the two nations and repeatedly pressed the point that the official instructions and appointments of the three named them as jointly and singly authorized to treat. Gerry evaded this deadly trap but remained at Paris after his colleagues' departure in the forlorn hope that new instructions would solve his dilemma. The abuse heaped upon him when he returned to a jingoistic America left him loyal to Adams personally but headed down a lonely road which led ultimately to the vice-presidency under James Madison.

The tone of this official dispatch suggests that perusal by the public may have been anticipated by the two Federalist envoys. It was widely reprinted after release by the President as one of the famous X, Y, Z dispatches.

. . . .Still animated by the same spirit which has dictated all their efforts to approach this republic, still searching to remove unfavorable impressions, by a candid display of truths, and a

SOURCE. Walter Lowrie and Matthew S. Clarke, eds., *American State Papers: Documents Legislative and Executive of the Congress of the United States, Class I, Foreign Relations,* Volume II, pp. 191-199.

frank manifestation of the principles which have really governed the United States, and still endeavoring thereby to facilitate the restoration of harmony between two nations, which ought to be the friends of each other, the undersigned will lay before you the result of their reflections on your letter of the 28th Ventose [March 18].

Whatever force you may please to allow their observations, the relative situation of the two republics, it is hoped, will not fail to convince you that they proceed from the most perfect conviction of their justice. You contend, citizen minister, that the priority of complaint is on the side of France, and that those measures, which have so injured and oppressed the people of the United States, have been produced by the previous conduct of their government.

To this the undersigned will now only observe, that if France can justly complain of any act of the Government of the United States, whether that act be prior or subsequent to the wrongs received by that Government, a disposition and a wish to do in the case what justice and friendship may require, is openly avowed, and will continue to be manifested.

Your complaints against the United States may be classed under three heads: 1st, the inexecution of their treaties with France; 2dly, the treaty of amity, commerce, and navigation, formed with Great Britain; 3dly, the conduct of their Government since that treaty. . . .

1st. From the commencement of the war, the American tribunals have, in effect, pretended to the right of taking cognizance of the validity of prizes brought into the ports of the United States by French cruisers. You have not been pleased to state a case in which this right has been asserted, and the undersigned are persuaded that no such case exists.

Far from asserting it, the Government of America has expressly disclaimed it. Mr. Jefferson, the then Secretary of State, in his letter to Mr. [Gouverneur] Morris of the 16th of August, 1793, which letter was laid before the French Government, declares, "that the United States do not pretend any right to try the validity of captures made on the high seas by France, or any other nation, on its enemies. These questions belong, of common usage, to the sovereign of the captor, and, whenever it is necessary to determine them, resort must be had to his courts. This is the case provided for in the 17th article of the treaty, which says, that such prizes shall not be arrested, nor cognizance taken of the validity thereof; a stipulation much insisted on by Mr. Genet and the consuls, and which we never thought of infringing or questioning. . . ."

But the United States have deemed it an indispensable duty to prevent, so far as they could prevent, the practice of hostility against nations with whom they were at peace, within their own limits, or by privateers fitted out in their own ports. . . .

They could not refuse to one belligerent power those rights of ordinary hospitality which were enjoyed by others, which the common usages of nations permit, and which were forbidden by no particular treaty. Such refusal would have been manifestly partial, and a plain departure from that neutral position in which the United States found themselves, and which good faith, integrity, and their best interest impelled them religiously to maintain. . . . They have refused shelter in their ports to the prizes made on the French republic, or to the ships of war belonging to the enemy and accompanying such prizes.

They have permitted ships of war, not bringing prizes with them, to remain in their ports without instituting tribunals to inquire whether such ships have at any time captured French citizens or French property. The reasoning on which this decision was founded, and which appears to the undersigned to have been conclusive, will not now be repeated. It has been detailed in several letters from the Secretary of State of the United States to the minister of France in Philadelphia. The undersigned will only observe, that the construction supposed to be just, and for that reason actually put upon the article, is believed to be more favorable than the literal construction to the interests of France. . . .

The undersigned will now consider what you have stated with respect to the treaty of amity, commerce, and navigation, formed with Great Britain.

You complain, citizen minister, in very strong terms, of the deception alleged to have been practiced with respect to the objects of Mr. Jay's mission to London, and also of the contents of the treaty which that mission produced. You are pleased to observe that it was then said that Mr. Jay had been sent to London, only to negotiate arrangements relative to the depradations committed on the American commerce by the cruisers of Great Britain. By whom, citizen minister, was this said? Not by the President in his message to the Senate announcing the nomination of Mr. Jay; nor by the then Secretary of State, in communicating to Mr. Fauchet the subject of that mission. The documents with respect to this assertion have been stated, and have been fully commented upon. It has been fully demonstrated that the American Government did not seize this occasion to practice a deception so unnecessary, so foreign to its well known character, and which could produce only mischief to itself. As you have in no degree weakened the testimony which is relied on as disproving this allegation, or produced any sort of evidence in support of it, the undersigned cannot but mingle some degree of surprise with the regrets they feel at seeing it repeated, accompanied with the charge of that 'dissimulation' of which all who examine well the conduct of the Government of the United States will so readily pronounce it incapable. You also criminate the secrecy which attended the negotiation. To this complaint, formally insisted on, it was answered that so much of it as was material to this republic was immediately communicated to her minister; and that she had no right to inquire further, or to be dissatisfied that other objects were not disclosed; that it is not the practice of France, nor of any other nation, to communicate to others the particular subjects of negotiation which may be contemplated; and that no nation could be independent, which admitted itself to be accountable to another, for the manner in which it might judge proper to regulate its own concerns. . .

Passing to the treaty itself, you say that the small majority by which it was sanctioned in the two Houses of Congress, and the number of respectable voices raised against it in the nation, depose honorably in favor of the opinion which the French Government has entertained of it. But you must be sensible, citizen minister, that the criterion, by which you ascertain the merits of the instrument in question, is by no means infallible, nor can it warrant the inference you draw from it. In a republic like that of the United States, where no individual fears to utter what his judgment or his passions may dictate, where an unrestrained press conveys alike to the public eye the labors of virtue and the efforts of particular interests, no subject which agitates and interests the public mind can unite the public voice, or entirely escape public censure. . . . .

The third head of your complaints relates to the conduct of the Government of the United States since their treaty with England. You observe that as soon as the treaty in question had been put in execution, the Government of the United States seemed to think itself dispensed from the observance of any measure towards this republic, and you adduce in support of this general observation: 1st, the refusal to permit in the ports of the United States the sale of prizes made by French cruisers; 2dly, the invectives and calumnies against the French Government, its principles, and its officers, contained in certain journals and pamphlets published in the United States; 3dly, the speech of the President to Congress in May last.

1st. The Government of the United States does not permit the sale in their ports of prizes made upon England by the cruisers of France. The fact is admitted. To erect it into an offence, it becomes necessary to prove that this measure violates either the engagements or the neutrality of the United States. Neither is attempted. To show that it violates neither, had this been rendered necessary, would by no means have been deemed an arduous task. It will now only briefly be observed, that the 17th article of the treaty of commerce of the 6th of February 1778, which alone relates to this subject, so far from stipulating for the sale of prizes in the ports of either nation, limits itself to a declaration, that the captors shall have liberty to bring them into port, free from duties, arrests, and searches, and to depart with them to the places expressed in their commissions, thereby evidently contemplating the then existing regulations of this nation. . . .

2dly. . . . .The genius of the constitution and the opinions of the people of the United States, cannot be overruled by those who administer the Government. Among those principles deemed sacred in America, among those sacred rights considered as forming the bulwark of their liberty, which the Government contemplates with awful reverence. . .there is none of which the importance is more deeply impressed on the public mind than the liberty of the press. That this liberty is sometimes carried to excess, that it has sometimes degenerated into licentiousness, is seen and lamented. . . .However desirable those measures might be which might correct without enslaving the press, they have never yet been devised in America. . . .Without doubt this abuse of a valuable privilege is matter of peculiar regret when it is extended to the Government of a foreign nation. The undersigned are persuaded it never has been so extended with the approbation of the Government of the United States. . . .

3dly. You complain of the speech of the President made to Congress in May last. It denounces, you say, the Executive Directory, as searching to propagate anarchy and division in the United States. . . .The President of the Directory addressed the recalled minister [James Monroe] in the following terms: "In presenting today to the Executive Directory your letters of recall, you give to Europe a strange spectacle. France, rich in her liberty, surrounded with the train of her victories, strong in the esteem of her allies, will not abase herself by calculating the consequences of the condescension of the American Government to the suggestions of its ancient tyrants. . . ." This official speech, addressed by the Government of France to that of the United States, through its minister, charges that government with condescensions to the suggestions of its ancient tyrants, speaks of the crafty caresses of certain perfidious persons. . .and desires the minister to assure, not his *Government,* but the *good people* of America, that they will always have the esteem of France, and that they will find in the French people that republican generosity which knows as well how to grant peace as to cause its sovereignity to be respected. . . .

When this speech. . .came to be considered in connexion with other measures; when it came to be considered in connexion with the wide spreading devastation to which their commerce was subjected, with the cruel severities practiced on their seamen, with the recall of the minister of France from the United States, and the very extraordinary manner in which that recall was signified by him both to the Government and people, with the refusal even to hear the messenger of peace deputed from the United States for the sole purpose of conciliation, it could not fail to make on the American mind a deep and serious impression. It was considered as too important to be held from the Congress, by that department of the Government which is charged with the duties of maintaining its intercourse with foreign nations, and of making communications to the legislature. . . .

The undersigned have now, citizen minister, passed through the complaints you urge against the Government of the United States. They have endeavored to consider those complaints impartially, and to weigh them in the scales of justice and truth. . . .The President of the United States has said, "If we have committed errors, and these can be demonstrated, we shall be willing to correct them; if we have done injuries, we shall be willing, on conviction, to redress them." These dispositions on the part of the Government have been felt in all their force by the undersigned, and have constantly regulated their conduct. . . .

The undersigned observe, with infinite regret, that the disposition manifested to treat with the minister who might be selected by this Government is not accompanied with any assurances of receding from those demands of money, heretofore made the considerations on which alone the cessation of hostility, on American commerce, could be obtained. . .You have signified, citizen minister, that the Executive Directory is disposed to treat with one of the envoys, and you hope that this overture will not be attended. . . with any serious difficulty. . . .The result of a deliberation, on this point, is that no one of the undersigned is authorized to take upon himself a negotiation, evidently intrusted by the tenor of their powers and instructions to the whole. . .It is hoped that the prejudices, said to have been conceived against the ministers of the United States, will be dissipated by the truths they have stated. If in this hope they shall be disappointed, and it shall be the will of the Directory to order passports for the whole, or any number of them, you will please to accompany such passports with letters of safe conduct, which will entirely protect, from the cruisers of France, the vessels in which they may respectively sail. . .

3

President Adams Fans the Fires
Public Letter of John Adams to the
Soldier-Citizens of New Jersey, May 31, 1798

Spontaneously and in customary fashion, groups of every description throughout the United States met the disclosure of French duplicity and bullying—for so they regarded Directory foreign policy—by endorsing letters of support for the administration in what appeared to be a crisis that could lead to outright war. Some were on the President's desk prior to the arrival of John Marshall from France in June, but Marshall became the central figure in the celebration of national independence and defiance that reached its crescendo in the summer and early autumn of 1798. Adams was determined to create strong support for his policies and strong Federalist, or proadministration, majorities in the Congress and state legislatures. He gave himself unsparingly to the work of writing out literally hundreds of inflammatory replies to the flood of letters which reached him at Philadelphia or at his home in Quincy where he remained for weeks because of the sickness of his wife. He insisted throughout his life that America needed unity and that only shock treatment such as these letters could achieve it. On July 14, Bastille Day, Federalist leaders in informal caucus came close to agreeing to a declaration of war, and it was in this atmosphere that the Alien and Sedition Acts were conceived. Dozens of letters similar to these may be found in the ninth volume of Adams's published works or in the microfilm edition of the Adams Family Papers.

Among all the numerous addresses which have been presented to me in the present critical situation of our nation, there has been none which has done me more honor, none animated with a more glowing love of our country, or expressive of sentiments more determined and magnanimous. The submission you avow to the

SOURCE. Charles F. Adams, ed., *The Works of John Adams,* 10 volumes, Boston: Little, Brown and Co., 1850-1856, Volume IX, p. 196.

civil authority, an indispensable principle in the character of warriors in a free government, at the same moment when you make a solumn proffer of your lives and fortunes in the service of your country, is highly honorable to your dispositions as citizens and soldiers, and proves you perfectly qualified for the duties of both characters.

Officers and soldiers of New Jersey have as little occasion as they have disposition to boast. Their country has long boasted of their ardent zeal in the cause of freedom, and their invincible intrepidity in the day of battle.

Your voice of confidence and satisfaction, of firmness and determination to support the laws and Constitution of the United States, has a charm in it irresistible to the feelings of every American bosom; but when, in the presence of the God of armies and in firm reliance on his protection, you solemnly pledge your lives and fortunes, and your sacred honor, you have recorded words which ought to [be] indelibly imprinted on the memory of every American youth. With these sentiments in the hearts and this language in the mouths of Americans in general, the greatest nation may menace at its pleasure, and the degraded and the deluded characters may tremble, lest they should be condemned to the severest punishment an American can suffer——that of being conveyed in safety within the lines of an invading army.

4

The Federalist Case for Alien and Sedition Laws
Fisher Ames to Christopher Gore, Dedham, Massachusetts, December 18, 1798

Popular reaction against the alien acts and against the Sedition Act in particular grew strong between July 1798, when they were enacted, and 1800, when the Jeffersonian Republicans made them a focal point of opposition in the turbulent elections of that year. Generally speaking, Americans, and especially their historians, have condemned them with such vehemence that it has become difficult for students of the period to understand how political leaders could defend them. But of course they did, and only by bearing in mind the sudden explosion of French armed might, the introduction of terror on a mass scale, and the continuous intrigues of French agents in America itself can we comprehend the state of mind which led the Federalists into acts which recoiled upon them. Whether rational or not, fears of a French invasion were commmon among them, and even the better legal minds such as those of Adams, Hamilton, and Marshall admitted a need for controls, whatever their reservations about the specific acts introduced in Congress.

Ames's letter to a confidential friend provides a specific instance of what they wished to eliminate or control. Dozens of similar examples may be easily discovered in the correspondence of Federalist leaders from the middle states and the South as well as New England where the shadow of old England living under similar legislation fell most sharply.

Your letters would be valuable if they were not scarce, as they are; and mine would be cheap if I did not labor so much to make them plenty. The scene you survey, and your place near the point or fulcrum of the British power, make me greedy for the news you

SOURCE. Seth Ames, ed., *The Works of Fisher Ames,* 2 volumes, Boston: Little, Brown and Company, Volume I, pp. 245-248.

send, or the comments that explain it. My seat in my chimney-corner compels me to generalize my ideas, and to bore you with essays, instead of amusing you with intelligence. . . .

The struggle with our Jacobins is like the good Christian's with the evil one. It is no amusement to the bystander, and is barren of events for description. Besides, one cannot tell how much others have gone into detail in their letters to you, nor what parts of our drama excite your curiosity, and to write every thing is impossible.

These are my apologies for being dull. When the despatches from our envoys were published here, the Jacobins were confounded, and the trimmers dropt off from the party, like windfalls from an apple-tree in September——the worst of fruit, vapid in cider and soon vinegar. The wretches looked round, like Milton's devils when first recovering from the stunning force of their fall from Heaven, to see what new ground they could take. The alien and sedition bills, and the land tax, were chosen as affording topics of discontent, and, of course, a renewal of the popularity of the party. The meditated vengeance and the wrongs of France done by our treaty [with Britain] were less spouted on. And the implacable foes of the Constitution——foes before it was made, while it was making, and since——became full of tender fears lest it should be violated by the alien and sedition laws. You know that federalists are forever hazarding the cause of needless and rash concessions. John Marshall, with all his honors in blossom and bearing fruit, answers some newspaper queries unfavorably to these laws. George Cabot says that [Harrison Gray] Otis, our representative, condemns him *ore rotundo,* yet, inconsistently enough, sedulously declares his dislike of those laws. G.C. vindicates J.M., and stoutly asserts his soundness of federalism. I deny it. No correct man—no incorrect man even—whose affections and feelings are wedded to the government, would give his name to the base opposers of law, as a means for its annoyance. This he has done. Excuses may palliate—future zeal in the cause may partially atone—but his character is done for. . . .False federalists, or such as act wrong from false fears, should be dealt hardly by, if I were Jupiter. . .The theory of the Feds is worse than that of the *antis,* in one respect. They help the government at a pinch, and then shout victory for two seconds—after which, they coax and try to gain the *antis,* by yielding the very principles in dispute. The moderates are the meanest of cowards, the falsest of hypocrites. The other side has none of them, though it abounds in every other kind of baseness. Their Guy Fauxes are no triflers. They have energy enough to vindicate the French, and, if opportunity favored, to imitate them. They stick to the cause, and never yield any thing that can be contested, nor even then, without a more than equivalent concession. They beat us in industry, audacity, and perseverance; and will at last meet us in the field, where they will be beaten.

There is no describing the impulse which they have given their party to decry these acts. They have sent runners everywhere to blow the trumpet of sedition. One David Brown, a vagabond, ragged fellow, has lurked about in Dedham, telling everybody the sins and enormities of the government. He had been, he said, in all the offices in all States, and knew my speculating connection with you, and how I made my immense wealth. I was not in this part of the country, otherwise I should have noticed his lies—not to preserve my reputation, but to disarm his wickedness. Before I returned from my trip to the westward, he had fled, and a warrant to apprehend him for sedition was not served. . . .There is at least the appearance of tardiness and apathy, on the part of government, in avenging this insult on law. But the judge and attorney think all is done right. The government must display its power *in terrorem,* or, if that be neglected, or delayed, in earnest. So much irritable folly and credulity, managed by so much villany, will explode at last; and the issue will be tried, like the ancient suits, by wager of battle.

I think the clamor against the alien law, a proof that the party has chosen to make one, and that it makes no odds on what the choice falls, an equal clamor being excitable on one as much as on another subject. The [safety of the republic] so plainly requires the power of expelling or refusing admission to aliens, and the rebel Irish, and negroes of the West Indies so much augment the danger, that reason, one would think, was disregarded by the Jacobins, too much even to be perverted. Kentucky is all alien; and we learn that the Governor, Gerard, has made a most intemperate address to the legislature of that State, little short of a manifesto. This is said to be echoed by the legislature. In that case, the issue must be tendered and tried. The gazettes will, no doubt, explain the fact to you more fully than I can at present.

I hear that one of our trio [of envoys] says, that he [Gerry] could not, with *any safety* refuse compliance with the demand to disclose the X,Y,Z of the Paris business. Can any words express the *merit* of the man, who can now plead his fears as his apology? Were I entrusted by a great nation, and called to act on a great stage, I should pray God to give me courage to defy a thousand deaths in such a case. . .Will not Europeans note such facts, and, if they feel a spirit of candor, say for us, that we are yet new in our independence, and that the notions of shame and honor, though not factitious in their origin, are so in their application? Our public men, they will say, will soon learn when they ought to lose life sooner than honor.

5

The Virginia and Kentucky Resolutions Condemned,

Sedition Act Defended

John Marshall and Henry Lee,

Address of the Minority in the

Virginia Legislature, 1799

In January 1799 the Virginia legislature rejected a series of resolutions expressing confidence in President Adams and his handling of the crisis with France by a vote of 68 to 97. Madison's famous resolutions had been endorsed by Virginians only a few weeks previously. An anonymous pamphlet appeared at once protesing both actions, condemning state interposition, and defending the Sedition Act which had produced them. The sixteen-page Address had been attributed to John Marshall, chiefly by his biographer, Albert J. Beveridge, and to Governor Henry Lee, chiefly by librarians. Until more

SOURCE. [John Marshall and Henry Lee]. *Address of the Minority in the Virginia Legislature to the People of that State; containing a Vindication of the Alien and Sedition Laws,*[Richmond, Va., 1799]

evidence is found, it appears wise to conclude that each had a hand in producing it. The selection printed here is in the style of Marshall and he, rather than Lee, is presumed to have written it since the argument is legal and constitutional.

Most defenses of the Sedition Act rested upon its reform of common law procedure in cases of seditious libel, namely, that the truth or falsehood of the charge became the decisive factor, but it is noteworthy in this instance that the law was defended almost exclusively on the basis of its constitutionality and its conformity with the English common law tradition. Marshall made his opposition to the law known in running for election to the House of Representatives declaring it unnecessary and politically inept. He avoided pleading the case of national self-preservation or raison d'etat frequently resorted to later in the case of the Sedition Act of Woodrow Wilson's administration or President Roosevelt's handling of Japanese-Americans after Pearl Harbor. Jefferson and his associates feared and resented Marshall's insistence that English common law remained in force where statutory law was silent, a Federalist position which assumed government powers of great elasticity. Four months later Marshall was elected to Congress by the citizens of Richmond.

. . .All abridgment of the freedom of the press is forbidden, [by the Third Amendment] but it is only an abridgment of that freedom which is forbidden. It becomes then necessary, in order to determine whether the act in question be unconstitutional or not, to inquire whether it does in fact ABRIDGE the freedom of the press.

The act is believed not to have that operation, for two reasons.

1. A punishment of the licentiousness is not considered as a restriction of the freedom of the press.
2. The act complained of does not punish any writing not before punishable, nor does it inflict a more severe penalty than that to which the same writing was before liable.

If by freedom of the press is meant a perfect exemption from all punishment for whatever may be published, that freedom never has, and most probably never will exist. It is known to all, that the person who writes or publishes a libel, may be both sued and indicted, and must bear the penalty which the judgment of his country inflicts upon him. It is also known to all that the person who shall libel the government of the state, is for that offence punishable in the like manner. Yet this liability to punishment for slanderous and malicious publications, has never been considered as detracting from the liberty of the press. In fact the liberty of the press is a term which has a definite and appropriate signification, completely understood. It signifies a liberty to publish, free from previous restraint, any thing and every thing at the discretion of the printer only, but not the liberty of spreading with impunity false and scandalous slanders, which destroy the peace, and mangle the reputation, of an individual or of a community.

If this definition of the term be correct, and it is presumed that its correctness is not to be questioned, then a law punishing the authors and publishers of false, malicious and scandalous libels can be no attack on the liberty of the press.

But the act complained of is no abridgement of the liberty of the press, for another reason. It does not punish any writing not before punishable, nor does it inflict a heavier penalty than the same writing was before liable to.

No man will deny, that at common law, the author and publisher of a false, scandalous and malicious libel against the government or an individual, were subject to fine and imprisonment, at the discretion of the judge. Nor will it be denied, that previous to our revolution, the common law was the law of the land throughout the United States.

We believe it to be a principle incontestibly true, that a change of government does not dissolve obligations previously created, does not annihilate existing laws, and dissolve the bonds of society; but that a people passing from one form of government to another, retain in full force all their municipal institutions, not necessarily changed by the change of government. If this be true, then the common law continued to be the law of the land after the revolution, and was of complete obligation even before the act of our assembly for its adoption. Whether similar acts have been passed by the legislature of other states or not, it is certain that in every state the common law is admitted to be in full force, except as it may have been altered by the statute law. The only question is, whether the doctrines of the common law are applicable to libels against the government of the United States as well as to libels against the governments of the particular states. For such a distinction there seems to be no sufficient reason. It is not to a magistrate of this or that description that the rules of the common law apply. That he is a magistrate, that he is cloathed with the authority of the laws, that he is invested with power by the people, is a sufficent title to the protection of the common law. The government of the United States is for certain purposes as entirely the government of each state, chosen by the people thereof, and cloathed with their authority, as the government of each particular state is the government of every subdivision of that state; and no satisfactory reason has been heretofore assigned why a general rule common to all, and punishing generally the malicious calumniators of magistrates, should not be as applicable to magistrates chosen for the whole, as those chosen for its different parts.

If then it were even true that the punishment of the printer of malicious falsehoods affected the liberty of the press, yet the act does not abridge that liberty, since it does not substitute a harsher or severer rule of punishment than that which before existed.

On points so extremely interesting, a difference of opinion will be entertained. On such occasions all parties must be expected to maintain their real opinions, but to maintain them with moderation and with decency. The will of the majority must prevail, or the republican principle is abandoned, and the nation is destroyed. If upon every constitutional question which presents itself, or on every question we choose to term constitutional, the constructions of the majority shall be forcibly opposed, and hostility to the government excited throughout the nation, there is an end of our domestic peace, and we may for ever bid adieu to our representative government. . . .

At a time when all ought to unite in repelling every evidence of the existence of division in the United States, on which division our enemy calculates, and with her knowledge of which has had the presumption to upraid us, it cannot but inflict a deep wound in the American mind to find the commonwealth of Virginia, exhibiting through her legislature, irresistable testimony of the degrading charge; nor will the embittering reflection be softened by the declaration of a determination to repel foreign invasion, which is occasionally interspersed in those proceedings. Hatred to government is unapt to beget a disposition to unite in its defence, and more probably would project other schemes, coupling defence from invasion with change of political system. The result of which might be union with the invader, for the purpose of accomplishing a *delectable* reform. . . .

6

Hamilton's Plans for Strengthening the Union
Alexander Hamilton to Jonathan Dayton, New York, February 1799

This letter written by Hamilton out of concern for the Virginia and Kentucky Resolutions and the rumblings of insurrection in the southern states is not a favorite of sympathetic Hamilton biographers. The context within which he wrote must be borne in mind, however. Hamilton had been called back into service by Washington and was exhausting himself in determined effort to recruit, provision, and train an army. Exaggerated accounts of Virginia rebelliousness and the collection of armaments were being circulated. Jonathan Dayton of New Jersey was Speaker of the House throughout the Fifth Congress, June 1797 to March 1799. Although violently anti-British in 1794, he had come to support the administration in its handling of the Whiskey Rebellion and the Jay Treaty. In a less detailed letter of similar tone to Senator Theodore Sedgwick of Massachusetts, Hamilton suggested moving troops across Virginia to test the degree of southern opposition to the laws.

An accurate view of the internal situation of the United States presents many discouraging reflections to the enlightened friends of our government and country. Notwithstanding the unexampled success of our public measures at home and abroad—notwithstanding the instructive comments afforded by the disastrous and disgusting scenes of the French Revolution—public opinion has not

SOURCE. Henry C. Lodge, ed., *The Works of Alexander Hamilton,* 12 volumes, New York: G.P. Putnam's Sons, 1904, Volume X, pp. 329-336.

been ameliorated; sentiments dangerous to social happiness have not been diminished; on the contrary, there are symptoms which warrant the apprehension that among the most numerous class of citizens, errors of a very pernicious tendency have not only preserved but have extended their empire. Though some thing may have been gained on the side of men of information and property, more has probably been lost on that of persons of a different description. An extraordinary exertion of the friends of government, aided by circumstances of momentary impression, gave, in the last election for members of Congress, a more favorable countenance to some States than they had before worn; yet it is the belief of well-informed men that no real or desirable change has been wrought in those States. On the other hand, it is admitted by close observers that some of the parts of the Union which, in times past, have been the soundest, have of late exhibited signs of a gangrene begun and progressive.

It is likewise apparent that opposition to the government has acquired more system than formerly, is bolder in the avowal of its designs, less solicitous than it was to discriminate between the Constitution and the administration, and more open and more enterprising in its projects. The late attempt of Virginia and Kentucky to unite the State Legislatures in a direct resistance to certain laws of the Union can be considered in no other light than as an attempt to change the government.

It is stated in addition that the opposition party in Virginia, the headquarters of the faction, have followed up the hostile declarations which are to be found in the resolutions of their General Assembly by an actual preparation of the means of supporting them by force, that they have taken measures to put their militia on a more efficient footing—are preparing considerable arsenals and magazines, and (which is an unequivocal proof how much they are in earnest) have gone so far as to lay new taxes on their citizens. Amidst such serious indications of hostility, the safety and the duty of the supporters of the government call upon them to adopt vigorous measures of counteraction. It will be wise in them to act upon the hypothesis that the opposers of the government are resolved, if it shall be practicable, to make its existence a question of force. Possessing, as they now do, all the constitutional powers, it will be an unpardonable mistake on their part if they do not exert them to surround the Constitution with more ramparts and to disconcert the schemes of its enemies. The measures proper to be adopted may be classed under heads.

First. Establishments which will extend the influence and promote the popularity of the government. Under this head three important expedients occur. *First.* The extension of the judiciary system. *Second.* The improvement of the great communications, as well interiorly as coastwise, by turnpike roads. *Third.* The new institution of a society with funds to be employed in premiums for new inventions, discoveries, and improvements in agriculture and the arts.

The extension of the judiciary system ought to embrace two objects: one the subdivision of each State into small districts (suppose Connecticut into four, and so on in proportion), assigning to each a judge with moderate salary; the other, the appointment in each county of conservators or justices of the peace without judicial powers. Both these descriptions of persons are essential, as well to the energetic execution of the laws as to the purposes of salutary patronage.

The thing, no doubt, would be a subject of clamor, but it would carry with it its own antidote, and when once established, would bring a very powerful support to the government.

The improvement of the roads would be a measure universally popular. None can be more so. . . . The institution of a society, with the aid of proper funds, to encourage agriculture and the arts, besides being productive of general advantage, will speak powerfully to the feelings and interests of those classes of men to whom the benefits derived from the government have been heretofore the least manifest.

Second. Provisions for augmenting the means and consolidating the strength of the government. A million dollars may without difficulty be added to the revenue. . . . The direct taxes ought neither to be increased nor diminished. Our naval force ought to be completed to six ships of the line, twelve frigates, and twenty-four sloops of war. More at this juncture would be disproportionate to our resources, less would be inadequate to the ends to be accomplished. Our military force should, for the present, be kept on its actual footing; making provision for a re-enlistment of the men for five years in the event of a settlement of differences with France—with this condition, that in case of peace between Great Britain, France, and Spain, the United States being then also at peace, all the privates of the twelve additional regiments of infantry, and of the regiment of dragoons, not exceeding twelve to a company, shall be disbanded. The corps of artillerists may be left to retain the numbers which it shall happen to have, but without being recruited until the number of officers and privates shall fall below the standard of the infantry and dragoons. A power ought to be given the President to augment the four old regiments to their war establishment.

The laws respecting volunteer companies, and *eventual army* [reserve or provisional army] should be rendered permanent, and the Executive should proceed without delay to organize the latter. . . . The institution of a military academy will be an auxiliary of great importance. Manufacturies of every article, the woolen parts of clothing included, which are essential to the supply of the army, ought to be established.

Third. Arrangements for confirming and enlarging the legal powers of the government. There are several temporary laws which, in this view, ought to be rendered permanent, particularly that which authorizes the calling out of the militia to suppress unlawful combinations and insurrections.

An article ought to be proposed, to be added to the Constitution, for empowering Congress to open canals in all cases in which it may be necessary to conduct them through the territory of two or more States, or through the territory of a State and that of the United States. The power is very desirable for the purpose of improving the prodigious facilities for inland navigation with which nature has favored this country. It will also assist commerce and agriculture, by rendering the transportation of commodities more cheap and expeditious. It will tend to secure the connection, by facilitating the communication between distant portions of the Union, and it will be a useful source of influence to the government. Happy would it be if a clause could be added to the Constitution, enabling Congress, on the application of any considerable portion of a State, containing not less than a hundred thousand persons, to erect it into a separate State, on the condition of fixing the quota of contributions which it shall make toward antecedent debts, if any there shall be, reserving to Congress the authority to levy within such State the taxes necessary to the payment of such quota, in case of neglect on the part of the State. *The subdivision of the great States is indispensable to the security of the general government, and with it of the Union.*

Great States will always feel a rivalship with the common head: will often be supposed to machinate against etc., and in certain situations will be able to do it with decisive effect. The subdivision of such States ought to be a cardinal point in the federal policy, and small States are doubtless best adapted to the purposes of local regulation and to the preservation of the republican spirit. This suggestion, however, is merely thrown out for consideration. It is feared that it would be inexpedient and even dangerous to propose, *at this time,* an amendment of the kind.

Fourth. Laws for restraining and punishing incendiary and seditious practices. It will be useful to declare that all such writings, etc., which at common law are libels, if levelled against any officer whatsoever of the United States, shall be cognizable in the courts of the United States. To preserve confidence in the officers of the general government, by preserving their reputations from malicious and unfounded slanders, is essential to enable them to fulfil the ends of their appointment. It is, therefore, both constitutional and politic to place their reputations under the guardianship of the courts of the United States. They ought not to be left to the cold and reluctant protection of State courts, always temporizing, and sometimes disaffected. But what avail laws which are not executed? Renegade aliens conduct more than one of the most incendiary presses in the United States—and yet, in open contempt and defiance of the laws, they are permitted to continue their destructive labors. Why are they not sent away? Are laws of this kind passed merely to excite odium and remain a dead letter? Vigor in the executive is at least as necessary as in the legislative branch. If the President requires to be stimulated, those who can approach him ought to do it.

7 FROM
Stephen G. Kurtz
President Adams Chooses Peace

There would have been a continuation of naval warfare well beyond 1800 had France chosen to continue her hostility toward the United States. Clearly, the governing Directory on advice from Talleyrand weighed self-interest in the scales with war and reversed policy. The United States, as the smaller power, could not force France to the negotiating table against her will, but by floating a well-armed fleet of frigates and sloops-of-war in a short space of time and by concentrating it in the West Indies where French vessels could be attacked most effectively, the President was able to exert maximum pressure. Yet his conduct of negotiations with France appeared to be politically inept, even suicidal, and most Federalists violently opposed him. Why he acted as he did and why he chose to make his decision known sooner than many circumstances seemed to dictate is the subject of the brief article which follows. It reveals the intimate relationship of domestic tensions to foreign policy decisions as well as the role of military and naval power in Federalist thinking about those decisions.

President Adams split the Federalists into openly hostile factions when he named William Vans Murray to treat with France in February 1799. The peace mission of 1799-1800 seriously weakened the structure of the party, but it led ultimately to the termination of an alliance that had proven dangerous to American interests, and it was Adams' own conviction that it had prevented a test of American federalism that might well have ended in disunion. In later life he repeatedly claimed that his conduct of foreign relations as President had been his greatest public service, "the most splendid diamond in my crown," as he put it in 1815.

SOURCE. Stephen G. Kurtz, "The French Mission of 1799-1800: Concluding Chapter in the Statecraft of John Adams," *Political Science Quarterly,* Volume LXXX, No. 4 (December 1965), pp. 543-557. Reprinted by permission of the *Political Science Quarterly.*

That Adams should pass over his constitutional writings, his parliamentary leadership in the struggle for independence, and his foreign diplomatic service during the seventeen-eighties, indicates that he regarded his conduct of peace negotiations in 1799 and 1800 as a master-stroke of statecraft, one of his own creation and execution.

An examination of the domestic as well as foreign pressures which influenced his conduct and careful consideration of the timing of his actions leads to deeper appreciation of his assessment. It is maintained here that Adams viewed the foreign and domestic crises of his administration as inseparable, that his peace decision was dictated largely by concern over internal unrest, that in responding positively to Talleyrand's overtures Adams continued to regard war as a likely possibility, and that the eight-months' delay between Murray's nomination and the sailing of the other two members of the mission was deliberate on Adams' part and owed nothing to the backstairs intrigues of cabinet officers. Adams waited until October to order the departure of Ellsworth and Davie because of unexpected delays encountered in completing the three squadrons of the Caribbean fleet. He did not lose direction of the negotiation to the Hamiltonian faction or its partisans within the cabinet.

I

In his message to Congress of December 1798 Adams declared that the administration would be prepared to settle differences with France when official assurances of her willingness to treat with any minister selected by the United States government had been received. Until that time, he concluded, defense measures would be pressed: "An efficient preparation for war can alone insure peace." When a few weeks later Adams decided that Talleyrand had provided such assurance through an exchange of letters between Pichon, the French charge, and Murray, the American Minister, at The Hague, he named Murray to the Senate as minister plenipotentiary: but Adams did not rule out the possibility of declaring war or slacken efforts to float a battle fleet at any time during the course of negotiations. "Our operations by sea and land are not to be relaxed in the slightest," he told Secretary of State Pickering in August 1799. "On the contrary, I want them animated with fresh energy." As late as the summer of

1800 Adams requested that John Marshall, Pickering's successor, place the question of declaring war upon France before the cabinet for discussion prior to his return to the capital.

By the time that Talleyrand turned the initiative back to the United States, Adams had taken advantage of his position to direct the building of the nation's defenses and to inflame public opinion against the French government. The powers granted the President under the Constitution were found sufficiently flexible to achieve the administration's goal of peace with honor in spite of division within the Federalist party, the threat of sectional cleavage represented by the Virginia and Kentucky Resolution, and the threat to the independence of the executive which Secretary Pickering posed in bringing Washington, Hamilton, and C.C. Pinckney into cabinet discussions in the fall of 1799. In spite of his subsequent reputation as a weak President, Adams proved bold in his conduct of foreign relations. He had developed a doctrine of executive power since 1776 which was as close to monarchical as American conditions would allow. In the third volume of his *Defence of the Constitutions of Government of the United States of America* (1787) Adams had written:

"The parties of rich and poor, of gentlemen and simplemen, unbalanced by some third power, will always look to foreign aid. . . . Whig and Tory, Constitutionalist and Republican, Anglomane and Francomane. . . . will serve as well as Guelf and Ghibelline. The great desideratum in a government is a distinct executive power of sufficient strength and weight to compel both these parties in turn to submit to the laws."

Nor was Jefferson wrong in viewing Adams as the leader of what he termed the "monocrats" and the basic cause of party division as disagreement over executive power.

It is clear that from the beginning of his administration Adams was aware of the loyalty which Pickering, Wolcott, and McHenry felt toward Alexander Hamilton. If he had not known of it, which seems inconceivable, he had well-meaning friends to warn him. A few weeks after his inauguration he replied to such a notice from Elbridge Gerry: 'Pickering and his colleagues are as much attached to me as I desire. I have no jealousies from that quarter." Adams showed by the private instructions which he gave to John Quincy Adams at the time of the latter's appointment as Minister to Prussia, however, that he was not prepared completely to trust Pickering: "Continue your practice of writing freely to me, more cautiously to the officer of State." Secretary of the Treasury Wolcott was told by Adams that there existed a natural antagonism on the part of Congress that would attempt to weaken the President's powers by encouraging cabinet officers to operate independently of his control. He pointed to a tax bill which, in his opinion, had granted entirely too much latitude to Wolcott as a case in point. "That policy will be pursued," Adams stated, "until we have a Quintuple or Centuple Executive Directory."

II

Whether Adams was wise in retaining Washington's secretaries is another question; his belief in the necessity of developing a permanent or semi-permanent civil service dictated it, and the difficulties which his illustrious predecessor had met in attempting to fill low-paying cabinet posts were clear enough. That a "three-vote President" might hesitate to face the same humiliating search is worth considering. Adams operated much more independently of the cabinet than had Washington. He followed precedent in asking for their written advice upon important questions, but there is no indication that he paid much attention to the opinions of his secretaries when his own opinions were contrary. Adams expected little more of them than that they write the routine dispatches and reports of their departments. Study, as well as experience, had shown him that an executive must make his own decisions, and most important to an understanding of his relations with his advisers, Adams had taken from his reading in Cicero, Tacitus, Machiavelli, Bolingbroke, and his other mentors a rule of operating with maximum secrecy. "The unity, consistency, promptitude, secrecy, and activity of the whole executive authority," he commented to Gerry in 1797, "are so essential to my system of republican government, that without them there can be no peace, order, liberty, or property in society." He explained to John Marshall, who replaced Pickering in the Spring of 1800, that in pretending to no firm opinion himself on a matter under discussion, he was able to extract honest opinions from subordinates. Although Adams had made it clear in his December 1798 message that a second mission might be dispatched should French policies change, his secretaries were given no intimation that he had decided to take the step prior to the eighteenth of February when Murray's name was submitted to the Senate. The President admitted to his wife, who was as surprised as others, that he had deliberately kept the decision to himself.

III

Most high-ranking Federalists regarded the decision as idiotic, a result of his solitary deliberation. "If any good results from it," Chief Justice Francis Dana of the Massachusetts Supreme Court commented to an English correspondent, "he will be entitled to the honour exclusively. His friends foresee none and deprecate nothing more seriously than a revival of diplomatic connections with France while under the influence of revolutionary principles." Dana frankly admitted his hope that the embassy would fail. If so, he concluded, " . . . it would create neither surprise or regret among the Federalists, who deem every procrastination a public blessing." Pickering, who dated his falling out with Adams from the moment of Murray's nomination, surmised that the President had kept his own counsels because of a bargain with the Jeffersonians, a promise of support in 1800 in return for the necks of McHenry and himself and a new French mission. Others saw in the peace move the insidious influence of Elbridge Gerry, who was known to have been in private conclave with the Adamses at Quincy. Although initially angered by Gerry's conduct during the first peace mission, Adams did not repudiate him or reject the report which Gerry gave of a change of policy at Paris, a nagging problem that ripened gradually into a major source of friction between the President and the Secretary of State.

Adams showed no confidence in the ability of his secretaries to deal with foreign affairs. His vanity and his habit of lecturing on the immense value of personal experience in foreign embassies only exacerbated feelings which his secrecy in important questions both reflected and created. That Talleyrand's use of Murray and Pichon as intermediaries was acceptable diplomatic form, Adams knew from his experience at Paris in 1781; Pickering could not accept it any more than McHenry could the President's insistence that recruiting a large standing army would prove an unnecessary danger and expense. Beneath the surface frictions, however, lay a fundamental divergence of viewpoint on the nature of the crisis itself. To Adams, the undeclared war with France was but one episode in the chronic situation which Americans had faced since the Revolution—that of avoiding dependence upon either of the great powers. As he expressed it to former Governor Thomas Johnson of Maryland, the basic aim of American foreign policy was "to avoid becoming a mere satellite to a mighty power," a danger that was as great from Britain as from France. Washington, writing to Lafayette on Christmas day 1798, expressed the same apprehension:

"That there are many among us, who wish to see this country embroiled on the side of Great Britain, and others who are anxious that we should take part with France against her, admits of no doubt. But. . . . the Governing powers of the country, and a large part of the people are truly Americans . . . . unwilling under any circumstances. . . . to participate in the politics or contests of Europe."

IV

By 1798 many leading Federalists, including the Secretary of State, had forgotten the lessons of the American Revolution in their antagonism toward the French Revolution and its American champions. The defense measures, tax increases, and security acts adopted in 1798 had produced a major crisis in American federalism and a threatening division which was reflected in the Virginia and Kentucky Resolutions. Although historical investigation has uncovered little that suggests preparation for armed rebellion on the part of Republican leaders in 1798 or 1799, Federalist eschatology insisted upon it. In the eyes of many Federalists, it has been remarked, the Republic seemed to have reached senility while still in its infancy.

Hamilton was convinced that Virginians contemplated armed revolt, and to all intents and purposes he commanded the United States Army. In January and February 1799 Hamilton's apprehension was so great that he pointed to reports of military preparations by the Virginia government and proposed strengthening the Alien and Sedition Acts, enlarging the jurisdiction of federal courts, the division of the southern states into smaller territorial units, and a movement of federal troops southwestward in order, as he put it, "to put Virginia to the test of resistance."

Characteristically, Fisher Ames, even as New England was reacting most violently against the French, saw the spirit of "Jacobinism" increasing on all fronts and called upon the executive to take steps to combat it. Jonathan Mason, also of Massachusetts, lamented that the Fifth Congress had failed to declare war, a step which, as he saw it, would be the most effective way of dealing with internal security; while the most pessimistic utterances were made by Francis Dana: "I pray Heaven I may be mistaken when I declare it as my expectation that if we do not have a foreign war, a civil war will be the lot of Americans and possibly both." Even the sanguine Jefferson harbored fears of violence and cautioned his political lieutenants against doing anything that could give the national government reason for moving troops into the South.

Tensions were increased precisely because France was believed to be incapable of transporting troops to American shores by virtue of Nelson's remarkable victory at Aboukir Bay, news of which reached Philadelphia in November 1798. "We are not afraid of a French invasion this winter," Adams wrote in reply to one of many congratulatory letters he had received. To exultant Federalists the way now seemed open to an even closer understanding with Britain than had developed since the conclusion of the Jay-Grenville negotiations of 1794. Evidence of cooperation undreamed of during Washington's administration had recently crossed the President's desk in the form of a convention concluded by British and American agents and Toussaint L'Ouverture, the ex-slave whose rebel forces had broken France's hold on the Island of Santo Domingo. A dispatch from Rufus King, American Minister in London, reached Adams on January 17 in which it was announced that Toussaint had agreed to open ports under his control to British and American vessels while closing them to French privateers. A subsequent dispatch announced that the British ministry had ordered its chief agent in Santo Domingo, General Maitland, to Philadelphia with full powers "to adjust a plan concerning St. Domingo." The American Minister added that George III had been generous in his praise of Adams' statesmanship and had asked repeatedly when the United States could be expected to declare war upon France.

The Federalist majority in Congress, over bitter Republican protests, responded warmly by authorizing trade with any former

French possession whose local authorities promised to refrain from attacks upon American shipping. Simultaneously, Congress also suspended commerce between the United States and the French Republic. President Adams signed the new legislation six days before naming Murray to resume diplomatic relations with France.

The situation in the early weeks of 1799 had become dangerous in Adams' judgment: the dominant faction in Congress welcomed closer cooperation with England despite the danger represented by her naval ascendancy, and, while admitting their concern over a clash between state and national authority, supported a large army officered by Federalists with no prospect of an invader in sight. The guarantee from the French government that he had insisted upon arrived in January 1799, a promise by Talleyrand that an American envoy would be received with dignity and honor. The reports of Gerry, Murray, John Quincy Adams, George Logan, and Joel Barlow from Europe indicated a change at Paris favorable to peace. Washington's brief note accompanying the Barlow letter testified to his belief in a general longing for peace. But in his own accounts of the mission, Adams insisted that in his conduct of foreign relations in 1799 and 1800 domestic unrest had been uppermost in his mind.

In a letter to John Jay written in November 1800 Adams pointed out that only among what he termed "a faction who have been laboring and intriguing for an army of fifty- thousand" had the peace decision been an unforgivable lapse. The peace mission and the reduction of the army, he stated, were intimately bound together. Adams wrote an explanation of his decision in 1801, a reply to Hamilton's attack upon him of the previous year, that was not published until 1809 in the *Boston Patriot.* He declared that had the French crisis not been relieved.

". . . it was my opinion then, and has been since, that the two parties in the United States would have broken into civil war; a majority of all the states to the southward of the Hudson River, united with nearly half New England, would have raised an army under Aaron Burr; a majority of New England another under Hamilton."

To John Taylor in their exchange of letters in 1814, he wrote:". . . we have had Shay's, Fries's, and I know not whose rebellion in the western counties of Pennsylvania. How near did Virginia and Kentucky approach in the last years of the last century?" Finally, in 1815 he pointed once more to the pressure of potential civil war:

"To dispatch all in a few words, a civil war was expected. The party committed suicide; they killed themselves and the national president (not their president) at one shot, and then, foolishly or maliciously, indicted me for the murder. . . . My own mission to France. . . I esteem the most splended diamond in my crown. . . "

V

In acting to break the domestic tension, Adams responded to a fear of states'-rights sentiment that he had harbored for years. "If the superiority of the national government is not more clearly acknowledged," he wrote in 1791, "we shall soon be in a confusion which we shall not get out of for twenty years."

Adams' solution to the problem of rising tensions, however, was not that of the Hamiltonian Federalists, who made no effort to conceal their anger. At the insistence of a Senate deputation the mission was enlarged with the addition of Chief Justice Oliver Ellsworth and Patrick Henry. A few weeks later, Governor William R. Davie of North Carolina was named in place of Henry, who declined. The President then packed his bags for a trip to Braintree where he remained from March until October. The failure of Ellsworth and Davie to depart until November has been repeatedly explained as the result of intrigues on the part of Secretaries Pickering. Wolcott, and McHenry, the Hamiltonian stalwarts in the cabinet. To explain the mission in terms of conspiracy is to suggest that while Adams remained at the side of his stricken wife, a cabal of Federalists, who wished to prolong hostilities or bring on a declaration of war, worked through Secretary Pickering to frustrate the President's policy. It is pointed out that mail was held up, orders questioned, and confidential information widely disseminated. According to such a construction, it was only when Navy Secretary Stoddert warned him that Adams awoke and, hurrying to the temporary capital at Trenton, broke with Pickering and ordered the departure in mid-October. If this interpretation is accepted, it is necessary to take a view of Adams that suggests dereliction of duty, premature senility, or worse. It also rests upon untenable assumptions: that Adams was unaware of attempts to delay the mission, that these attempts caused the eight-months' delay, and that Adams himself wished negotiations to commence as promptly as possible.

Brtain's supremacy on the sea presented the prospect of being drawn tightly into her orbit, a situation that Adams, like Washington before him, believed dangerous to American interests. Nelson's victory on the Nile had released a mechanism whose movement threatened to result in what would have amounted to an Anglo-American alliance, a joint-expedition against Spain's American empire, and the fulfillment of Hamilton's military and imperialist dreams. A declaration of war early in 1799 pointed toward the ascendancy of "the feudalists," as Elbridge Gerry called them; a gesture of peace toward France promised the relaxation of internal unrest and the frustration of military adventures.

Adams' behavior between February and October 1799 indicates strongly that he considered the nomination of Murray premature in terms of diplomacy and that he had no intention of hastily beginning to negotiate. Patrick Henry was certainly a strange choice if speed was a consideration: he had twice before refused federal appointments pleading advancing age, and, as could be anticipated, the exchange of letters alone consumed several weeks. Governor Davie was not notified of his appointment until June and was instructed to remain silent about departure plans until the Directory had sent a specific guarantee to treat with the three men named. The exchange of letters between Murray in the Netherlands and the Paris government covering this point was not completed until the middle of May and not sanctioned by Adams until August. On September 10 Davie took leave of the North Carolina legislature and did not reach Trenton, the yellow-fever season capital, until early October. The correspondence between Adams and Pickering during this period reflects neither urgency nor anger on the President's part.

Furthermore, the reasons for holding up the mission which were advanced by Pickering were respected by Adams. Benjamin Stoddert, about whose loyalty there has never been question, pointed out to Adams that the Murray nomination had hurt relations with England and that the Anglo-American commission making awards to former Loyalists and British merchants under Article VI of the Jay treaty was at loggerheads:

"No doubt their commissioners have for a long time been soured, and have in some instances acted as if it were their desire to plunge the two nations into war. If England insists on a quarrel, however we may lament the calamity, we need not fear the result if our own people are satisfied that the Government has acted in all instances right."

Secretary Pickering pressed for delay on the basis of discord at Paris and the rise to power of Napoleon which Federalists saw as the first step toward a Bourbon restoration. Adams dismissed the restoration possibility but agreed with Pickering that it would be wise to delay: "The revolution in the Directory, the revival of the clubs and private societies in France, and the strong appearance of another reign of democratic fury seem to justify relaxation of our zeal for the sudden departure of the envoys." Two weeks later he wrote Stoddert: "I have no reason nor motive to precipitate the departure of the envoys." As late as September he informed Pickering that when he arrived at Trenton there would be ample time to decide what should finally be done about the mission. He added that from his own experience he knew late October to be a safe time for ocean travel. Stephen Higginson, federal naval agent and shipbuilder at Boston, reported that there were rumors among Adams' friends who had visited him at Quincy that the President had doubts about dispatching the mission at all.

Finally, what lay behind the long delay was the President's conviction that the defense of American rights must rest upon naval power, the keystone of Adams' realpolitik. He had been the warmest advocate of American naval power since the seventeen-seventies. "Floating batteries and wooden walls have been my favorite system of warfare for three and twenty years," he wrote to the Boston Marine Society in the fall of 1798. But, he added, "I have had little success in making proselytes." The principal theater of war between the United States and France was the Caribbean and, after Nelson had eliminated the possibility of transporting a French army to America, could have been nowhere else. Although a nation of limited resources the United States was capable of building a fleet that could deal France's trade with the West Indies a crippling blow in the judgment of both Adams and

Stoddert. "The sixty or eighty French privateers out of Guadaloupe must be very small and trifling." Adams commented to Stoddert in August. "We shall be very indiscreet if we depend upon the British to defend our commerce and destroy French privateers. We must depend on God and our rights as well as the English."

The foreign policy of neutrality was fragile without the means of protecting America's rapidly expanding ocean commerce. Adams acted upon the assumption that the only chance of ending French attacks upon United States shipping rested upon her fears of the power to retaliate. What was needed in 1799 was time, time to complete the three squadrons authorized for operations in West Indian waters. The leisurely manner in which Adams dealt with his correspondence with Pickering in 1799 stands in marked contrast to the haste and careful attention to detail which he gave to his communications with Secretary Stodder. Copies of their letters found in the "Letterbooks" in the Adams Family Papers as well as those printed in the fourth volume of *Naval Documents Related to the Quasi-War between the United States and* France abundantly testify to the deep concern which Adams and Stoddert shared for the completion of naval vessels. Unexpected construction problems and severe epidemics of yellow-fever in the summers of 1798 and 1799 had slowed efforts in government yards and in Stoddert's office which had to be moved twice from Philadelphia to Trenton.

It was not until September 1799 that the Secretary could report the squadrons fit for sea duty. The first, under the command of Captain Silas Talbot of the U.S.S. Constitution, was ordered to rendezvous off Santo Domingo; the second, under Daniel McNeill, to Surinam off the Guiana coast; and the third, commanded by Richard V. Morris, to Guadaloupe. Each was to have consisted of a frigate and five brigs, but Stoddert's final orders of September 9 show that both the Surinam and Guadaloupe flotillas would be incomplete for several weeks. The date for each group to rendezvous at its station was October 10, the day of Adams' arrival at Trenton where he at last issued orders for the departure of Ellsworth and Davie. He did so over the protests of Pickering, Hamilton, and Ellsworth, all of whom argued that news from Europe indicated an impending victory for the Coalition and the restoration of the monarchy in France.

In the months that followed, Napoleon and Talleyrand gave scant attention to the relatively inconsequential problem of American relations. Adams awaited the result anxiously, convinced that France would be guided largely by considerations beyond his control, by the outcome of European battles and diplomacy but also by advice which he was certain American Republicans would supply with their eyes upon Jefferson's election. Renewal of hostilities was possible, he told his secretaries in the summer of 1800, for he feared that France would attempt to maneuver the envoys into repudiating the terms of the Jay Treaty with England. Defense preparations would not be relaxed until an acceptable treaty had been signed and ratified as long as he remained President. All that the American government could do to influence the outcome was being done.

The Americans at Paris met with a three-man commission headed by Joseph Bonaparte and pressed for reparations amounting to twenty million dollars as well as recognition of the legality of the abrogation of the treaties of 1778 and 1788. By the Treaty of Morte-fontaine, however, the United States assumed the claims of its own citizens as the price of severing the French alliance. While Adams waited, he doubted. "These Federalists may yet have their fill at fighting," he commented to John Trumbull in September 1800. "They may see our envoys without peace, and if they do, what is lost? Certainly nothing, unless it be the influence of some of the Federalists by their own imprudent and disorganizing opposition and clamor. Much time has been gained."

POSTSCRIPT

John C. Miller, the Decline of the Federalists

As a result of the elections of 1800 Jefferson and the Republicans assumed political power nationally as well as in states and localities which had been strongly Federalist but a few months previous. By 1815 or 1820 many men of Federalist sympathies remained actively engaged in political and economic life, but to all intents and purposes there was no national party reflecting the old Federalist faith. Why the Federalists lost control and lost ground so rapidly in the last months of the Adams administration is apparent when one considers the antipathies of national leaders, the disregard of party decision-making on the President's part, and the violent cleavage caused by the Federalist response to France's challenge. In the Alien and Sedition Acts and in convictions arising out of the Sedition Act, the Federalist leaders badly miscalculated the temper of America; in internecine quarrels over the provisional army and over appointments to military ranks, they wasted their strength; and in taxing the citizenry for things that appeared of dubious value once the reaction to the X,Y,Z Affair had cooled, they lost their standing among the agricultural majority without whose support no party could stand.

On the other side of the coin is the imprint of Jeffersonian party organization and management: towns and counties were lost, often by very narrow margins, in 1800 simply because the Republicans had built more efficient organizations. Finally, it may be asked whether Federalists did not share viewpoints about society and man's place in it that had come to be archaic by the dawn of the nineteenth century, for instance, a marked degree of hostility to the heady notions of equality and democracy which their spokesmen communicated by indirection even when they did not overtly

SOURCE. John C. Miller, *The Federalist Era, 1789-1801,* New York: Harper and Row, Publishers, Incorporated, 1963, pp. 108-116. Copyright (C) 1960 by John C. Miller. Reprinted by permission of Harper & Row, Publishers, Inc.

proclaim them. In this selection from his brief history of the Federalists from the adoption of The Constitution to Jefferson's inaugural, John C. Miller summarizes their basic values.

The leaders of the Federalist party were lawyers, merchants, and large landowners. But the leadership did not faithfully reflect the composition of the party as a whole. Manifestly, there were not enough landed magnates, businessmen, and professional men in the United States to form a political party; had not Federalism attracted the votes of the farmers and the town artisans, it never would have attained power in the United States. The party appealed especially to the more prosperous farmers living near the cities and engaged in growing cash crops. In Lancaster County, Pennsylvania, for example, there were a number of farmers of the Federalist persuasion worth from fifty to several hundred thousand dollars. Even in New England, the merchants, lawyers, and shipowners who constituted the nucleus of the party leaned heavily upon the well-to-do farmers and the Congregational clergy.

Being men of wealth and high social position, the Federalist leaders fell easily into the assumption that there was a close connection between the ownership of property and the possession of the talents necessary to the efficient administration of government. The men who had made good in trade, speculation, and the professions were the proper custodians of the national welfare; they alone possessed the ability, wisdom, sobriety, public spirit, and love of good order upon which the success of all government, and especially republican government, depended. It was plain at least to the Federalists that the people of the United States could ensure their happiness and prosperity only by accepting the principle that "those who have more strength and *excellence,* shall bear rule over those who have less." Surely the frankest politicians who ever graced the American scene, the Federalists made no pretence of being other than what they were: upper-class Americans who had a natural-born right to rule their inferiors in the social and economic scale. Even within the party itself, the rank and file were never permitted to indulge the pleasing illusion that they were the social equals of the leaders. Particularly in the northern cities, good society was coeval with the Federalist party: a gentleman was a Federalist but, unhappily, it did not follow that every Federalist was a gentleman.

Despite the fact that Federalism sought to carry over the aristocratic bias of colonial society into the Republic, it did not represent the last stand of an old order. Rather it marked the first concerted effort on the part of the business and professional class, together with prosperous landowners, to arrogate to themselves direction of the nation's affairs. Having already solidified their economic position, the Federalist merchants, lawyers, speculators, bankers, and landowners undertook to put in practice the maxim that those who owned the country ought to run it.

In part, it was upon the necessity of making the United States a first-rate power that the Federalists based their claim of a right to rule. Under the Articles of Confederation, they argued, national security had been jeopardized by a weak and inefficient central government — an experience which ought to have taught Americans that their peace, happiness, and safety depended upon establishing a powerful national government and giving the full measure of confidence to those best qualified to administer it. Accordingly, the Federalists tried to inculcate in the American people a love of the Union which subordinated local interests to the good of the whole nation and put the welfare of the United States over loyalty to any foreign country whatever. "I would wish my countrymen to feel like Romans, to be as proud as Englishmen," said Gouverneur Morris; "we are neither Frenchmen nor Englishmen, we are Americans." The Federalists were the champions of an ideal without which the Republic could not have endured.

During the period of their ascendancy, the Federalists constantly inveighed against the "pernicious," the "baleful," the "abominable" doctrine of states' rights. Here, they exclaimed, was the eternal enemy of national prosperity and greatness, the opening wedge for demagoguery, foreign intrigue, and civil war. At this time, of course, the Federalists were not aware that the time would come when they embraced this hateful thing and acclaimed it a refuge against Jeffersonian Democracy.

The Federalists were wedded to a philosophy of human nature which proved more enduring than their nationalism: in the end, these patricians were left with little except their contempt of the people. To a considerable degree, this attitude was derived from the struggle between creditors' rights, and majority rule which had been waged in the states during the period of the Articles of Confederation and which had seriously undermined the optimistic faith in human possibilities that had illuminated the Declaration of Independence. Viewing human nature through a glass darkly, the Federalists recoiled from what they saw: instead of being temperate, wise, and virtuous, mankind in the mass seemed to be actuated by cupidity, envy, and malice. "The most ferocious of all animals, when his passions are roused to fury and un-controlled, is man," said Fisher Ames. "Men are often false to their country and their honor, false to duty and even to interest, but multitudes of men are never long false or deaf to their passions." "The many," said George Cabot, "do not think at all" — they were purely creatures of feeling. Ames and Cabot believed that this assessment was the product of a candid and dispassionate examination of human nature. The leaders of the Federalist party were not merely politicians — they were students of psychology who had mastered, to their own satisfaction, what in the eighteenth century was called "the science of human nature."

Men being what they were, the Federalists concluded that government must be rendered capable of resisting the passions of the people. "The delusions of democracy, like other delusions of the human mind," it was pointed out, "cannot be resisted by reason and truth alone. . . . Reason will not answer — reason will not protect your houses, ships and stables from thieves. You must have for protection the controlling *fear of God and Fear of Govern-ment.*"

In the democratic state, as the Federalists viewed it, no one feared either God or government; instead, popular majorities ruled without let or hindrance and the soverein people gave free reign to every whim and desire, however transitory and injurious to the public welfare. Federalists prided themselves upon being Fighters against Democracy: in their eyes, none were more worthy of honor than those who did battle against egalitarians and demagogues. In 1801, Noah Webster boasted that he had spent "the largest part of eighteen years in opposing Democracy." He thought that if the American people understood their true interests, they would gratefully commemorate his efforts to save them from that slough of despond.

In combating democracy and all its works, the Federalists supposed that they were upholding the cause of freedom. Their purpose, as they conceived it, was to save the country from the despotism produced by "popular delusion, injustice and tyranny." They proclaimed themselves to be the friends of "temperate liberty"—not the kind which came like a whirlwind effacing established institutions and leveling distinctions, but the mild, benignant variety which cast the mantle of the law over the rights and property of every individual. "American liberty," said Fisher Ames, "calms and restrains the licentious passions, like an angel, that says to the winds and troubled seas, be still." True freedom, they pointed out, could not be enjoyed unless some rights were curtailed: "Honest men must submit to the force that is necessary to govern rogues. . . . To make a nation free, the crafty must be kept in awe, and the violent in restraint." In their own eyes, the Federalists were the true heirs of the American Revolution: the patriots of 1776, they said, had never defined liberty as the privilege of a mob to do as it pleased. Tyranny, they knew, bore many faces, and they were resolved to fight it whether it came in the guise of King George and his ministers or the American populace.

In keeping with their view of human nature, the Federalists did not credit the mass of the people with sufficient intelligence to make themselves a threat to the established order. In themselves, the people were nothing; it was only when they were set in motion by demagogues that they became dangerous. In short, the people needed leadership — and they found it, the Federalists lamented, in the most unscrupulous, self-seeking, and unprincipled members of society. "The republicanism of a great mass of people," said Fisher Ames, "is often nothing more than a blind trust in certain favorites, and a less blind and still more furious hatred of their enemies." The trouble was that the people were unable to distinguish between their true friends and enemies; as a result, democracy became the rule by the worst passions of the worst men in the community.

The mark of a demagogue, in the Federalists' opinion, was not only that he gave the people an inflated sense of their own importance but that he set the poor against the rich. To the

Federalists, the central theme of history was the struggle between the opulent members of the community and "the discontented and factious at the head of the poor. . . . The jealousy of the rich is a passion in the poor which can always be appealed to with success on every question, and . . . the engine by which a giddy populace can be most easily wrought on to do mischief." Chancellor Kent summoned history to prove his contention that "there is a constant tendency in the poor to covet and to share the plunder of the rich; in the debtor to relax or avoid the obligations of interest; in the indolent and profligate to cast the whole burden of society upon the industrious and virtuous; and there is a tendency in ambitious and wicked men to inflame those combustible materials." Federalists agreed that "the poor we have always with us," but they could not say as much for the rich: exposed to assaults of ignorance and poverty, the rich seemed to have but a slim chance of survival in a democratic state.

As for warning the people to beware of the wiles of demagogues, the Federalists feared it was wasted effort. For one thing, the people seemed incapable of resisting the blandishments of these seducers of unquiet souls: a few honeyed words and they were ready to yield all. In the second place, the Federalists were inclined to regard demagogues as an inevitable concomitant of freedom: "The more free the citizens," they said, "the bolder and more profligate will be their demagogues." Since poverty was also regarded as an inescapable by-product of freedom, it seemed to the Federalists that in the United States demagogues would never want materials upon which to work. Already, mourned Noah Webster, the "preposterous doctrine of equality" had "stripped old men of dignity and wise men of their influence."

In a democracy, the Federalists believed that the normal course of events was from disaster to catastrophe. Bad as was majority rule, they did not suppose that it was the last word in abominations. Men could not long endure the chaos produced by popular majorities which did the bidding of demagogues: the only good that Federalists could say of democracy was that it was soon over. In itself, democracy was merely a way station on the way to the Inferno: in Fisher Ames's words, "like death, it is only the dismal passport to a more dismal hereafter." That hereafter was the despotism of one man whose mission it was to put an end to freedom, including the freedom of the majority to do as it pleased.

And for this service, the dictator was hailed by the people as their savior — as indeed he was, for he had saved them from their worst enemy, themselves.

There was no danger that a Federalist would be mistaken for a demagogue. Federalists prided themselves upon their disdain of "the vile love of popularity": even if political office depended upon it, they swore that they would not truckle to the people. They repeatedly declared that they would rather be right than be popular, and it is indicative of their state of mind that they believed it was rarely possible to be both. "I have frequently been the servant of the people, always their friend," said Gouverneur Morris; "but not one moment of my life their flatterer, and God forbid that I ever should be." In 1797, Rufus King accounted it a paradox that the people were "less wrong than their government, which, everywhere seems to be destitute of both wisdom and courage."

The Federalists were careful to distinguish between democracy and republicanism. At the same time that they expressed their detestation of democracy, they professed veneration for republicanism. They regarded democracy as the uncontrolled will of the people operating through the government, whereas republicanism imposed restraints upon the power of the people, taught respect for law and order, and discriminated between liberty and licentiousness.

Despite their abhorrence of democracy, Federalists admitted that it was an integral part of every well-ordered government. But — and upon this point Federalists were especially emphatic — it was not the whole of government. Their ideal was a "mixed government" composed of democracy, aristocracy, and monarchy poised in such delicate equilibrium that no single element could make itself dominant over the government. The branch allotted to the people was the House of Representatives — and this, said the Federalists, was all any people who wished to be truly free had a right to ask. For if the democratic part of the government succeeded in making itself supreme — and the Federalists believed that it was the nature of democracy to grasp at all power — despotism resulted.

Thus the Federalists were willing to acclaim the people sovereign but not to invest them with the plenitude of authority usually attached to that title. Government of the people they could accept, but not government by the people. Instead of the people ruling the government, the Federalists wished to see the government rule according to the Constitution. The people, in short, were to reign but not to rule, that important function being reserved for "the choice sort of people," sober and discreet men, seasoned by wealth and education and dedicated to keeping the passions of the populace within bounds. To whom else could this description apply but to the leaders of the Federalist party? And, in fact, as organizers and managers of businesses and banks, the Federalists brought skills to the government which it sorely needed; even their enemies admitted that they were men of rare constructive administrative ability. During their tenure of power, no Federalist officeholder was found guilty of malfeasance.

In essence, the Federalists' doctrine was that men cannot live by liberty alone; order and stability were often in conflict with the popular will, and in such instances order and stability must prevail. The real danger to liberty, from their point of view, came from the people themselves: where the people were all-powerful, liberty perished. Nor did they deny the converse of this maxim: where the government was all-powerful, liberty was extinguished. They were not advocates of an omnipotent government; their ideal was a government capable of moderating "the unruly passions of men" but at the same time limited in its powers. For while the Federalists looked to the general government for protection against the"rapacious democrats" in the states, they did not ignore the possibility — and, after 1796, a very real possibility it was — that the democrats would gain control of the general government itself. Unlike Edmund Burke, the great English conservative, they did not consecrate the state — there was too much danger that it would fall into the wrong hands.

Beset by democrats, demagogues, and disorganizers, the Federalists looked upon the President as their rock of salvation. To him they gladly assigned the responsibilities of leadership in both foreign and domestic affairs. "It is upon the Executive we depend for the execution of the laws and for general protection," declared a Federalist congressman. He is "the cement of our Union, the representative of the whole people." A Federalist was expected to construe the powers of the President broadly and to defend his prerogatives against legislative encroachment. In this regard, Fisher Ames set a model for his party: it was said that Ames seldom spoke without casting aspersions upon the House of Representatives and bestowing praise upon the President.

Nevertheless, when it came to strengthening executive powers, many Federalist congressmen experienced a sharp conflict of loyalties. On the one hand, they were eager to erect the Presidency into a tower of strength against "popular licentiousness"; on the other hand, *esprit de corps* attached them to their own particular branch of the government. For the most part, however, the fear that the rule of Congress would mean the triumph of democracy — "it will play the mob at last," Fisher Ames predicted — kept Federalist members of Congress loyal to the executive. Not only did they look with equanimity upon the aggrandizement of the executive — they cheerfully abnegated powers of Congress in order to ensure that he did not want authority.

Experience had taught the Federalists that the principal work of government must be in neutralizing "the follies and vices of men." Nevertheless, they did not take a wholly negative view of the functions of government; besides holding down the lid on the democratic caldron, they expected government to act in behalf of the business interests of the country by means of tariffs, bounties, and other aids. As British subjects, Americans had learned the advantages as well as the disadvantages of mercantilism; and now, emancipated from British control, they wished to perpetuate the advantages of that system. "Government," they said, "is formed to promote the general good, and that government is best which tends most directly to that end."

BIBLIOGRAPHY

A great many of the printed primary sources needed for a study of the Federalists have been cited throughout this volume and will not be listed again. A basic list of books covering the period from 1780 to 1800 should certainly include the following: on the Confederation period, Merrill Jensen, *The New Nation* (New York, 1950), and on the entire period from 1789 to 1815, the two volumes in the New American Nation Series, John C. Miller, *The Federalist Era* (New York, 1960), and Marshall Smelser, *The Democratic Republic* (New York, 1968); on the diplomacy of the Federalists, Alexander DeConde, *Entangling Alliance: Politics and Diplomacy under George Washington* (Durham, N.C., 1958), and *The Quasi-War: the Politics and Diplomacy of the Undeclared War with France, 1797-1801* (New York, 1966), and Bradford Perkins, *The First Rapprochement* (Philadelphia, 1955); on the Adams administration, Manning J. Dauer, *The Adams Federalists* (Baltimore, 1954), and Stephen G. Kurtz, *The Presidency of John Adams* (Philadelphia, 1957); and on the Federalists after 1801, David H. Fischer, *The Revolution of American Conservatism* (New York, 1965); James M. Banner, Jr., *To the Hartford Convention* (New York, 1970), Samuel E. Morison, *Harrison Gray Otis* (Boston, 1969), and Shaw Livermore, Jr., *The Twilight of Federalism* (Princeton, 1962); and for a comprehensive treatment of the entire period, Edward Channing, *History of the United States*, 6 volumes (New York, 1905-1925), Volume IV. The student who reads these dozen works will be well into the subject; the more recent of them contain excellent bibliographies which will show him where to probe further.

Additional reading according to the chronological scheme of this text should include the following: *Chapter I*, Gordon S. Wood, *The Creation of the American Republic, 1776-1787* (Chapel Hill, 1969); Clarence L. Ver Steeg, *Robert Morris* (Philadelphia, 1954); Douglas S. Freeman, *George Washington*, 7 volumes (New York, 1948-1954),

Volume V; Richard H. Kohn, "The Inside History of the New-burgh Conspiracy: America and the Coup d'Etat," *William and Mary Quarterly,* 3rd ser., XXVII (April 1970); Worthington C. Ford, ed., *Journals of the Continental Congress* (Washington, 1906), Volume XXIV; and the Syrett and Cooke edition of *The Papers of Alexander Hamilton* (New York, 1962), Volume III. *Chapter II,* on the framing and adoption of the Constitution, Charles Warren, *The Making of the Constitution* (Cambridge, 1947) remains a reliable basic work which may be compared with Robert A. Rutland, *The Ordeal of the Constitution: the Antifederalists and the Ratification Struggle, 1787-1788* (Norman, Oklahoma, 1966) and the work of Jackson T. Main previously cited. An important study critically examining the famous thesis of Charles Beard is Forrest McDonald, *We the People* (CLicago, 1963), while essential points in the controversy over adoption of the Constitution are ably discussed in Cecilia Kenyon, "Men of Little Faith: the Anti-Federalists on the Nature of Representative Government," *William and Mary Quarterly,* 3rd. ser., XII (January 1955); Stanley Elkins and Eric McKitrick, "The Founding Fathers: Young Men of the Revolution," *Political Science Quarterly,* LXXVI, No. 2 (June 1961); and from the biographical point of view, in the outstanding work of Irving Brant, *James Madison, Father of The Constitution, 1787-1800* (Indianapolis, 1953). It is also helpful to compare the famous *Federalist Papers* with a collection of opposing essays found in Morton Borden, ed., *The Antifederalist Papers* (Lansing, Mich., 1965).

The development of a strong and cohesive Hamiltonian faction and, subsequently, Federalist Party units on the regional and state levels, may be traced in Harry M. Tinckom, *Republicans and Federalists in Pennsylvania, 1790-1801;* (Harrisburg, Pa., 1950); John A. Munroe, *Federalist Delaware, 1775-1815* (New Brunswick, N.J., 1954); Norman K. Risjord, "The Virginia Federalists," *Journal of Southern History,* XXXIII (November 1967); Henry M. Wagstaff, "Federalism in North Carolina," *James Sprunt Historical Publications ,* IX, No. 2 (Chapel Hill, 1910); George C. Rogers, *Evolution of A Federalist: Williams Loughton Smith of Charleston* (Columbia, S.C., 1962); and in the South generally in an uneven work, Lisle A. Rose, *Prologue to Democracy* (Lexington, Ky., 1968). For the rise of the Federalists in New England and New York, the printed sources are abundant, but one essential source, often cited as a secondary work because of its title, is George Gibbs, *Memoirs of the Administrations of Washington and John Adams* (New York, 1846), an excellent collection of letters of New England Federalists.

Readings bearing upon the contents of *Chapters IV and V* should include Broadus Mitchell, *Alexander Hamilton and the National Adventure* (New York, 1962), especially strong on the Whiskey Rebellion; the headnotes concerning the Neutrality Proclamation in Syrett and Cooke, *Papers of Alexander Hamilton,* Volume XIV; John R. Howe, "Republican Thought and the Political Violence of the 1790's," *American Quarterly,* XIV (Summer 1967); Felix Gilbert, *To the Farewell Address* (Princeton, 1961); Samuel F. Bemis's two studies, *The Jay Treaty* (New York, 1923) and *The Pinckney Treaty* (New York, 1926); and the indispensable *American State Papers, Foreign Relations,* Volume I.

Chapter VI dealing with the split among the Federalists and their role in opposition to Jeffersonian policies may be expanded by study of the works of DeConde, Perkins, Dauer, Kurtz, Fischer, Banner, and Morison cited previously. The outstanding work on the Alien and Sedition Act is James M. Smith, *Freedom's Fetters* (Ithaca, N.Y., 1956), and a great deal may be learned about Federalist party organization — or the lack of it — by examination of Noble E. Cunningham's companion works, *The Jeffersonian Republicans, 1789-1801* (Chapel Hill, 1957) and *The Jeffersonian Republicans in Power* (Chapel Hill, 1963). Henry Adams's nine-volume volume *History* is now available in abridged paperback edition, and his Documents Relating to New England Federalism, 1800-1815 (Boston, 1877) remains an essential reference work on the reaction to the Embargo and the background of the Hartford Convention. See also Edmund Quincy, *Life of Josiah Quincy* (Boston, 1867). A model study of state politics during the Jeffersonian era which reveals much about Federalism is Carl R. Prince, *New Jersey's Jeffersonian Republicans, 1789-1817* (Chapel Hill, 1967), and a recent article by Victor Sapio throws considerable light upon the vitality of Federalism in Maryland, "Maryland's Federalist Revival, 1808-1812," *Maryland Historical Magazine,* 64 (Spring 1969).

Biographies of many Federalist leaders should also be consulted beginning with David H. Fischer's *Revolution of American Conservatism,* previously cited; also in alphabetical order, the biographies of John Adams by Page Smith (1962), Gilbert Chinard (1933), and the still valuable account written by his son, John Quincy Adams, and grandson, Charles Francis Adams, in the first volume of *The Works of John Adams*. Zoltan Haraszti, *John Adams and the Prophets of Progress* (Cambridge, 1952) is a superb intellectual study of reactions to the eighteenth-century Enlightenment. Fisher Ames has recently been given full biographical treatment in Winfred E. A. Bernhard, *Fischer Ames* (Chapel Hill, 1965) and the Delaware Federalist leader, James A. Bayard, in Morton Borden, *The Federalism of James A. Bayard* (New York, 1955). Biographies of Hamilton appear with regularity. Especially recommended are the two-volume study by Broadus Mitchell, previously cited, and John C. Miller, *Alexander Hamilton, Portrait in Paradox* (New York, 1959). The editorial notes written by the editors of *The Papers of Alexander Hamilton*, fifteen volumes to date, are superb. For King, see *Robert Ernst, Rufus King* (Chapel Hill, 1968); for Pickering, Charles W. Upham, *Life of Timothy Pickering*, 4 vols. (Boston, 1873); and for a brief study of his foreign policy, Gerald E. Clarfield, *Timothy Pickering and American Diplomacy, 1795-1800* (Columbia, Mo., 1969). Biographies of several important southern leaders remain to be written, but those now available include Marvin R. Zahniser, *Charles Cotesworth Pinckney* (Chapel Hill, 1967); George C. Rogers, *William Loughton Smith*, cited above; and the seventh volume of Douglas S. Freeman's monumental life of Washington, completed after Freeman's death by J. A. Carroll and M. W. Ashworth. Of the post-1800 Federalists, John Marshall is undoubtedly the most important. The standard biography for fifty years has been the four volume work by Senator Albert J. Beveridge (1916-1919). Careful study, however, reveals the deficiencies as well as the remaining value of this work. It is recommended with reservations. An excellent study, *The Jurisprudence of John Marshall* by Robert K. Faulkner (Princeton, 1969), contains a fine essay on Marshall's vision of America which is strongly recommended.

Finally, it is always of great value to study the opposition, and the understanding of Federalism that any serious student aims to achieve cannot be accomplished without giving equal time to Jefferson, Madison, Gallatin, and the other Jeffersonian Republican leaders. The eighteenth-century setting within which the history of Federalism is worked out is ably provided by Robert R. Palmer in his *Age of the Democratic Revolution*, 2 vols. (Princeton, 1959, 1964).